THERE'S A dog IN THE HOUSE

NANCY CHWIECKO
AMY FERNANDEZ

Designed by Garret Voorhees, www.garretvoorhees.com
Typeset in Chronicle and Whitney, by Hoefler & Frere-Jones

First Published in 2010 by Design Dog Press, www.homedesignfordogs.com
Published and Printed in the USA
ISBN: 978-0615-39585-2
Library of Congress Control Number: 001650657

The photographs have been compiled from many sources. Permission was obtained for all of the photographs and is noted on each photograph. All other photographs are owned by the author.

COVER PHOTOS
TOP Collection of Nancy Chwiecko
BOTTOM Lindsay Karl, www.lindsaykarl.com

DEDICATION

Many factors contribute to a happy, comfortable home, but none more so than the presence of loved ones. This book is dedicated to my sister Carol, who flawlessly combined her love for her dogs and her creation of a beautiful home. (Amy Fernandez)

And for Bob Landau, who never met a dog he didn't love.

ACKNOWLEDGMENTS

Sincere thanks to all who helped make this book possible, my friends and family. Special thanks to my husband Rich for his generous support and great cooking. No one could ask for a better partner. And to my sister and nieces: Kristin, Melissa and Jessie Landau, for their support.

Thanks to all the wonderful people I have met in the dog world:
My agility teacher and friend, Helene Juice, Chance of a Lifetime Dog Training; my agility dog training buddies, Anne, Diane, Linda and Andrea. Without any of them, I would still be in dog kindergarten!

Thanks also to those who gave me advice or helpful information for this book:
Annie Brody (Camp Unleashed)
Dr. Katherine Houpt, DVM (Animal Behavior Clinic, Cornell University)
Leea Foran (Foranimals, Lenox, MA)
Sue Auger (Denali Obedience School)
Angella Avallone, (Bandit's Bathhouse)
Dr. Michelle Rosenbaum, DVM
Mitch Frankenburg, (Paw House Inn, Rutland, VT)
Judy Ostrow, author
Tom Paddock (Paddock Oriental Carpet)
Charles Lewis, AIA
Robert Eggleston, AIA.

Thanks to Barb Miller for editing early versions of the book and to Diane Doran for reading and editing the final version of the book.

And especially to all the dogs that I have shared my life with, past and present:
Heidi, Bogie, Bona, Max, Molly, Nellie, Sumo, Teddy, Mitzi, Maggie, Joey and Quinn. There is a special place in my heart for the three Dobermans I have been honored to live with, the best teachers and product testers in the world: Haiku, Willa and Lena. (Nancy Chwiecko)

Foreword

I was honored to be asked to write a short foreword to *There's a Dog in the House* by Nancy Chwiecko and Amy Fernandez. I had been familiar with Amy's meticulously researched and beautifully written books and essays, and I was not to be disappointed by her collaboration with interior designer and proud dog owner, Nancy Chwiecko. The authors have written a comprehensive and user-friendly guide to creating the very best domestic environment for our dogs. Every practical design option is considered, with in-depth research on a myriad of materials and their potential suitability for dogs, whether in small city apartments or big houses in the country.

These chapters, which range from such topics as dog behavioral issues, building maintenance and home repair and construction, reflect a deep understanding of animal behavior, balancing what dogs need and want with what is practical for today's homes. An extensive and detailed resource list is provided for each chapter.

This book is an impressive and comprehensive study of how we live with our dogs, their physical and emotional needs, and how we can create the best environment for a safe, healthy and happy life with them. *There's a Dog in the House* is an invaluable resource and a pleasure to read. It is a "must have" for those fortunate enough to enjoy the companionship of a dog.

WILLIAM SECORD

Introduction

ABOVE AND OPPOSITE The significance of the family dog is
reflected in these studio portraits taken between 1850 and 1910.
It is interesting to note that photographers commonly used
furniture as a prop for posing the dog.
Photos from the collection of Nancy Chwiecko

REALISTIC EXPECTATIONS

We love our homes and aspire to make them as comfortable and responsive to our needs as we can. Much of who we are is wrapped up in them. Increasingly we also desire to share this environment with our beloved dogs. It is estimated that upwards of 45 million US households now include one or more dogs. The challenge is to create an environment that fosters harmony with our dogs while respecting the different needs of people and pets. The fact that human and canine needs are generally compatible has been the basis for thousands of years of happy coexistence. But, the dog's role has changed. Today it is commonplace for our dogs to live in our homes, something that was highly unusual just 50 years ago. Dogs may have been provided with regular food and shelter in a barn, shed or dog house but they were rarely invited to share the comforts of our homes.

Today, dogs have moved into our lives on a very intimate level. They sit on our furniture, cuddle up in our beds, use our bathtubs, and sometimes dine at our tables. No longer the privilege of diminutive lapdogs, your Golden Retriever Molly or Rottweiler Max shares these comforts as well. Contracts from breeders, shelters and rescue groups routinely stipulate that dogs must be housed indoors, and from a cultural standpoint, treating your dog like a family member has become a sign of enlightened, compassionate ownership.

This change has led to better understanding of the human/canine bond, but it has created an entirely new set of co-habitation issues. We dream of living in perfect harmony with our pets, but dogs stubbornly cling to the idea of being dogs. As much as we love them, they shed, chew, mark territory, track in mud, and show no interest in the aesthetic or hygienic aspects of home design. A dog may patiently cooperate to have his feet wiped and dried before entering the house, but there is no sense in hoping for the day when he will perform this chore on his own in order to spare the new carpeting.

Many novice owners fondly imagine a peaceable kingdom with their pets politely sharing the comforts and amenities. This vision usually undergoes a drastic revision when reality clashes with imagination. Puppies have a knack for making that happen sooner rather than later. Trying to strike a balance between a puppy's curiosity and exuberance and your desire for an orderly home can lead to a radical reevaluation of ideal home design. This ideal home might have stainless steel furniture and concrete floors with a drain in the middle. The dog might enter the house through the canine equivalent of an automatic car wash for a rinse and wash cycle, then move to the next chamber to be dried, brushed and fluffed. There would be no chance to shake water everywhere and muddy paws would never touch the door frames, the windows or floors.

Wait a minute; this is starting to sound an awful lot like a kennel or a zoo! As a rule, dogs are quite adaptable and, since the time we dwelled in caves, they have been content as long as they are in our company. But living in a kennel is not the choice of most dogs or humans.

Should we design our homes to look like a kennel? Or a car wash?

BENEFITS OF DOG OWNERSHIP

Dogs will unquestionably modify your home environment. Is it worth it? Most dog owners would respond with an enthusiastic yes without hesitation. In the past 20 years numerous studies have confirmed the positive impact dog ownership has on human mental and physical health.

DOGS:
- can help lower blood pressure
- increase social interactions between humans

DOG OWNERS:
- have lower cholesterol levels
- especially the elderly, cope better with stress and are less lonely
- have a higher one-year survival rate following heart disease
- feel more secure and less afraid of becoming a victim of crime
- are more apt to engage in regular exercise
- who suffer from life threatening or chronic disease show a reduction in stress and depression and improved ability to cope

CHILDREN
- with dogs adjust better to serious illness and/or death of a parent
- with dogs learn compassion
- exposed to dogs during the first year of life have a lower frequency of allergies and asthma

Even without these documented benefits, many of us choose to share our homes with dogs simply because we relish their company.

GETTING IT RIGHT FROM THE START

Working with a professional can open up a world of design possibilities and innovative solutions. However, they are trained to evaluate these issues from a human perspective. It's up to you to critique their suggestions for feasibility in a home with dogs. Take the time to make your needs clear but always back this up with your own research and decisions. Someone unfamiliar with living with dogs can easily underestimate your needs or assume that you are exaggerating when you request certain design features.

For instance:
- Even small dogs can wreak havoc on gates or railings if they are not securely anchored to a structural element rather than drywall.
- Railings may need to be installed with the rails closer together than even building codes dictate to prevent small dogs and puppies from squeezing between the bars.
- A designer may assure you that a particular surface is durable or "easy to clean". But that term is relative. It may be durable if foot traffic consists of two or three people on a daily basis. Eight, sixteen or more dog feet running across it may have a different effect. Be prepared to research materials and ideas.
- Designers may not be aware of potential hazards of materials or furnishings. For example window treatment cords, even those that are cut or separated can wrap around a dog's leg or neck.
- Designers may not be aware of dog behavior that could create issues or problems. If your Rottie tends to have strong guardian response, glass doors and large picture windows are not going to make life easier.

In response to the growing interest in eco-friendly homes, many designers recommend replacing rugs or carpets with natural fibers such as cotton or sisal that are naturally dyed. While natural fibers sound better from an environmental perspective, unless they are organic, they will contain dangerous pesticides and processing chemicals. Natural dyes used to color them will run if they become wet.

See Resources for information on where to find an architect, interior designer or contractor.

HOME SECURITY

Dogs have protected hearth and home for thousands of years and this time honored reason is just as valid today. It doesn't matter what type of dog you have; or whether the dog has been trained for this job. Almost every dog will instinctively detect intruders and sound the alarm. Police, security experts and former burglars acknowledge that thieves routinely avoid homes with dogs and multiple dogs are most effective. A thief might consider subduing or diverting one dog, but very few will risk contending with multiple dogs. If you don't have the wherewithal to cope with five Dobermans, take heart. Two or three Toy Poodles are an equally effective deterrent.

EVALUATING PRODUCTS AND ELEMENTS

The importance of selecting appropriate materials, finishes, furniture and other interior products is critical to you and your dog's wellbeing. Interior products that are most appropriate will be compatible with your lifestyle, your environment, the type of home you live in, your family, pets and your job.

To achieve the most appropriate design solution for your home many criteria must be examined. They include cost, aesthetics, durability, maintenance, lifespan, health, safety, physical comfort, codes, regulations, and sustainability.

All of these criteria are easily understood, but a few of them jump to the forefront when sharing your home with a dog. Durability, maintenance and cost are probably high on the list of most dog owners. Health, safety and environmental considerations are increasingly important to dog owners.

Durability and lifespan are paramount considerations when designing a home with dogs in mind. Maintenance and cleaning might rank as the second most important criteria to dog owners. While many designers and manufacturers make claims about durable and maintenance free products, nothing lasts forever and everything needs maintenance. Dog owners appreciate elements that are easily cleaned, not easily destroyed, and look good for as long as they live in their home. Durable, long-lasting materials usually cost more initially, so it's important to recognize materials that will live up to their promise.

In recent years attention has focused on health and safety relative to the interiors of buildings. In the past most attention centered on fire safety and preventing injuries within the home. Fire safety is a big consideration because dogs may respond in unexpected ways to a fire. Inadequate home design also increases the odds that your dog might play a role in causing injuries like falling or tripping.

Sustainable design is a practice and philosophy meant to minimize our impact on the environment and to sustain the earth for future generations of all species. In order to be considered sustainable, designs should reflect a harmonious balance with the environment. For example building materials, finishes, furnishings and their by-products should:

- not deplete the earth's natural resources or endanger habitat
- be free of hazardous substances that are introduced into the ground, water or air
- result in minimal or zero waste
- not threaten or burden future generations (ex., toxic chemicals or excessive landfill contributions)
- be reduced, reused, and/or recycled

Many products are now certified as sustainable to help ease the selection process. And luckily, there are many guides available that help address these issues.

The Resources at the end of the book contains valuable information on where to find specific items or information found throughout the book. It is conveniently listed by chapter.

CHAPTER 1

The Logistics of Living with *Canis familiaris*

Dogs happily and comfortably live in the messiest household as long as their basic needs are satisfied. But you must be honest about what you are willing to deal with. No matter what you read or hear, a dog is going to change your life. These changes are generally positive but some are more challenging including: damage to your possessions, disruption in your routine, or changes in your home territory. Realistically, you can look forward to sharing a satisfying home environment with your perfect canine soul mate as long as you are willing to do some advance research. Preparing for a harmonious life with the canine species includes finding the right dog and understanding canine behavior.

Needless to say, good grooming, training and socialization will minimize many potential cohabitation issues but the first rule of creating a happy human/canine living space is to choose your dog wisely. Yes, it is possible to keep a pack of Great Danes in a studio apartment and raise Chinese Cresteds in Alaska. But arrangements like this require a substantial commitment and tremendous modifications to your lifestyle. Whether you are looking for your first dog or already own one, knowing what to expect from a particular breed or mixed-breed will help determine some specific design requirements.

IDENTIFY YOUR DESIGN CHALLENGES
- Can your home and lifestyle accommodate your dog of choice?
- Do you own your house or rent it?
- How much time do you spend at home?
- How large is your home?
- Are you a fanatical housekeeper?
- Does your home's style reflect this behavior?
- Would some areas be off limits to the dog?
- Is the rest of your family equally interested in having a dog?

All dogs share some basic care requirements that are bound to impact your home environment. Adequate room to run and play is only one canine space requirement. Some breeds may require pricey modifications to your living space such as air conditioning, double fencing, a bigger, less economical car to transport them, or a fully equipped grooming area.

BEHAVIORAL DESIGN CONSIDERATIONS
A dog's physical needs are hard to overlook but mental needs often have a far greater impact on daily life. A large portion of training is directed towards discouraging normal dog behaviors like barking, jumping, digging, and chasing.

Breeds with strong instincts to hunt, herd, or guard will display behaviors associated with these jobs. For example, a Miniature Dachshund may seem like an ideal choice for a senior citizen. But Dachshunds are hunters. They are alert and vigilant which translates to a strong propensity to bark, chase and dig. Instincts can be modified and redirected through training but they cannot be eradicated from a dog's brain. Proactive, effective design offers the best solutions for both dog and owner. Every breed has its own particular suite of instinctive and normal behaviors such as guarding, barking and predation. Normal behaviors often quickly turn into

Dogs, like humans, vary in their tolerance for dirt. Some breeds, like the Doberman Pinscher and Shiba Inu are known for fastidious habits. If you are a meticulous housekeeper, you will be happiest with a breed that is equally fussy and clean. And it goes without saying that breeds known to drool, shed, and track in copious amounts of dirt will not be a good match for your lifestyle.

nuisance behaviors if we allow it. Many of the behaviors that regularly lead to problems can be effectively managed by good home design. See Chapter 12 for design solutions for behavior problems.

SOCIAL BEHAVIOR

Dogs need grooming, exercise, training, and health care, all of which pale in comparison to their need for companionship. Although the concept of pack mentality is often misunderstood or used to justify a good deal of human and canine misbehavior, it is essential to canine happiness. Recognizing this psychological need makes it far easier to understand many dog behaviors and effectively address them through home design. Pack behavior is a survival system that depends on strict adherence to cooperative strategies for procuring food, defending territory, and raising young. Domestication altered or eliminated the need for most of this behavior, but not the underlying triggers. Dog packs lack the definitive structure of wolf society because dogs rarely need to worry about survival. It may be obsolete but dogs remain pathologically attached to this ancestral security blanket. Puppies always sleep in a pile, and this preference usually carries over into adulthood. Dogs pile together and maintain physical contact even when this sleeping arrangement is uncomfortable, and the best spot is always near their pack leader. This explains why it is difficult to discourage dogs from sleeping in bed with their owners. While this arrangement is common with modern dog owners, they often fail to recognize it as a source of competition in multiple dog homes.

In addition to the challenges posed by a human home environment, domestic dog packs usually include multiple species, (i.e. dogs, humans, cats) and very often, more than one dominant individual. Despite simplified media portrayals of canine pack behavior, it remains hard to define. For instance, in a multiple dog home one dog may be in charge of defending the territorial perimeter of the backyard and another may step in to supervise during mealtime. Status may be contingent on which room of the house they are in, or which article of furniture they happen to be lying on. This arrangement may be complicated but canine society is usually calm, although the reasons for this may be difficult to accept from a human standpoint. Unlike us, dogs have no desire for individuality or independence. They comfortably occupy subordinate roles within our hodgepodge group of humans and animals as long as they feel assured of the security and stability signified by pack acceptance. A stable home environment is a key part of this, but most of all, successfully living with a dog requires a commitment to integrate him into your daily life.

It may be simpler to relegate your dog to a backyard, kennel or dog room but you and your dog will pay the price as he develops maladaptive strategies to cope with the resulting insecurity, loneliness and boredom. In addition to social needs a wide range of canine motivations and needs stem from instincts. These vary by breed but they should be a major consideration when choosing a dog and designing an appropriate shared living space.

While dog professionals often have 10 or more dogs, there seems to be a threshold for the number of dogs that individual humans can tolerate in the average household. Statistics indicate that nearly 75 million dogs live in American households. Many homes have 2 or more dogs in them. Most municipalities have a cap on the number of dogs allowed; often that number is 3 or 4.

CANINE SENSES AND PERCEPTIONS

When given the choice, dogs will select and modify specific areas of their territory for sleeping, eating and eliminating. Every dog is territorial to some extent, but they react to spaces in very distinct ways based on a combination of early training, socialization and breed specific sensory patterns. Large open and empty spaces may make some dogs uncomfortable. Others don't like small enclosed spaces and become noticeably agitated when they are placed in a crate or asked to go through an agility tunnel. Every dog has quirks but design solutions will be far more effective if they address the parameters of the canine senses as well as your dog's individual personality.

VISION

Our most critical perceptions of our environment come via sight. It's therefore difficult to refrain from evaluating canine design elements this way. Human and canine eyes are designed for very different functions. Our vision accommodates the fact that we are most active in the daytime. Canine vision is great for its original use, finding and catching prey. Dogs have excellent ability to spot movement and incredibly good night vision. Most experts agree that dogs can see colors in the yellow, blue and gray wavelengths. This would be similar to a human with red-green colorblindness, meaning that the red would be seen as yellow, green as white and blue/green or blue/red as grey. They also have less than one tenth of our ability to focus on objects and discern detail. This varies by breed but most dogs can only see at 20 feet what a person might be able to see easily at 75 feet. Because they have trouble focusing at close range they may not notice something on the floor in front of them unless they smell it or it moves. They compensate by using their noses and paws to investigate small objects.

The dog's skull shape provides a much wider field of vision which aids in seeing both predators and prey. A wider field of vision sacrifices a dog's binocular vision, making their depth perception more limited than ours. But the biggest difference to keep in mind is the canine vantage point. Even the tallest dog will see your home from a very different perspective than you do. Vision is an important design consideration, but from a canine perspective, other senses are far more critical.

HEARING

Compared to us, dogs have excellent hearing. They detect faint sounds, higher frequencies and can localize sounds far better than humans. This poses design challenges that are often underestimated. Dogs bark at things our ears cannot detect. For instance, you may not notice the rusty squeak every time your front gate is unlatched because your attention is drawn to your dog's ballistic barking to warn you of a possible intruder. Sneaking around the house is also nearly impossible if there is a dog in residence. They respond instantly to significant household sounds like the tinkle of car keys and the hum of the can opener.

SMELL

Dogs are born with only two well developed senses, touch and smell. Their sense of smell is their primary means of learning and communicating and this remains true throughout their lives. The canine olfactory sense is far superior to anything we can imagine and definitely deserves more attention from the perspective of canine home design. Understanding the olfactory sense from a canine point of view helps us to select appropriate finishes, remove odor trapping items and recognize environmental lures that may encourage certain behaviors.

Smell profoundly influences every aspect of a dog's behavior especially his relationship to the environment. Selective breeding has produced variations in dogs' visual and auditory acuity as well as individual reliance on these senses. Despite these differences, all dogs are olfactory communicators. Their sense of smell is estimated to be 100,000 times greater than our own. They can analyze odors and pick out one particular scent among many, and detect minute dilutions of odors. Some breeds, like Bloodhounds, have been selectively bred to have an especially keen olfactory sense, but from a human perspective, it is difficult to imagine this sense on any level.

We notice when something smells bad in our home, especially if it happens to be dog related, and our major efforts are geared towards eradicating these odors from the environment. Dogs perceive odors from a completely different perspective. They use their noses to navigate, communicate and understand their environment in a very detailed way. They also rely on this sense to learn far more about us than we realize.

Because they are built to receive and process so much olfactory information, their perceptions about the world are constructed primarily from information and memories of smells, similar to the way that our brains retain visual images. The number of olfactory receptors in the canine brain is comparable to the number of visual receptors in a human brain. They not only spend a lot of time seeking and analyzing scents, they devote considerable effort to producing them. Keep this in mind when you invite a canine to share your living space.

Dogs possess skin, scent and sweat glands that produce a variety of odor-packed oily and watery secretions. These glands are distributed all over their bodies, especially on the head and face, around the base of the tail and on their feet. Their location provides a lot of insight into characteristic canine behaviors, such as the propensity for vigorously rubbing their heads and feet on the furniture (or you). This is not entirely an affectionate gesture. It's a means of delineating territory.

Olfactory signals have the advantage of being species-specific. They are always uniform, instantly recognizable within the species but unrecognizable to outsiders (like us). They are also extremely message-specific. Unlike visual and auditory signals, olfactory signals diffuse slowly through the environment. They cannot be immediately turned on or off, and their message lingers long after any encounter. This makes them especially suitable for communicating territorial boundaries. It will also vastly complicate housetraining if you are not careful about cleaning up all traces of urine odor after your dog has an accident. These scents also explain why well mannered dogs suddenly begin marking their territory like graffiti artists when they detect an unwelcome visitor.

Faint traces of urine odor provide ongoing temptation for territorial leg lifting. Although dogs will instinctively keep their small den area clean, they have an equally strong impulse to saturate their territory with their own scent. They will repeatedly mark spots with a familiar scent, and will also target new or unfamiliar objects in their territory. From a canine perspective, peeing on anything with an alien smell including a brand new rug or chair is an appropriate security measure. After the new item has been in your house for a few days, it absorbs scent molecules from the environment and the scent marking urge will wane. On the other hand, if you are not vigilant and the dog manages to repeatedly mark a new item it may become a habitual target thanks to the smell.

Underestimating the extent to which dogs are influenced by this sense also leads us to overlook the role of food as a behavioral trigger. If your dog is easily aroused by food smells, being in the kitchen can cause an adrenaline rush. Another common problem is dumpster diving. Dogs learn new habits in many ways but operant conditioning is high on the list. The urge to investigate is rooted in their survival instinct. Sniffing something interesting in the garbage and tipping it over to find last week's moldy ham sandwich is comparable to hitting the jackpot in Vegas. Like gambling addicts, most dogs only need one good payoff to start this cycle. Hiding the trash is rarely effective. Never underestimate a dog's ability to sniff out concealed items. Frequent emptying of garbage and paying close attention to where food and garbage are stored will reduce foraging behaviors.

TASTE

In contrast to their sense of smell, the canine sense of taste is very weak. Dogs have only about one sixth the taste buds of a human. Most are clustered at the tip of the tongue and it is estimated that three quarters of them stop functioning by age ten. This helps to explain their willingness to taste and consume strange things. A moldy sandwich is not the ideal diet but it is fairly benign compared to some of the things that dogs eat. They have fatally ingested bones, knives, forks, aluminum foil, scouring pads, corncobs, coins, jewelry, and medications to name a few. Four paws and a nose low to the ground puts them in close contact with the world around them but the canine method of tactile exploration is quite different from ours. The canine equivalent of human fingertips is the tongue. If a dog wants to thoroughly investigate an interesting surface, this is the tool that comes out of the toolbox. Needless to say, this can lead to quite a bit of trouble. Preventing accidental consumption of dangerous items is a major part of puppy-proofing, but for many dogs, it becomes a lifetime challenge. Curiosity can lure dogs to lick and chew novel surfaces and textures. Nubby wool upholstery is often recommended as a good choice for pet owners, but it can also be a magnet for a curious dog. Many are also obsessed with licking interesting finishes off of wood furniture or peeling textured wallpaper. Tassels and fringe are universally irresistible. If you have design features like this in your home keep an eye on them when your dog arrives. If you already have a dog, you may want to avoid adding them.

TOUCH

This sense is easier to relate to because dogs and humans respond in much the same way. We find touch equally pleasurable. Puppies use their tactile sense to maintain contact with their littermates and their dam from the moment of birth. Most dogs never lose this survival based fondness for physical contact, using it to reaffirm their connection to their pack. Some enjoy it so much that they will seek it out, to the point of becoming a nuisance, known as attention seeking behavior. This is easily avoided if we are cognizant of its reward value. That can be difficult because many of us get into the habit of petting our dogs to calm our nerves and relieve stress.

Dogs also use their front paws to investigate, which can be mistaken for touching. The sensitivity of the canine paw is nowhere near that of the human hand. If a dog wants to manipulate an object he usually uses his nose. But many dogs are capable of using their paws in impressive ways to investigate the environment and this must also be kept in mind when designing. Dogs with long legs and hare feet, (more elongated paws) can be incredibly skilled at grabbing objects, opening doors, and scaling fences. If your dog has an inquisitive mind paired with these anatomical advantages, you may want to avoid certain types of fixtures, fencing or hardware.

Dogs are built for competitive eating. Their digestive tract, from one end to the other is designed to accommodate huge amounts of food as quickly as possible, digest it rapidly, and if necessary, fast for long periods until the next meal arrives. Compared to us, dogs have a poorly developed sense of taste and savoring their food is never the primary goal of a meal. Their teeth are designed to grab and tear rather than chew, and the muscular canine esophagus sends large chunks of partly chewed food on to the stomach. This increases the possibility of ingesting foreign objects but dogs can also vomit at will. Their internal philosophy tells them to eat first, think later and this reflexive ability provides one level of protection against bad food decisions. But it will not protect an insatiable dog from everything he might encounter in the average home. That is your job.

CHAPTER 2

What the Dog Needs and Wants

Designing spaces for living with our dogs should mirror the methods used to design spaces for human habitation. Design is a problem solving process that begins with two basic questions: What do you need? And what do you want?

Since we can't ask our dogs these questions we must rely on observation, experience and creative imagination. Creative exercises such as envisioning the space from the dog's perspective is not only fun; they help you to better understand your dog. How does your dog see, smell, hear and feel the environment from his vantage point? What temptations are in his range? What obstacles block his path? What dangers does he face in his home environment? These are some of the issues that shape the homes we share with our dogs.

Designing your home to accommodate both species sounds great but where do you begin? The easiest solution is to start from scratch in order to perfectly accommodate this complicated range of needs for both. This might include radiant heat in the floor, central vacuuming, electrical outlets placed high on the walls, good lighting and plenty of windows for natural light and ventilation, a laundry sink or raised bathtub for grooming, outdoor faucets with hot and cold water and at least one separate entry leading to a secure enclosure. And that's just for starters.

Of course, for most of us, reality is quite a bit different. We have already chosen a living space, moved in, customized and decorated, and then decided to share it with one or more dogs.

WHAT DOES YOUR DOG SEE AND SMELL?
Dogs see our homes from a completely different physical perspective. There may be temptations, obstacles and dangers that we don't see from our vantage point.

The image of the hearth on the right is at eye level for a small dog, while the view of the stove at left is what a 20" high dog might see.

This is somewhat more challenging but good design can help, provided you are willing to participate in the process. You can become aware of new materials and design solutions by simply taking the time to notice them. The next time you visit your vet's office check out the materials and ask some questions. For example, if the flooring looks good, ask how long it has been there and how easy it is to maintain?

Like any roommate, dogs move in with plenty of stuff and immediately start revising your routine and your home unless you step up to the plate first. Effective home design makes your life comfortable and enjoyable. Your dog care routine should fit seamlessly into this goal. You need to address a few key elements to make this possible. "How, where and when" should be decided for every aspect of your dog's routine before you bring him home. This schedule always needs a bit of tinkering, but a dog is guaranteed to turn your home into chaos if you jump into this project without a plan. The primary issues are feeding, sleeping, eliminating, grooming, exercise, and mental stimulation. If you have done your breed specific research, you have some concept of what is needed for each aspect of routine care. Lastly, you will need appropriate storage for all of your dog related items. For specific information on design ideas and how to manage your home environment refer to subsequent chapters.

FEEDING

Smart feeding combines optimum nutrition, economy, convenience, and reinforcement of desired canine behavior. This doesn't happen automatically. Good eating habits result from good health, good training, and a good environment. The number of daily feedings changes throughout a dog's life. A puppy may need to be fed three or four times daily. By adulthood this may be cut back to one or two meals, and again readjusted to meet the changing nutritional needs of a senior dog. Regardless of the schedule, every routine involves storage, preparation, consumption and clean up.

Dogs do best if fed controlled amounts at specific times rather than having constant access to food. Regulating the time and amount makes it easier to control your dog's weight and monitor his overall health. Meal time can also be used as a training opportunity to reinforce good behavior.

FEEDING MANAGEMENT

Feeding multiple dogs requires more time, space, and food and most importantly good leadership. Different size dogs may require different quantities of the same food, different combinations of kibble and canned food, or special supplements. This can literally turn into a free-for-all canine brawl by the time the food is ready. Mealtime can be a cause of serious dog fights but an effective pack leader can orchestrate a communal dinner without problems. The simplest solution is to feed them separately. Put each dog in a separate room or crate before you start preparing the food and don't let them out until you have picked up the empty dishes. Pay attention to their behavior as they eat. A dog may leave half of his food because he is intimidated, not because he is full. While most dogs wolf

IS YOUR DOG FRIGHTENED OF CLIMBING STAIRS?
Stairs can be intimidating for any dog. Some have more difficulty going down, while others have trouble going up. The photos above are both taken from the approximate eye level of a toy dog. At this height stairs can be as imposing as the ancient temple stairs at Angkor Wat in Cambodia, shown immediately above.

down their food, some dogs eat very slowly, especially seniors, disabled dogs or puppies.

DOG DISHES

Dishes for food and water should be durable and easy to clean. Heavy ceramic or weighted dishes are more spill resistant but a young child or elderly adult may have trouble carrying a large ceramic bowl to fill or clean it. The best choice is stainless steel. It travels well and can be used indoors or outdoors. Keep in mind that metal bowls tend to heat up more quickly in the sun, and a dog's tongue can freeze to metal in winter. Stainless steel dishes are available in heavier weights and designer colors. A rubber rim on the bottom will help prevent the dish from sliding around as the dog eats but these rubber rims are not securely attached and can melt into a disgusting gooey mess in the dishwasher. A better option is to place a rubber mat under the bowl.

Glass and ceramic bowls are chosen by dog owners because they are aesthetically pleasing and heftier than stainless steel. If you choose either buy only those that are labeled food and microwave safe. Neither may tolerate freezing temperatures. Glass and ceramic bowls are breakable. An excited dog can easily break one and more than one dog has been rushed to the emergency room from a laceration caused by a broken dish. Collapsible, portable bowls made from plastic or nylon lined with plastic are handy for travel. They can be easily stored in a purse, backpack or glove compartment in your car. Before packing for a trip confirm that your dog willingly eats and drinks from them. If you have space, his customary bowls are preferable.

The value of raised dishes to prevent gastric torsion (bloat) has been discounted by recent research. However they may be useful for dogs with throat, neck, back or joint problems. If a feeding platform is the right choice for your dog options range from custom wood or metal versions to a simple overturned plastic dishpan. The platform should be sturdy with a non-slip surface or recessed spaces to hold the bowls securely. The bowl should be removable and all parts easily cleaned. If the platform was recommended by your vet ask her what the best height would be but in general it should be between the bottom of the chest and base of the neck.

Plastic bowls have become very common in the past 20 years. They are inexpensive, lightweight and fairly durable but:

- Plastic is not uniformly food safe—use only plastic bowls designated as such.
- Some breeds can develop contact dermatitis from plastic dishes leading to fading pigment of the nose.
- Plastic is inevitably chewed or scratched. Dogs can ingest pieces of chewed plastic and scratches retain bacteria, causing sanitation problems.

The pets in this household have fresh water on demand. The HDuo™ unit can be seen in the back corner of this kitchen.
Courtesy of The Livable Home Store: www.thelivablehomestore.com

WATER

Your dog's water should come from the same clean, potable source as your drinking water. Water should be available to a dog at all times. A thirsty dog will not hesitate to drink out of muddy puddles, birdbaths, toilets, or a pond and ingest toxic biological agents and chemicals.

Automatic watering systems range from bubbler-stop devices, to those that can be hooked up to your water system. One simple type consists of a large bottle of water inverted on a stand and water is fed by gravity into the dog bowl. This is inexpensive, but large water bottles can be difficult to manage. More complicated on demand watering systems can be attached to either outdoor hose bibs or indoor plumbing. This may require a plumber.

The simplest on demand system is a drip water bottle which hangs upside down on the side of a pen or crate. The dog accesses water by touching the end with their tongue. Many dogs must be trained to drink from a drip water bottle. During weaning, puppies are taught to drink water by their mother. Typically they learn to lap water from a dish. However, generations of commercially raised dogs often do not have the opportunity to learn this skill because the cages are fitted with water bottles. Keep this in mind if you bring home a pet shop puppy. The fact that water is available does not guarantee that the puppy knows how to drink from a dish. For more on clean drinking water see Chapter 4.

SLEEPING

Dogs have long known what we all suspect, sleep is essential to health and happiness. They spend a good deal of time sleeping or reclining. This varies by breed, age, weather, and activity level but averages about 14 hours per day. Your dog will need a safe, comfortable space for daytime lounging and nighttime sleeping.

New dogs and puppies should be confined at night for safety. Unless you plan for this, you can find yourself living with a nocturnal rambler. Dogs sleep in cycles: 16 minutes asleep, five minutes awake. The canine sleep cycle normally includes more frequent but shorter periods of wakefulness than humans. However, dogs easily adapt to our sleeping schedules. Most puppies object to the idea of sleeping alone and/or sleeping through the night. Acceptance usually includes some protesting for the first few nights. These issues can be minimized if you place the puppy's crate or pen near your bed. You may lose a night or two of sleep but it will provide reassurance and help him adapt more quickly.

A recent AKC survey shows that 21 percent of dog owners have their dogs sleep in bed with them. Sleeping with dogs for warmth has been documented in many cultures for centuries. Dogs and humans have coevolved to perfect this arrangement for thousands of years. In Mexico, Central and South America, sleeping with hairless dogs was a means of keeping warm without the benefit of central heating or warding off malaria when the mosquitoes feasted on the dogs instead. Today, comfort and companionship are the main motivations and with a little planning, this is possible for all parties involved. For more on beds and crates refer to Chapter 7.

Many owners are tempted to take a new puppy to bed but this can be dangerous unless you are a light sleeper. Even a large puppy can be smothered by a human rolling over on top of him or injured if accidentally knocked off of the bed. Until he is trained a puppy will wake often during the night for bathroom breaks. Unless you wake up to deal with this, you may find an unwelcome surprise on the bed.

ELIMINATION

Dogs are naturally reluctant to soil their sleeping area but that is the extent of their instinct in that department. When confronted with wider territory the natural canine inclination is to thoroughly scent mark everything. Discouraging this desire is one example of how training can override natural instinct. The difficulty in accomplishing this varies but sensible home design will always make the job easier. For ideas on indoor and outdoor dog potties see Chapter 8.

There is no right or wrong housetraining method. Any method can be effective from dog doors to paper training as long as you follow a few simple rules. These apply to all dogs introduced to a new home regardless of age.

- Put the dog on a consistent feeding and elimination schedule.
- Restrict access to most of your home.
- Supervise like a hawk to prevent accidents from happening.
- Crate or confine the dog when unsupervised.
- Never punish a dog for mistakes.
- Always reward the dog immediately for eliminating in the proper location.
- Clean up accidents immediately and thoroughly.

DOG WASTE

Picking up dog poop is not a glamorous job but it is necessary. Dog waste on lawns, roads, sidewalks, driveways and in parks will eventually mix with rain water and end up in ground water and surface water such as rivers and lakes. One Maltese may not seem like a public health issue but consider the math for 75 million dogs on a daily basis and you can begin to understand the outcome. Approximately 20,000 tons of dog waste is produced every day. Total quantities of dog waste every year is measured in millions of tons.

In addition to polluting water, dog waste can harbor parasites and attract insects which can transmit diseases like cryptosporidiosis, giardiasis, and salmonellosis. Dog waste can be harmful to plants due to its high nitrogen content. From a more immediate standpoint, dog waste also contributes to odors, and can be a general nuisance if stepped in.

SCOOP IT

Pooper scoopers and poop bags are the simplest method for collecting dog waste. There are several basic types of pooper scoopers. The easiest to use is a two part system with a flat shovel and a scooped shovel or rake. Tong-like scoopers that are permanently connected are more difficult to use. Single scooper rakes or shovels are easier to carry but still require something to push the poop onto the scooper. Metal clean up tools are more durable than plastic scoops and rakes. Look for inexpensive, lightweight aluminum tools with long handles. Hanging them off the ground can help keep them out of a child's or another dog's reach. They don't have to be sterilized but they should be soaked in disinfecting solution or periodically rinsed and air dried to remove residual waste or they will attract flies.

Poop bag choices range from plastic food storage bags, biodegradable and flushable bags made for dog waste and more complicated drawstring style bags that can be held under the dog as he eliminates. Whatever type of bag you use the process is simple: turn it inside out, place it on your hand like a glove, turn it right side out and the poop is in the bag. Food storage bags are most commonly used but biodegradable bags that can be composted, buried or thrown away in your garbage are a more responsible choice. If dog waste is placed in a regular plastic bag and sent to a landfill it could, conceivably, remain entombed there for a long time.

FLUSH IT

The environmentally preferred way to deal with dog waste is to flush it down a toilet into a septic system or sewage treatment plant. The solution is fine if you have one small dog, trained to use an indoor elimination system. The waste produced by three dogs on a daily basis makes it difficult to handle in this manner unless you have a bathroom with outdoor access. Flushable poop bags make this process easier.

DIGEST IT

A more practical compromise is a mini septic system designed for dog waste. Waste is deposited in a covered container buried in the ground and mixed with water and enzymes to hasten decay. The waste decomposes and is reduced to a harmless, nutritious, organic liquid that leaches from holes in the sides and/or bottom of the container into the surrounding soil. Digester liquids must be added through the top periodically. Systems installed in clay and hard packed soils should be modified by placing the digester in a much larger hole and surrounding it with gravel and sand, similar to a raised bed septic system. In cold climates with temperatures under 40°F, digester use will be restricted to warmer months. DIY digesters can be made utilizing a large lidded plastic diaper pail or garbage can. Drill holes in the sides and completely cut out the bottom. Dig a hole deep enough to cover the can with only a couple of inches exposed at the top. Place gravel in the bottom, put the can in, put more gravel in and you are ready to go. You may need to add sawdust or chopped straw to aid in decomposition. It's best to place the digester in an out of way place. For multiple dogs you may need more than one digester.

BURY IT

The key to burying dog waste is to bury it within the most biologically active top layer of soil, 5″ to 12″ deep. Don't place it near water sources, vegetable or fruit gardens and children's play areas.

COMPOST IT

Composting dog waste is an idea that is promoted in areas of the world where dog waste is a major problem. In urban areas dog waste often ends up in the landfill or in urban parks and can create potential health hazards. Dog waste compost should never be used on fruit or vegetable gardens but it can be used for other plants.

> Fairbanks, Alaska is a small city with a big problem. With over 20,000 dogs, what to do with dog waste that was thrown in the landfill or rivers seemed an insurmountable problem. The city conducted research on large scale composting of dog waste and determined that it is possible to safely compost dog waste.

The concept of composting is very simple: combine a nitrogen source with a carbon source and periodically mix it. To make compost from dog waste the formula combines dog waste (nitrogen source) with sawdust or chopped straw (carbon source). This process will require a lot of dog waste to work properly. Otherwise you will have to add additional nitrogen,

This mini-digester is meant to be buried with only the lid showing above ground. *Courtesy of Doggie Dooley: www.doggiedooley.com*

such as grass clippings, to the mixture. The process can take place in a bin or hole approximately 3′h x 3′w x 3′l. Several companies make composting units that handle dog waste.

TOSS IT

Despite the fact that many municipalities do not permit the disposal of dog waste in trash collection systems, it is probably the most common disposal method. This is a dilemma because dog waste is a health hazard if disposed of in a landfill, but most municipalities do not provide an alternative solution. For this reason these laws are rarely enforced. If you live in an apartment, condo or urban setting with a small yard, you won't be able to bury it, or use a digester, but an indoor composting unit is a viable option.

Some cities have implemented a separate pick up for dog waste and permit the use of biodegradable bags. This trash will end up in a separate facility where it can safely decompose or be composted. A few cities have adopted the use of dog toilet stations with bags meant to be used in parks and public areas where people walk their dogs. The trash can then be kept separate and sent to separate facilities. The potential for large scale composting with this trash is also possible.

DOG WASTE REMOVAL COMPANIES

Dog waste removal services now exist in many urban areas. For a fee they clean up your yard on a daily, weekly or monthly basis. Most advertise on-line or have listings in the phone book.

TYPE	SMOOTH	SHORTHAIR	COMBINA-TION	DOUBLE COAT	LONGHAIR	WIRE	CURLY
BREED EXAMPLES	Miniature Pinscher Greyhound	Beagles Labrador Retriever	Cocker Spaniel Newfoundland	Pomeranian Samoyed	Maltese Afghan Hound	Jack Russell Fox Terrier	Poodle Bichon Frise
DESCRIPTION	Flat, Fine Variable Undercoat	Smooth, Sleek, Hard	Short on head and legs, slightly longer, thicker on body and profuse on chest, neck, ears, abdomen and tail.	Harsh outer coat, soft dense undercoat.	Fine with very little undercoat	Ranges from shaggy to flat and hard	Curly, low density
LENGTH	Short up to ½"	Short to 1"+	Varies	Varies	1"+	Varies	Medium to long
SHEDDING	Continuous	Continuous	Seasonal, loses abundant undercoat twice a year	Seasonal, loses abundant undercoat twice a year	Minimal	Minimal	Minimal
OILY	Minimal	Yes	Yes	Yes	No	No	No
GRIME/ODOR	None	Yes/Yes	Yes/Yes	No/Yes	No/No*	No/No	No/No**
BRUSHING FREQUENCY	Weekly	Weekly	Daily to weekly	Daily is best	Daily is best	Weekly***	Frequently
WEATHER PROTECTION	Minimal—need to be indoors more	Resistant to heat, cold and damp	Resistant to cold and damp. Heavier coats not heat tolerant	Maximum insulation	Minimal—need to be indoors more	Protective and dirt repelling	Harsh, curly coats will repel water and dirt. Cottony coats are dirt magnets
OTHER		Stiff fur difficult to remove from upholstery	Fur will mat, attract dirt and debris. Heavily coated feet track substantial dirt	Seasonal shedding can become year round if kept indoors	Dead fur remains trapped in the coat and eventually throughout your house	If clipped, wire coats soften and attract dirt and moisture more easily	Coat texture attracts dirt. These breeds are often thought of as hypo-allergenic

* Coat will collect dirt without frequent bathing

** Odor if not washed. Coat will attract dirt without frequent grooming

*** Require plucking or stripping to retain dirt repelling texture

**** Brushed and bathed frequently, trimmed every 4 to 6 weeks

Dog urine does not pose the logistical problems of solid waste removal but it will damage shrubbery, erode fence posts, attract bees and can create odor buildup. Dogs tend to favor specific spots and this can exacerbate these problems. To avoid brown spots in your lawn hose the area with water frequently to minimize damage.

GROOMING

A clean healthy dog, regardless of breed, should never have a detectable odor. Keeping your dog clean also makes for a cleaner home and this is especially important if your dog climbs on the sofa or sleeps in bed with you. If your home or your dog has a doggy odor, don't bother running out for the latest magic cleaning solution. Concentrate on keeping your dog cleaner or identifying the source of the problem through a veterinary exam.

Every dog requires regular grooming. Some breeds need only a few minutes per week to look good. Others require more due to their coat or physical structure. For instance, longhaired dogs may need to have their head coat tied up or trimmed.

Brachycephalic (short muzzled) breeds like Pugs and Bulldogs need their face wrinkles washed daily. Wirehaired and curly coated breeds require plucking or trimming in addition to brushing. Most owners start out grooming their puppy on the kitchen counter or coffee table. As the puppy grows and the job gets more complicated this arrangement becomes less convenient. It often leads to neglecting this chore. Make your life easier, and set up a doggy beauty shop at home. For more on appropriate bathing sinks, tubs and faucets see Chapters 4 and 8. To design an entire groom-room see Chapter 9.

Shedding is the biggest housecleaning challenge for most dog owners. Grooming can help keep shedding under control. Dog fur ranges from short to long, flat to dense, and coarse to silky. The appearance of a coat can give a misleading impression about its potential upkeep.

EXERCISE AND PLAY

Your dog's exercise needs and activity level will impact your home in many ways. All dogs need exercise but the amount and variety will be dictated by age, breed and size. Thanks to their boundless energy and curiosity, puppies tend to keep themselves well exercised and the biggest problem is safety. A fenced yard is a great way to get your dog outside on days when your time is limited, but this is not a solution that works equally well for all breeds.

Obviously the location of your home becomes more critical if your dog requires hours of daily outdoor exercise. Traditionally, it was assumed that every dog would be blissfully happy if given the opportunity to live on a farm or run freely. While some breeds need substantial daily outdoor activity, many do not. Dogs really do sleep 14 hours a day, including many breeds that are traditionally considered working dogs. On the other hand, many canine behavior problems are simply due to insufficient daily exercise. If these needs are met, the dog will be a model tenant.

Certain breeds are programmed to remain energetic and vigilant for a long period, but don't assume this based solely on size and working description. For instance, a Beauceron is expected to be on his feet working intensively for an eight hour stretch. No amount of training can override this instinct. A Pekingese is the classic example of a breed that is well adapted to a sedentary lifestyle. A Peke will relish his daily walk and happily spend the rest of the day quietly guarding his home. Superficially, a Pomeranian would seem to be equally well suited to that lifestyle. However, the Pom is descended from a large all purpose farm dog. They are reactive, energetic, hardy and a far cry from a Peke in terms of energy level.

Just like us, many dogs need motivation to keep fit as they get older. The time honored method is taking the dog out on a leash for walks. Depending on your dog's energy level this can range from once to several times daily lasting fifteen minutes to two hours.

If you have a dog with abundant energy, you may need to find someone to help manage his daily exercise needs such as hiring a dog walker, enrolling your dog in a daycare program or play group, or participating in dog sports.

Some dogs are very active indoors and, once again, size is never a reliable indicator. To a great extent, reactivity and energy levels are regulated biochemically. A breed's indoor activity level can have an enormous impact on your daily life and home design challenges. Working breeds like Mastiffs and Doberman Pinschers are active as puppies, but tend to settle down considerably as they mature. They are genetically programmed to be quiet and watchful guards. On the other hand, many terriers like the Jack Russell Terrier are constantly on the move. They are programmed to relentlessly search for vermin. Without adequate daily activity, this can translate into a companion that endlessly patrols your home, digs up flower beds, and barks out the window to alert you of every passing car.

If you have a backyard, a garage, a basement or even an extra bedroom, you have the potential to create a canine play area. This will not only encourage your dog to exercise, it reinforces the bond between you and your dog. An indoor play area can be the ideal solution when it's too hot, cold or wet outside. It can be valuable space if you are training a performance dog year round.

STORAGE

If your canine family grows or you become interested in one of the many dog related activities such as agility or flyball, you may find yourself dealing with an expanding collection of grooming supplies, training equipment and sundries. Attempting to consolidate dog paraphernalia is a common storage problem, often resulting in a hodgepodge of important grooming and training items for different dogs jumbled together. No one does this intentionally, but organization is challenging. You won't feel the real impact until an emergency arises and you find yourself madly sorting through old squeaky toys and dog brushes for an important medication or conversely searching for the essential squeaky in a minefield of dog coats. This problem grows exponentially unless you implement workable storage solutions from the get go.

The secret is the Principal of First Use Storage. Items should be stored according to how they are used and how often they are used. Rather than storing an item by a specific category or group it should be placed near where it will be used. For example, instead of devoting an entire closet to dog supplies, store grooming supplies in a drawer in the bathroom, medications and food in the pantry, leashes and collars in the entry closet, toys in the play room, and agility equipment in a storage shed. Items that are used most often deserve storage space that is more accessible. For instance, dog towels and emergency clean up supplies may need to be stored separately rather than in a group—one near the door, one in the car, one in the bathroom. Those that are used most often deserve storage space that is more accessible.

Since visibility and accessibility are equally important, storage should be organized into as many separate drawers, shelves, bins, etc, rather than consolidating them in one large drawer or shelf. Drawers are more accessible than shelves because you can immediately see the entire contents. Unfortunately, this only provides an advantage at a height below eye level. Above that point shelves work better. Drawer dividers and bins can help to organize similar objects. For example stack bins on shelves for vitamin supplements and sort them by dog rather than type. Bins with covers should be clear for visibility. Hooks or pegs are great for constantly used items such as leashes, dog coats and towels. Creating your own storage areas has never been easier thanks to the incredible range of DIY storage systems to choose from. A quick search for closet systems or storage on the internet will present many options, including systems you can design on line.

See Resources and subsequent chapters for products and more information.

CHAPTER 3

Health & Safety

Throughout history, dogs and cleanliness have been seen from differing standpoints. Some cultures, such as ancient Tibetans revered dogs. Tibetan Spaniels were considered highly valuable, kept in monasteries as "alert dogs" and bed warmers. Other cultures considered dogs unclean and couldn't imagine sharing a house with them, let alone their bed. In terms of contemporary culture, keeping dogs indoors is a relatively new idea. Until quite recently most dogs were expected to earn their keep guarding people, animals and homes. Used for hunting or as exterminators of vermin in the household, fear that dogs could spread fleas, mites or worms was a valid concern. Even fifty years ago it wasn't uncommon for dogs to have rabies, distemper or other contagious diseases.

Dogs and humans have come a long way in terms of sharing space. Thanks to advances in sanitation and vaccination we rarely consider the possibility of catching a disease from our dogs. How much should we worry about "germs" and sharing spaces with our dogs? Humans are not likely to get sick from their dog but anyone with a compromised immune system should follow a few simple hygiene rules: wash your hands after touching your pet, keep your home and your dog's environment clean.

The way we design our homes, the materials we choose to build it with and the methods we use to clean it all impact the health of human and canine inhabitants. Prevention of diseases focuses on a sensible approach and consultation with your veterinarian who can discuss appropriate vaccinations, tests and treatments for your dog. But it also includes cleanliness inside the home as well as the environment surrounding our homes. If you keep your dog indoors he will avoid unsupervised contact with other animals, including other dogs.

PARASITES, BACTERIA AND VIRUSES

A zoonose is any disease that can be transmitted between species. Zoonoses arise from microbial sources such as bacteria, viruses or parasites. The likelihood for contracting any of these diseases from your own dog is very low. Parasite transmission through environmental sources include: water, food, dog feces, and insects. Bacteria can be transmitted in the same ways as parasites but they can also be transmitted through blood, and other bodily fluids. Preventing water borne diseases is fairly easy. See Chapter 4 for more information on water. Prevention should focus on maintaining a clean environment, disposing of dog stools, and testing and filtering your water supply.

WILDLIFE

Whether you live in an urban, suburban or rural setting you will likely encounter wildlife. Dog lovers generally appreciate wildlife and find it easy to co-exist. However, some animals can become a nuisance if they enter your home or interact with your dogs. Frequent intruders include mice, birds, bats, squirrels, rabbits, rats, skunks, raccoons, and snakes. You may even encounter larger animals such as deer, coyotes and bear. Interestingly, some animals live close to their human neighbors completely undetected. Raccoons are often more common in urban settings than in rural settings. No matter where you live insects will invariably be a part of your environment. Concerns about wildlife include the spread of disease, such as rabies, distemper, leptospirosis, fleas and mange, although all of these can be prevented or controlled in dogs. Any mammal can contract rabies but raccoons and bats lead the list in terms of percentages. Animals are attracted to our homes in pursuit of two basic needs: food and shelter. Eliminate food sources and minimize sheltering opportunities and you may reduce wildlife encounters.

Food sources include dog food, bird seed, vegetable gardens, fruit trees, compost piles, dog feces and for some insects, blood. Eliminating food sources can be as simple as feeding your dog indoors and securely covering bins containing compost, dog waste and bird seed. If you feed your dog raw bones outdoors pick up and dispose of them immediately after consumption. If your yard is fenced consider placing compost bins and bird feeders outside of the fenced area. This will minimize dog/wildlife encounters and keep your dog from eating compost or bird seed. Fences around vegetable gardens and fruit trees can help eliminate larger wildlife. Larger predators, like coyotes, owls and hawks may consider your puppy or small dog as prey. If you live within predator habitat it is always best to supervise your dog while he is outdoors and NEVER leave him alone.

> Animals, such as rabbits, are a nuisance because dogs enjoy eating their droppings. These can contain harmful bacteria or protozoa, although they rarely cause severe illness. It can be impossible to keep rabbits out of your yard, even if it is fenced. A fairly large rabbit can squeeze through the holes in a chain link fence. Because rabbits are prey animals, dogs love to chase them. This may control the rabbit problem, but dogs can also escape from yards or get injured while pursuing rabbits.

Our homes and other buildings are often chosen as suitable shelter for rodents because they contain food and provide a safe haven from larger predators. In some cases predators, like snakes, enter our homes in pursuit of the mice, compounding the problem of uninvited wildlife. Outdoor landscapes can also become safe havens for wildlife. Shrubbery and plantings located near buildings are often used by mice, rabbits, snakes and skunks as shelter to keep cool and hide during warm weather. Any undisturbed place that provides cover has the potential to attract mice, chipmunks, snakes, fleas, bees and wasps. These include rock walls, lumber piles, firewood and even cars.

Keeping animals and insects out of your house requires a complete inspection of your home from inside and out and top to bottom. Animals will inhabit obvious and not so obvious spaces. Raccoons and starlings can be found living in roof eaves. Squirrels, chipmunks and bats can find easy access to attics, especially in older homes. A persistent raccoon can easily widen a small gap in a wall if he wants to get into a building. Once inside he can wreak havoc on a space. Inspect door and window screens for holes and gaps. Doors, and windows are most obvious but other locations include cracks in the foundation, holes in roof soffits and eaves and any place that a pipe enters in or out of the home, including electrical conduit, water and sewer lines, exhaust vents, AC units and TV cable lines. A mouse or a small snake can squeeze through an opening that is less than 3/8" in diameter. Often these openings are underground; be sure to dig around buried pipes for a complete inspection. If you find an opening there are several things you can use to fill it, depending on how large it is. Smaller openings can be filled with caulk or expanding foam insulation and larger ones may require wire mesh. Cut the mesh to overlap the opening, secure it and coat with expanding foam insulation. It is important to spray the holes from both sides of the wall if possible. Expanding foam insulation can be purchased at a D-I-Y store. These fixes may not be permanent, so inspection every year is necessary. Cover openings under porches and decks with lattice or wire fencing to exclude larger animals that like to den there. To rid your house of bats will require more work. Installing a "one-way bat door" will prevent bats from re-entering your home once they leave for the night. These must be installed only after babies are large enough to leave, otherwise they will die unattended by their mother. Once all bats have left for the year, usually in the fall, all holes should be covered to prevent bats from returning the following year.

Skunks deserve special mention because a dog/skunk interaction is a memorable one. Skunks often den under decks, porches or buildings and tolerate humans living in close proximity. Skunks, in particular, do not like loud music with a strong bass sound. Placing a radio near the den location at dusk can send them packing. Although they slow down in the cold months they are not true hibernators and are often seen outside when temperatures rise above 30°F. They are fairly slow moving, in part because they have a built in defense mechanism they readily use if threatened. Dogs are natural predators of skunks so it is not uncommon for dogs to be sprayed. Skunks can spray up to 15 feet. If your dog is sprayed by a skunk do not let him indoors until you are able to wash him off. The oils will permeate any porous surface and can be very hard to remove. While there are many home remedies that range from useless to dangerous a few good commercial remedies work and include Skunk-off®, Skunk-Kleen, and Nature's Miracle® Skunk Odor Remover. All are also recommended for cleaning clothing and surfaces in your home.

> Interactions between your dog and wildlife can be minimized by knowing when specific wildlife are active. Although you may see mammals during the day almost all are most active at night from approximately one hour before dusk until one hour after dawn. You can avoid problems by supervising your dogs after hours, turning on lights outdoors and fencing your yard. Go out the door before your dog does, and make a lot of noise.

INSECTS

Insect bites are a nuisance to both dogs and humans and can be a source of serious health problems. Fleas, ticks, mosquitoes, flies and mites can all cause illness ranging from allergic skin conditions to more serious bacterial or parasite infections such as Lyme disease or heartworm. If you live in areas where these insects and conditions are prevalent, have your dog tested yearly and use appropriate preventive treatments. While houseflies are known to carry bacteria, for most humans and dogs they are just a general nuisance. Houseflies are attracted to garbage, dog waste and food sources. Bees and wasps can cause serious allergic reactions and painful stings in both humans and dogs. Employ the following actions to minimize insects in and around your home:

- use screens on open windows and doors
- check screens for damage, gaps and holes
- fan exhaust and dryer vents are all potential sources of entry and may need to be screened
- keep yourself and your dog indoors during insect active times; mosquitoes are most active at dusk and dawn and in the shade; bees and wasps during warm weather, especially July through September
- remove potential habitats for bees and wasps: rock walls, lumber piles and unused objects such as buckets, and plant pots
- remove potential food sources

MOSQUITOES

Mosquitoes can transmit heartworm disease to dogs. Heartworm is a potentially fatal disease and should be taken very seriously. Anything that can hold stagnant water for more than a few days is potential mosquito breeding grounds. Gardens that encourage wildlife can actually be a good natural control of mosquito populations. Collectively, certain insects, birds, bats and fish are all effective predators of mosquitoes.

Mosquito control includes the following:

- eliminate shallow water features: bird baths, wading pools and water gardens, even tarps and tree holes are potential breeding grounds
- check and clean gutters to displace standing water
- bug zappers, black and ultraviolet lights are not effective against mosquitoes and may attract and kill beneficial insects
- mosquitoes are weak flyers, fans can work as a deterrent on a deck or open porch
- mosquitoes are more likely to breed in windless areas; they prefer stagnant water that is sheltered by grasses and other plants

FLEAS

Fleas are universally despised and can be nearly impossible to get rid of once they take up residence. Fleas prefer temperatures between 65–80F and humidity above 50%. In some areas of the country they are a seasonal problem while other areas deal with fleas all year long. There are hundreds of species of fleas including a dog flea, cat flea and human flea. The cat flea is the source of 95% of flea problems in the U.S. Where there is one flea, there are bound to be many more. Adult fleas spend their entire lives on their host but flea eggs and immature fleas can be anywhere that your dog normally spends time, including your carpet, the dog's bed, your bed, the car, and the yard. A flea eradication program should concentrate on those areas.

Prevention includes:

- selecting hard surface flooring such as wood, concrete, ceramic tile or linoleum
- avoiding soft surfaces that harbor fleas such as wall to wall carpet, textured upholstery and textile window treatments.
- cleaning, including vacuuming frequently.
- steam clean carpets twice a year

Do not assume that your dog has fleas simply because he is scratching; every dog scratches. Excessive scratching can be due to problems ranging from allergies to dry skin. To check for fleas in your home place a bowl of soapy water under a bright light in a darkened room. Fleas are attracted to the light and if they are lurking in your home, you will find a few in the bowl within a day or two.

FLEA INFESTATIONS

An effective program must target adult fleas on your dog as well as the immature fleas in your home. Since flea larvae will live off of organic debris, such as human skin scales, vacuuming furniture can be helpful. Vacuum floors and upholstery often, many dog professionals do this twice a day. Throw out the vacuum bag in a bin outside of your home. Further treatment may include washing all bedding, yours and your dogs, in hot water and drying in a hot dryer twice a week. Carpets and upholstery can be steam cleaned and treated with insect growth regulator (IGR) or insect development inhibitor (IDI) to break the flea life cycle once or twice per year. If your dog spends time outdoors you may also need to treat some parts of your yard. Areas with full direct sunlight are not going to harbor fleas. They gravitate to damp, cool, shady areas. Wildlife and stray cats are the major source of outdoor fleas. Despite your indoor control efforts, your dog will continue to be re-infested if he comes into contact with them. Topical flea treatments are the newest innovation in the ongoing battle. These will kill adult fleas on a dog within 48 hours and remain effective for several weeks. These products will not kill immature fleas in your home. Severe infestations may require professional help.

When a food source is available the life cycle of a flea can be as short as 21 days but when food is scarce flea pupae can survive up to 21 months. The pupae hatch into adult fleas in response to one or more of the following: heat, motion, vibration or an increase in carbon dioxide levels. In the absence of an animal host, fleas will feed on humans. Unsuspecting home buyers have moved into a new home to be greeted by hundreds of newly hatched fleas seeking a meal.

TICKS

Tick-borne diseases (TBD) caused by viruses, bacteria or parasites are transmitted to people and dogs from ticks. Most humans and dogs are infected during the spring and summer months. Although TBDs are more common in specific regions, most appear throughout the United States and include Babesiosis, Erlichiosis, Lyme, and Rocky Mountain Spotted Fever. There are many species of ticks, educate yourself about those in your area.

Ticks can be found nearly anywhere from thick forests to manicured suburban lawns. They thrive in moist environments and prefer tall grasses, bushes, trees and leaf litter. It is difficult to protect yourself and your dog completely from TBDs. Minimizing the risk includes having your dog tested yearly and treated with tick preventive. Check your dog's body on a regular basis. This is important after walking in thick tall grass or wooded areas. If you must walk your dog in the woods, try to walk only on established trails and keep your dog on the trails. Use a leash if necessary. Create a tick free zone in your yard by removing brush, leaf litter and keep the grass cut short and restrict your dog to this area.

BIRD MITES

Bird mites are tiny parasitic insects of birds and their young. When fledglings leave the nest the bird mites will seek other hosts. Often a trail of bird mites can be seen from the bird nest to your home. Humans and dogs can become temporary hosts; however, bird mites can't complete their life cycle on humans or dogs. Bird mite bites can cause intense itching. To prevent bird mite infestations remove bird nests on or near your home as soon as they are abandoned. It is a federal offense to remove active bird nests with eggs or birds in them. Safer treatments for killing mites, including boric acid and/or diatomaceous earth, can be used in attics and non-habitable spaces indoors. Horticultural dormant oils and insecticidal soap work well outdoors. Do not use anything directly on or near dogs, birds or nests. Human and dog bedding must be washed frequently with hot water and borax or hydrogen peroxide based soap. Wipe or spray bed sheets and dogs beds with rubbing alcohol or hydrogen peroxide. Rugs and carpet should be cleaned as well as walls and ceilings. Severe infestations may require professional help.

POISONOUS ANIMALS

Although parts of the world may have nothing more poisonous than bees and wasps some regions are home to poisonous lizards, salamanders, snakes, toads, frogs, spiders, and scorpions. Educate yourself about these animals in your particular area so you know what to do when you encounter them. You may need to train or restrain your dog to prevent confrontations with these creatures. Take precautions if you live in or are traveling to an area with poisonous animals. If your dog is a snake killer he can't be expected to know the difference between a non-poisonous snake in New York and a poisonous one in Texas.

PLANT HAZARDS

There are many plants that are considered toxic to dogs and can cause mild to severe symptoms, including death. The ASPCA has a website with a complete plant list and a 24 hour poison control center 888-426-4435 (fee based consultation available) www.aspca.org/pet-care/poison-control. A plant does not have to be poisonous to cause problems for you and your dog. Thorns, thistles and some seed pods can lodge themselves in a dog's foot pad, skin, ear, eye, mouth or nose. You may need to limit the areas where your dog is allowed to roam, if nettles, foxtails or thorny plants are prevalent.

INDOOR SAFETY

Dogs can become injured in countless ways through carelessness or freak accidents. It's impossible to prevent every possibility but common sense and a "child-proofing" approach to safety will prevent most accidents in the home. Child safety products, such as toilet locks and door locks can be found on-line or at stores that stock items for child safety.

> In general there are several things you should keep in mind to ensure your dog's safety:
>
> - know what hazards may lurk in your home
> - post pertinent phone numbers in a prominent location including: your vet, emergency vet, poison control (888-426-4435)
> - when you are engaged in any distracting activity like cooking, working, construction, maintenance, gardening, or doing a specific hobby know what your dog is doing or put him in his crate.
> - organization and storage are the best way to prevent the ingestion of a foreign object. If objects have a place to be stored they have a better chance of ending up there.

FALLS

Dogs can be injured by falling, accidentally slipping, ill advised jumping or being accidentally pushed by another dog or person. Tiny dogs and puppies can be seriously injured by a falling human. This often results from tripping over a little dog or falling while carrying one in your arms. Elderly dogs, small dogs and giant dogs may have more difficulty negotiating stairs or slippery floors, getting on or off a piece of furniture or in and out of a car. These accidents can result in broken bones, spinal injuries, concussions or worse.

Dogs can fall from windows, even when there are screens in place. Installation of a metal dog gate, or custom made grate is recommended if your dog is strong enough to knock the screens out. Falls into holes or bodies of water are more common than you might think. Dogs have been known to fall into basement window wells, excavated basements, fish ponds, swimming pools and sewer drains. These areas should be fenced off. Never assume that your dog will understand that something is dangerous.

STAIRS

Puppies and older dogs without previous experience climbing stairs need to be trained to use them. Dogs usually find down more difficult then up. While most dogs learn to use stairs and it becomes second nature to them, some develop stair phobias, usually after being frightened by slipping or falling on the stairs.

Stair treads themselves are often the culprit but landings or slippery floors at the bottom of the stairs can be problematic. Non-slip carpet runners or tread mats can alleviate this problem. Weakness, instability and balance disturbances can cause elderly dogs to slip and fall on the stairs. Carpeting stairs will add traction as well as cushioning in case of a fall. Thin or worn carpet may be just as slippery as bare stairs, especially carpet that covers the nosing. Since most people prefer bare wood treads for aesthetic reasons a good choice is to use carpet treads that leave the wood treads visible. These are typically 9″ x 28″ with a non-slip rubber backing to hold them in place. For added security a product called HOLD-IT For Rugs™ works well. It comes in a roll, like tape, with adhe-sive on one side and latex foam on the other side. Hold-It is adhered to the bottom of each carpet tread and then placed on a clean wood tread. Thus secured, the treads won't move even with multiple dogs running up and down the stairs.

Many dogs are fearful of walking on open riser stairs, that is, stairs that have no back and that you can see through. Open risers are more common on contemporary stairs, outdoors or on spiral stairs. Closing the backs of the risers will help avoid this problem, but this may not be possible on all stairs and it will likely require professional help. Dogs can be un-comfortable walking past open railings with widely spaced or horizontal members or railings made with thin wire, glass or clear plastic. Small dogs can break a leg simply by catching it in a railing. If your dog can easily fit his head through the openings between railings then the space is too wide. If you can't afford to replace the railings built with safer dimensions, consider covering them with wire or plastic mesh, plexi-glass or plywood panels. See chapter 10 decks, for more info on railing dimensions.

These plants are placed out of the dog's reach on a well designed plant shelf located in the entry/mud room.

OPPOSITE The countertop over the washer and dryer serves many purposes including a place to pot plants. An added bonus is the deep utility sink that makes it easy to wash a small dog or water plants.

LEFT The plant shelf viewed from the entry door. The plants also serve as a visual barrier between spaces.

ABOVE Plastic grating can keep your dog's nose out of your plant pot dirt. *Courtesy of Cardinal Gates: www.cardinalgates.com*

NON SLIP FLOOR AND STAIR SURFACES

Hard surface floors and stair treads can be altered to make them less slippery by applying durable non-slip finishes. Textured aggregates and additives, such as sand, pumice or rubber can be added to paint or clear coatings. Non-slip finishes and toppings include:

- textured floor paint for deck, garage, porch and basement floors.
- clear anti-slip finishes applied to indoor or outdoor hard surface and resilient floors.
- anti-slip, no-skid tapes that look and feel like sandpaper and work well on basement, attic or garage stairs.
- metal or rubber tread covers for outdoor use.
- decks and treads built with textured recycled plastic lumber.

When shopping for non-slip paints or additives, look for products with low or zero VOCs. Non-slip coatings are common in the boat building and repair industry, so if you can't find a suitable product in a local store, check out a marina store. Be careful when selecting boat building finishes. Many of them contain toxic chemicals such as epoxy. Epoxy coatings create an extremely durable floor finish but most epoxy paint has high VOCs and the vapors are hazardous to the user's health. The space should be fully ventilated for as long as a few weeks to adequately remove all of the gases. If you must use epoxy look for low VOC varieties. (See chapter 4 for more on VOCs).

Additional tips for avoiding slipping and falls:

- use ramps for short rises (2 or 3 risers) or for getting into and out of chairs, sofas, beds and cars
- use dog boots with rubber soles for traction
- keep dogs off high story balconies or decks
- cover railing with a protective barrier such as solid wood, chicken wire or garden fencing

FALLING OBJECTS

Books, plants, art objects, tools, and appliances are just a few of the things that could fall on your dog and hurt him. Depending on his size and the weight of the object this could have very serious consequences. A panicked dog can easily topple a TV or a computer if he becomes entangled in the cord, secure the cords out of the way. Assess storage areas, laundry rooms, and the kitchen. Put heavy objects behind doors or high enough out of the way, or low enough to prevent harm. Make sure plants are placed securely out of reach.

HOUSEHOLD CLEANERS AND CHEMICALS

The list of potentially harmful and deadly household cleaners and chemicals is fairly long. It is best to assume that any cleaner or chemical is harmful and should be kept out of your dog's reach. This includes obvious caustic substances like bleach, detergent, and, turpentine, poisons like bug spray and weed killer as well as less obvious items like, potpourri, toilet bowl cleaner, dryer sheets, and furniture polish. Provide secure storage areas for all of your household cleaners, chemicals, compounds and pesticides. Familiarize yourself with poisoning hazards.

Antifreeze deserves special mention as a particularly hazardous and deadly household chemical. Most poisoning occurs when some antifreeze is spilled on a garage floor or driveway and a dog licks it up. A tablespoon of antifreeze can kill an average size dog.

DROWNING

Dogs are most likely to drown in any situation where they can't get out of the water. Drowning hazards are not necessarily large or seemingly dangerous. Small dogs and puppies can drown in something as small as a bucket or toilet, but anything that contains water poses a hazard. Pay attention to your dog's whereabouts, minimize hazards, block access to potential water hazards, and learn canine CPR techniques. For more on swimming and water safety see Chapter 10.

ELECTROCUTION

From a canine perspective, electrical cords, Christmas lights, and chain lights look like great toys. Tugging on a cord will inevitably include biting and a dog can easily be electrocuted or start a fire. Electrical outlets can also be a potential electrocution hazard, but this is rare. The easiest solution is to cover electrical outlets and cords. Plywood or Homosote® panels can be placed against the wall in front of the outlet and/or cord. If you are designing a new home consider placing outlets out of reach – higher than normal. This is a bonus in spaces with horizontal surfaces such as desks because outlets will be more convenient for your use as well. Electrical outlet covers and safety plugs used to childproof a home can safeguard your dog too. Some puppies that normally ignore electrical outlets are attracted to outlet covers. Always supervise and be aware of your dog's propensities. While outlet covers are found in hardware and DIY stores, covers for electrical cords are more difficult to find. There is only one product that is specifically

Carpet stair treads are kept in place with HOLD-IT for rugs™. They do not shift or move and can be removed without damaging the wood treads.

Safety netting can be put over railings on decks or balconies to prevent falls or trapped heads. *Courtesy of Cardinal Gates: www.cardinalgates.com*

LIGHTING SAFETY

Fixed light fixtures, such as pendants or recessed fixtures are safer than freestanding table lamps or floor lamps in homes with dogs. There is less likelihood of chewed cords, strangulation from a cord or electrocution, let alone breakage when a dog catches a cord while running behind the sofa!

made to prevent pets from chewing on cords. CritterCord™ is a clear cover infused with a citrus scent to deter chewing. Citrus scent will deter some, but not all, dogs. Metal braided sleeving is a more effective solution and is made from stainless steel. It is commonly used to protect electrical lines and camera video equipment.

INGESTING FOREIGN OBJECTS

Pica is a somewhat common behavior and refers to the consumption of indigestible nonfood items like clothing, rocks, batteries, coins and just about anything else. Dogs will swallow these objects and their bowels become obstructed which may require emergency surgery. Puppies, like babies, have no hesitation about putting potentially dangerous items in their mouths and can choke as a result. Dogs engage in this behavior less often as they mature, but readily indulge when they find a sufficiently tempting item. This isn't limited to stray cough drops discovered between the couch cushions. Veterinary organizations actually run contests where members compare notes about the most incredible items they have surgically removed from the canine digestive tract. Children are more likely to have multiple items that are within a dog's reach like toys and clothes strewn on bedroom and playroom floors. Children's belongings are also more likely to smell like food, which encourages dogs to taste them. If you have children in your home it is important to be vigilant about picking up items. Teenagers, in particular, may need to be reminded to keep their room clean or keep their bedroom door closed at all times.

FIRE SAFETY

Do not assume that your dog will automatically be fearful of fire or recognize the danger of a hot oven or clothes iron. Fire safety preparation includes planning evacuation routes and training your dog. Plan multiple escape routes. Often dogs become habituated to only one or two doors in your home. Although this minimizes the possibility of escape, the dog may not readily run out of an unfamiliar door during an emergency. Therefore spend some time training your dogs to go through all of the exterior doors. At the very least, during a fire, you might have to pick up your dog to get him out to safety. Some dogs hate to be grabbed by the collar but during emergencies it might be necessary. Train your dog to accept this handling by gently grabbing his collar and rewarding him for cooperating.

Your escape plan must also include a way to confine your dogs after they are removed from the home. Fires trigger an instinctive fight or flight response. Dogs can panic and run right back into their burning home to seek safety. Others run into traffic or are never seen again. They may also bite well meaning rescuers. If you have a detached garage or shed, put your dog in there temporarily. Confine him to your car if nothing else is available. If you have multiple dogs store sufficient crates or leashes somewhere outside your home in case of an emergency.

See Resources for products and more information.

SAFETY TIP
RESCUE ALERT STICKERS

Rescue alert stickers for children and pets became popular over the past decade. In theory, they were a good idea. Firefighters responding to an emergency at your home would see the sticker and run inside to save your children and pets. In reality, fire departments and other rescue groups no longer pay attention to these signs.

A firefighter's primary job is to save humans. Although they often save pets, they risk their lives to do so. Many people don't bother removing these stickers when they are no longer relevant. As a result, they have become routinely ignored.

Air, Ground, Water & Light

Dogs can be divided into heat or cool seeking beings. Some love basking in sunshine or snoozing in front of a woodstove, others prefer sprawling on a cool floor or to laze in the shade. Dogs tolerate a range of temperatures but they all have a preferred comfort zone. The insulated coats of arctic breeds or large heat dissipating ears of desert breeds are examples of highly efficient systems for temperature regulation. The dog's primary means of thermoregulation is panting, which is far less efficient than sweating. If it is too cold they curl up, burrow down, and shiver. Without our assistance, blankets and sweaters are not an option. A long coat without a substantial undercoat provides little or no protection from cold. Conversely, a dog with short hair may not tolerate excessive heat. Coat density rather than length is the important factor to consider. Very few breeds are designed to tolerate extreme climates without taking shelter. It's our responsibility to ensure that our homes provide a comfortable environment for our dogs.

Like us, dogs can suffer from hyperthermia (heatstroke) or hypothermia (excessive cold). Heatstroke results from a rapid rise in body temperature and this constitutes a medical emergency. However, certain dogs experience a less dramatic response to excessive heat which can also take a toll on health. Breeds with short muzzles, such as boxers or pugs and dogs with breathing problems, like asthma, collapsing trachea or laryngeal paralysis are less able to cope with excessive heat. Two or three degrees in temperature rise can cause discomfort. Very large breeds, such as Mastiffs and St. Bernards have a high body mass ratio. For these breeds, body heat builds up quickly and dissipates slowly. Breeds with low body mass, thin coats, or very little body fat are most likely to become uncomfortable in a cold environment. Small breeds such as Chihuahuas and Yorkshire Terriers are known for their dislike of cold. However, larger dogs with thin coats or low body fat also have a low tolerance for cold. Indoors, this will probably not elicit a dramatic response like heavy panting when a dog is uncomfortably hot. A chilly dog will become inactive and seek a place to curl up. Keeping warm uses a lot of energy and the effort can take a toll on health, especially for dogs that are elderly or suffering from joint problems.

Before doing major renovations or building a new home consult an architect, engineer and/or HVAC professionals to:

- determine the most efficient and cost effective heating and air conditioning options
- orient your home site to best take advantage of sunlight, shade, and breezes.

HEATING, VENTILATION AND COOLING (HVAC)
WARM DOGS

There are many types of heating systems available and some are better suited to homes with dogs. In general heating systems are divided into two groups: central heating systems and unitary systems. Central heating systems heat an entire building while unitary systems, like a woodstove or space heater, heat one room. Central heating can further be divided into two groups: those that use water to distribute heat, such as hot-water baseboard, radiator or hydronic (liquid) radiant floor and those that use air to distribute heat, such as forced-air. In general, central heating systems are safer than unitary systems for homes with dogs in them because the heating elements are out of your dog's reach. Duct registers or baseboard convectors do not reach dangerous temperatures.

Forced-air systems use a fan to blow air throughout your house. Integrated filters trap dust, dander, hair and fine particles, which is a practical feature in a home with dogs. The major advantage of a forced-air system is the ability to easily and cost-effectively add air conditioning because the ductwork is already in place. A disadvantage is that forced-air systems can cause dry air, dry skin and troublesome scratching or incessant licking. Dry air can also irritate the nasal passages and throat of your dog, especially problematic for dogs with allergies, asthma or other breathing problems. A humidifier can help; ideal humidity is between 40% and 60%.

> Static electricity is created by friction between two materials with different compositions and is more prevalent in dry air. All dogs experience static charge but it contributes to tangles, mats and substantial coat damage in long coated dogs. It causes dog fur to cling to everything, making it more difficult to get rid of.
>
> A humidity level above 55% will greatly reduce static electricity. If you select a humidifier the best type is a central humidifier, as part of your HVAC system. There are many other types but you should only consider buying one if you are committed to daily cleaning of the unit. Improper maintenance increases the risk of bacterial and fungal growth.

Ductwork needs to be cleaned periodically, as often as 2 years or as infrequently as 10, or anytime you do major construction in your home. The only way to be certain is to have your ducts inspected every 2 to 3 years, especially in homes with multiple dogs.

Other suitable and quiet dog-friendly heating systems include hydronic radiant floor heating, and active and passive solar heating systems. The benefits of either system for a home with dogs are safety: no hot surfaces to come in contact with; and no indoor air pollution from dust, dander or gases. Hydronic radiant floor heating utilizes a heat source, such as a boiler, heat pump or solar collector to distribute heated water through tubing that is laid underneath a floor. The system radiates heat to objects that come in contact with the floor, including humans and dogs. Popular in animal shelters and kennels, it is an excellent choice for heat seeking dogs who relish lying on a warm surface. It has a tendency to overheat highly insulated and air-tight homes. Active and passive solar systems rely on the sun to heat a space. Passive systems capture sunlight through sun-oriented windows which convert the sun's energy to heat and warm the home's interior. Active systems are designed to heat water or produce electricity and use outdoor "collectors" that absorb sunlight and transfer this into energy.

Two important considerations in selecting a heating system are safety and maintenance. The primary concern is to protect your dog from potential burn and fire hazards. Radiators should be covered and wood stoves surrounded by barriers. Electric space heaters can become hot enough to cause burns. Dogs have caused house fires by pulling space heaters off of tables, chewing on the electric cords or urinating on the unit. Floating dog fur can cause sparks on space heaters that could lead to a more serious fire. Dog toys or bedding can accidentally come in direct contact with radiators, space heaters or baseboard convectors. This limits the general effectiveness of the unit and is a fire hazard. Woodstoves or fireplaces create fine particles and dust that can irritate throats and exacerbate allergies and asthma in both humans and dogs.

COOL DOGS

Methods to keep your home and your dog cooler include fans, passive ventilation, shading and air conditioning. From an environmental viewpoint the best way to cool your house is passively and naturally.

COOLING STRATEGIES INCLUDE:

- strategically placed trees
- awnings
- low-E windows
- operable windows to regulate temperatures
- indoor or outdoor window treatments
- installing radiant barriers
- a light colored roof
- insulated walls and roof
- replacing old appliances
- unplugging unused electronic devices
- using fluorescent or LED lamps
- using AC only when needed
- cleaning AC filters monthly
- using exhaust fans in kitchens, bathrooms and laundry rooms

Fans don't cool the air, but they can remove warm air from a space or draw cooler air into a space. A whole house fan is a good example of removing warm air. Whole house fans, large fans centrally located between the upper ceiling and the attic floor, draw cool air from lower locations up and out through roof vents. The fan on a central HVAC unit can also draw cool basement air up into the rest of the house.

COOLING SYSTEMS

Air conditioning (AC) is essential for some dogs, and for others it is an appreciated luxury. Unfortunately, providing this comfort for our dogs is not always easy or economical. Like heating systems air conditioning systems are divided into two broad categories, central AC systems and unitary systems. All units work on the same principal: they cool air by extracting heat from a specific area. Central AC systems deliver cool air through a system of ducts to cool an entire building. There are two types: a split system or a packaged unit. The split system consists of an outdoor compressor/condenser and an indoor air-handling unit. A packaged unit houses everything outdoors. Central AC is quiet, convenient and more efficient than room air conditioners. For your dog, it provides comfort and freedom of movement throughout the entire home.

Ductless mini-split systems are similar to central AC split systems but they have several indoor units and no ducts. The advantage is that each indoor unit has its own thermostat. You will only need to cool a space when your dog is in it. Because there are no ducts these units are good for homes that do not have central forced-air systems.

Unitary systems consist of window or wall units, and portable room units. Window units are easiest to install into a double hung window, portable room units require placing a flexible hose out a window or wall opening. These units are great for renters or for those who cannot afford the price of central AC. Before buying one, establish that your home can meet the unit's power requirements. These units tend to be noisy and the filters need to be cleaned at least once a month. Window AC units make your house more vulnerable to burglars.

ENERGY RATINGS FOR AC

Air conditioning units are rated based on how much energy they use. Energy Efficiency Ratio (EER) and Seasonal Energy Efficiency Ratio (SEER) are two rating systems. For Central AC select units with a SEER over 13, and for room units an EER over 10 is best. Energy Star® rated units will reflect these values.

INDOOR AIR QUALITY AND INDOOR POLLUTION

The average American spends 90% per day indoors either at home or at work. In today's world our dogs spend more time in our home than we do. Home indoor air quality has a direct impact on your dog's health and comfort. Indoor air has diminished for many reasons that include energy efficient buildings and biological and chemical pollutants. Pollutants have been linked to numerous health problems in humans. It is not yet known how pollutants impact dogs, but the best course of action is to err on the side of caution.

TIPS FOR BETTER AIR

- humidity levels below 50% in your home will discourage mold and other bacterial growth
- ventilate high moisture areas, such as bathrooms, kitchens and basements
- avoid carpeting in damp or moist spaces such as bathrooms or basements
- kill mold with a weak bleach and water mixture
- maintain HVAC systems, change or clean filters regularly
- avoid products that contain formaldehyde, PVC or high VOCs
- keep your home clean, vacuum regularly
- groom your dog regularly

Eliminating or minimizing the source of pollutants such as dust, pollen, tobacco smoke, and pet dander can improve indoor air quality. Ventilation is the best way to maintain fresh air indoors and to truly eliminate odors and most pollutants. If ventilation is not possible an air cleaner can help. Ventilation is either passive or active. Passive ventilation can be as simple as opening a door or window. Active ventilation uses a mechanical device to move air out, such as an exhaust fan in a kitchen. Electric window openers can be added to new or existing casement, awning or skylight windows. When the temperature climbs indoors some automatically open and then close when the temperature drops or if it rains. This could be an excellent way to ventilate and cool a space whether you are home or not. Those windows should be small casement or awning windows placed high or above other windows to minimize dog escapes or destructive behaviors such as shredding window screens.

Air cleaners remove particles and some may also remove gases and odors. Two forms of air cleaners are recommended for homes with dogs: air filters and UV sterilization. Air filters work when particles are trapped as air flows through the filter. Panel filters, reusable filters and pleated filters made from foam, paper, fiberglass or textiles are commonly used on exhaust fans, portable AC units and central HVAC systems. If using one of these filters select the highest efficiency filter with a MERV (Minimum Efficiency Reporting Value) rating above 10. Maintain equipment properly and clean or replace filters regularly. Clogged and dirty filters will reduce the equipment effectiveness and use more energy. Mold spores can attach to filters used in moist locations.

The ideal filter for a home with dogs is a High Efficiency Particulate Air (HEPA) filter because they can remove dander, allergens and 99.9% of all particles larger than .3 micrometers in diameter. A pre-filter can improve the lifespan of a HEPA filter. HEPA filters are dense so they require more energy to move air through them. They can be used with conventional forced-air HVAC systems, portable units or vacuum cleaners.

Activated charcoal or carbon filters are also a good choice because they can remove odors from the air. Like other filters they can be used with HVAC systems, portable units, vacuum cleaners or exhaust fans.

UV sterilization is common in water treatment and can be used to clean air. A high-energy fluorescent lamp is placed within the air flow of a building, typically as part of the central HVAC system. As the air flows past the UV lamp it kills microorganisms such as bacteria, viruses and some mold. These units have been successfully used in hospitals and veterinary clinics and would work well in homes with multiple dogs.

AVOID negative ion and ozone generator air purifiers. They are dangerous to humans and dogs because they produce ozone that can irritate the lungs, causing coughing, chest tightness and shortness of breath. Even low amounts of ozone can be problematic.

POLLUTANTS

Biological pollutants, living or dead organisms are extremely common in our homes. Many of these things are invisible to the naked eye. Examples include mold, pollen, dust mites, animal dander and microbes such as bacteria, parasites or viruses. Both humans and dogs can suffer allergic reactions or infection as a result of exposure to biological pollutants. See chapter 11 for more on allergies.

Environmental conditions such as high humidity and poor air circulation contribute to the growth of biological pollutants and certain materials, such as carpet, actually attract and trap them. Minimizing the use of thick or textured textiles can help prevent the growth of biological pollutants.

PLANTS AS AIR CLEANERS

Plants are known to add oxygen to the air, filter impurities out of the air and charge airborne particulates so they become fixed to other surfaces. Recent scientific studies have shown that plants might help clean indoor air but it would take hundreds of houseplants to effectively do this in a 1500 square foot home. A more promising approach in research is concentrating on hydroponic systems in which air is drawn through the root zone of plants in a growing medium.

MOLD

Mold is found in warm, damp spaces like basements and bathrooms. Leaky faucets, roofs or periodic flooding and wooded locations all contribute to mold growth. Mold is brought indoors from outside when spores are blown in through windows or tracked in on clothing and shoes. It thrives on plant and other organic material but can be found on synthetic products such as carpet. Toxic mold produces "mycotoxin" that can be deadly in large quantities. "Toxic molds" or "black molds," are not always visible, but signs include: musty smells, rotting wood, surface discolorations, and a constant need of humans to clear their throats due to irritation of the nasal and mucous membranes. Toxic mold can damage the brain, kidneys, and liver, as well as cardiovascular, nervous, and immune systems. In minor cases mold can be removed using detergent and water or a weak bleach solution, one cup bleach to one gallon of water. In severe cases professional help is necessary.

Our dogs spend more time in our homes than we do making them more susceptible to the effects of poor indoor air especially from mold, carbon monoxide poisoning and VOCs.

CHEMICALS, GASES AND VOCs

Common chemical indoor air pollutants include carbon monoxide, PVC, radon, and volatile organic compounds (VOCs). Carbon monoxide can kill or cause severe chronic damage. It is an odorless, tasteless and invisible gas. Any appliance or heating unit that uses carbon based fuel produces carbon monoxide as a by-product. Carbon monoxide poisoning can creep up on a person or dog without warning and will have a greater impact on whoever spends the most time in your home. Exposure can be acute or chronic and causes nausea, dizziness, headaches and possibly death. Symptoms of acute exposure occur immediately or within a few days. In chronic cases low levels of carbon monoxide exposure occur over a long time period. If you suspect that either you, or your dog, have been exposed to carbon monoxide move to fresh air immediately and seek medical help.

Symptoms of carbon monoxide poisoning in dogs:

- drowsiness
- lethargy
- weakness and in-coordination
- bright red color to skin and gums
- trouble breathing
- coma
- chronic exposure may cause exercise intolerance, abnormal gait and abnormal reflexes

Fortunately, there are steps you can take to detect and prevent this silent killer. Install carbon monoxide detectors on each floor of your home, one should be close to where you sleep. Purchase only detectors that have been tested by a reliable organization such as Consumers Union or Underwriters Laboratories. An alarm that plugs in and has a battery for backup in case of power failure is also a worthwhile investment. Most detectors have expiration dates, and must be checked and replaced periodically. Purchase one with a digital readout that constantly displays the levels, you may notice when levels start to rise before it becomes a problem.

SAFETY TIP

While carbon monoxide detectors are important, and required in some states, they are not a substitute for proper installation, use and maintenance of equipment.

- Have your furnace inspected, cleaned and maintained on a yearly basis.
- Use gas appliances that vent directly outdoors.
- Never use gasoline powered equipment indoors.
- Never heat your house with a gas range or oven— even during a power outage.

VOCs

Substances that readily evaporate at room temperature are called "volatile organic compounds." Volatile Organic Compounds (VOCs) are emitted as gases from certain solid and/or liquid materials. "Volatile" describes chemicals that evaporate easily into the air at varying rates, organic refers to chemicals that contain carbon, and most are made from fossil fuels. VOCs form toxic vapors which contribute to poor indoor air quality. VOCs can create smog, produce odors, be inhaled or absorbed through our skin or seep into water supplies. Although we normally consider synthetic chemicals as the source of VOCs, natural elements such as mold or cleaning ingredients such as pine or citrus oil are also culprits. VOCs are found in thousands of household items including paint, plywood, adhesives, insulation, synthetic fabrics, and cleaning products. Not all VOCs are harmful.

Health problems associated with VOCs depend on the concentration and amount of the chemical, the personal physical characteristics of the individual, route of absorption and the exposure time. Immediate symptoms include: eye, nose and throat irritation, difficulty breathing, headaches, rash, dizziness, fatigue, confusion, and nosebleeds. Long term exposure to VOCs may contribute to more serious illness including major organ damage, cancers, neurological problems and reproductive disorders. Typical indoor VOCs levels are two to ten times higher than outdoors and many products contain more than one chemically caused VOC. TVOCs or Total Volatile Organic Compounds refers to the total number of VOCs in a given air sample. This is a cumulative result of different chemicals evaporating from furnishings and products into the atmosphere of your home. MVOC refers to Microbial Volatile Organic Compounds. MVOCs are produced by certain types of molds. Professional testing is available to determine the levels of VOCs in your home.

> Known carcinogens found in buildings and construction materials:
>
> - Arsenic
> - Benzene
> - Asbestos
> - Cadmium
> - Radon
> - Tobacco Smoke
> - Vinyl Chloride (PVC)

POLYVINYL CHLORIDE (VINYL, VINYL CHLORIDE OR PVC)

PVC is one of the most prevalent materials found in buildings today. It is used in plumbing pipes, electrical conduit, flooring, wall-coverings, furniture and accessories. The known hazards of PVC are mostly associated with the manufacturing process and the plasticizers (softeners) used to make it pliable. Exposure raises the risk of liver, brain, lung and blood cancers. Neurological damage has also been documented. It is not completely known what the risks are once it is fabricated into a product. Many countries have already banned plasticizers

used to make PVC pliable. These additives have been shown to cause toxicity and biochemical changes in the kidneys and liver, lower sperm counts, and abnormal development. They are found in vinyl dog toys and softer vinyl flooring. When particles from vinyl flooring are freed through scratching or chewing this can create a health risk for you and your dog. While it may not be necessary to remove vinyl products from your home, if possible avoid them.

CONTAMINANTS OF WATER, GROUND AND AIR

Radon is an invisible, odorless radioactive gas produced by the breakdown or decay of uranium. It occurs naturally in rock formations and soils and can seep into buildings through cracks in the foundation or through mechanical openings. It can contaminate groundwater, affecting water supplies and is also found in fairly high concentrations in building materials such as granite countertops. Tightly enclosed spaces permit radon levels to build up to values much higher than outdoor levels. Radon is the second leading cause of lung cancer in humans, and dogs can also develop lung cancer from radon. Exposure does not cause immediate symptoms and most people are unaware of a problem until a member of their household is diagnosed with lung cancer. Therefore it is important that every home be tested for radon. Radon mitigation can be accomplished in new and existing homes and should be done by a qualified radon mitigation contractor. Mitigation isolates the radon gas source and vents it directly outdoors. Once the process is complete you and your dog can lively safely within your home as long as your system has a monitor and/or you retest for radon every two years following mitigation.

Lead is a well documented environmental hazard and is found in building materials. Lead paint produced prior to 1978 is the primary cause of lead poisoning in dogs and humans. Other lead sources include: curtain weights, some ceramic dishes, pipes, and batteries. It is primarily released into the air through combustion from cars, power plants and manufacturing. Once airborne it can travel long distances before settling in the soil and migrating to water sources. Dogs can come into contact with lead by ingesting contaminated water or soil but accidental ingestion of contaminated food and water is a common route of exposure. Puppies and young dogs are more susceptible primarily because of their curiosity and chewing habits. Urban dogs, like urban children, are more likely to have higher concentrations of lead in their blood. Symptoms in dogs include gastrointestinal problems, nervous system dysfunction and anemia. Lead poisoning can be treated but the prognosis is better if caught early.

Mercury is a toxic substance found in an assortment of household items such as batteries and fluorescent lamps. Before 1992 it was widely used in paint. Dogs can accidentally ingest mercury from old thermometers, batteries, and electrical items. Mercury is also found in higher concentrations in larger, older predatory fish at the top of the food chain, like tuna or grouper. In the body, mercury accumulates at a rate higher than it is lost through a process known as bioaccumulation. In humans and dogs it can cause renal failure, gastrointestinal disorders and neurological problems.

Zinc is a necessary nutritional element for both humans and dogs, but it can also be a source of poisoning causing gastro-intestinal distress, anemia and pancreatic damage in dogs. Hazardous household items containing zinc include galvanized coatings on fences, crates, hardware, coins or skin preparations.

Arsenic in the form of Chromated Copper Arsenate (CCA) is a preservative and pesticide, added to lumber used in decks and exterior construction. In 2003 it was phased out of residential use and was replaced by two alternative wood preservatives: Copper Azole and Ammoniacal Copper Quaternary. CCA still exists in numerous homes in the form of older decks. Arsenic exposure is most likely to occur from breathing the sawdust, or direct contact from treated wood. Arsenic poisoning symptoms in dogs include skin problems, gastrointestinal disorders, and in severe cases, death. Dogs, because of their innate chewing habits, and their closer proximity to deck floors face a higher risk for arsenic toxicity. They will often lick themselves, further exacerbating the problem. Arsenic leaches out of treated lumber into the surrounding environment, in particular the soil near a structure such as a deck. Contaminated soil can pose the same hazard as the original material itself. Dogs that dig, or lie in the soil increase their exposure. It is important not to leave toys, especially chew toys, in this area. Specially developed plants can be used to remove arsenic from the soil. (See Resources). Alternatives to treated lumber include recycled plastic composite wood and cedar.

SAFE WATER

Dogs can live without food for days but will suffer ill effects very quickly without clean, safe water. For most of us a supply of water requires nothing more than turning the nearest faucet in our homes. Water that flows from household faucets usually comes from surface water (water that has run off from streams, rivers, lakes, etc.) and is collected in reservoirs, or from ground water (water that has filtered through the ground, such as rain water) that is extracted by means of a well. Unless it comes from a well, it is passed through a water-treatment facility for testing and treatment before it reaches your faucets.

Well water is regulated in the sense that most municipalities issue a certificate of occupancy only after the water passes minimal tests. After that it is the homeowner's responsibility to have their well water tested. The frequency of testing depends on the depth of the well, past problems, and health status of individuals who regularly drink this water.

While we are very lucky to have the luxury of ready access to treated water, it's not always as safe and healthy as it should be. In fact, recent research suggests that tap water often contains a plethora of naturally-occurring and man-made contaminates, including heavy metals, industrial chemical pollutants, and substances intentionally added to water supplies to kill bacteria, adjust pH, and eliminate cloudiness. Pesticides, chlorine, and lead in drinking water are of special concern and have been linked to everything from cancer to heart disease. Pesticides compromise water quality, particularly in heavily-farmed areas. Chlorine has long been added to public water supplies to kill disease-causing bacteria, however, the levels of chlorine in drinking water today can reach dangerously high levels.

In addition to chemicals and metals, water can also contain biological contaminants, such as viruses, bacteria, and parasites, including E-coli and nitrates (which can enter a water supply from poorly maintained septic systems), coliform bacteria, and protozoa such as Cryptosporidium, Giardia and coccidian. These pathogens can cause a variety of gastric upset and can be deadly for people or dogs with compromised immune systems. Some, like coccidian may have little impact on a healthy dog, but can be fatal to a puppy. Protozoa enter the water system primarily from fecal contamination.

Many times, water can look and taste fine but still be contaminated. For this reason it is a good idea to have your water tested annually. Testing should be conducted by an independent party, not someone who is in the business of selling you a water filtration or water treatment system. There are two basic categories of water treatment systems: Point-of-Use (POU) such as a single tap and Point-of-Entry (POE) for a whole house. If you need a water filtration or treatment system, it will be necessary to buy and install the correct type. This will

WATER TREATMENT SYSTEM OVERVIEW

TYPE	BASICS	REMOVES/REDUCES	POE	POU
Activated Carbon Filter	Highly absorbent carbon in filter attracts and traps impurities	Bad tastes, odors such as chlorine, heavy metals: lead, copper, mercury and more		X
Distiller	Boils water and re-condenses purified steam	Heavy metals: lead, mercury, copper, arsenic and more	X	X
Reverse Osmosis	Membrane separates impurities from water	Protozoa: Cryptosporidium, Giardia, heavy metals, sodium and more	X	X
Ultraviolet Sterilization	UV light kills micro-organisms	Bacteria, viruses, parasites and mold. (may not kill 100% of these)	X	X
Cation Exchange Softener	Softens hard water, requires space for a resin tank and a brine tank	Calcium and Magnesium	X	

vary according to where you live, the water source (municipal vs. well) and the type of contamination and condition, i.e. soft vs. hard. There are many systems and none of them will remove everything. For example activated carbon filters can remove metals such as lead and copper and UV light systems are good at removing bacteria and some viruses. To determine the correct system it is important to contact a water purification specialist in your area. Eliminating minerals through "softening" is a very common procedure in homes today. Softening could be beneficial in a home with dogs because it can make bathing more effective. It reduces the quantity of soap used while improving lathering and removal and can alleviate dry skin. On the other hand, the "softening" process adds sodium to your water. The quantity will vary depending on your water. Reverse osmosis (RO) can remove sodium from water and an RO system could be added if appropriate for your situation.

Bottled water is often recommended to prevent brown staining on a dog's coat caused by mineral laden water. Although bottled water does not come under the same scrutiny as tap water and can be contaminated, most bottled water is safe to drink.

LIGHTING

Humans are diurnal animals, that is, we are more active during the day and our eyes are more adapted to daylight. Dogs are cathemeral or arrhythmic, meaning they are active during both day and night and therefore have good vision in a wide range of light levels. Since the dogs visual system is built for the practical purpose of finding, killing and eating prey their lighting needs are less specific and more adaptable. Dogs sleep during both day and night and lighting does not seem to impact their sleep patterns. Dogs have adapted well to the human need for light. Three types of light are part of the human environment: natural, daylight and artificial. The sun, moon, stars and fire, are considered natural light. Daylight comes from the sun, but windows, skylights and solar tubes play a key role in bringing light to our spaces. Incandescent, fluorescent, LED, and HID are some examples of artificial light. Dog/human related activities require light and most of us are not very critical about the source or quality. And this is a mistake. Good light is not only important for careful work; it has a huge impact on our perceptions and mental wellbeing. Lighting focuses attention, guides us through a space and provides security by enhancing visibility, illuminating hazards, or removing us from danger. Lighting design has become a very important part of creating dynamic and comfortable interior spaces for humans and their dogs.

The best approach for designing lighting is to determine what your lighting needs are. Is it for a specific task, to illuminate a particular feature, for security or just so you can move through a space? Try to visualize where you want the light to fall. Not all spaces need to be evenly lighted but it is important to avoid abrupt changes in light level. For example if you are moving from a very dark space into a very bright space your eyes will not adjust immediately and you could be temporarily blinded by the change. While dogs have excellent versatility in adapting to light levels, their eyes still have to adapt.

LIGHT AND HEALTH

Many species are biologically affected by natural light thanks to our innate biological clock that regulates sleep and waking which is known as circadian rhythm. Other physiologic processes are controlled including body temperature, blood pressure and the release of hormones. This clock depends on the natural light cycle within any given 24 hours—the cycle of day and night. Sunlight, or UV light is important for the health and wellbeing of dogs just as it is for humans. In humans and dogs, lack of sunlight will disrupt the circadian rhythm and can cause Seasonal Affective Disorder (SAD). It is most common in humans who live in hemispheres more closely situated to the poles. People with SAD may become depressed and fatigued. Dogs with SAD develop a specific pattern of hair loss usually involving the flanks. Dogs (and humans) may benefit from light therapy which consists of doses of high levels of light intensity during the waking hours to help set or adjust the circadian rhythm. UV light is necessary for dogs to synthesize Vitamin D through their skin. To accomplish this it's important to take your dog outside at least once a day for a few minutes.

See Resources for products and more information.

FLICKERING LIGHTS

Research indicates that dogs see the flickering lines in a TV and may see flickering in fluorescent lights. While it is known that rapidly flickering lights can cause epileptic seizures in humans it is not clear whether this is true in dogs. Fluorescent lights are also notorious for buzzing ballasts which may be disruptive to dogs as well.

CHAPTER 5

The Kitchen and Dining Areas

Generous overhead lighting

Extracting vent fan

Refrigerator with freezer drawer below

Hard surface countertop

Deep sink with goose neck faucet and sprayer

Bistro style seating with metal legs

Porcelain tile floor

This kitchen has many dog friendly attributes that can be easily adapted into any new kitchen or renovation. *Courtesy of Heritage Custom Cabinetry: www.heritagecabinetry.biz (P. Leach)*

The kitchen is the busiest and, at times, the messiest room of the house. Durable, washable and hygienic surfaces are essential. Along with all daily human activities, dogs typically eat in the kitchen and dog food, supplies and medications may be stored here. Your dog may bathe or sleep in the kitchen as well. Increasingly dog owners also use their kitchens to prepare homemade and raw diets. Kitchens are rarely designed with a particular lifestyle or family in mind so it is important to consider your dog's needs when reorganizing, renovating or building a new kitchen.

Every dog owner wants a kitchen floor that is durable and easy to clean and countless choices seem to fit this bill. Porcelain ceramic tile takes top honors for durability and stain resistance. It is also aesthetically pleasing, easily maintained and works well with radiant floor heating systems. Other good choices include non-porcelain ceramic tile, concrete, terrazzo and stone. Ceramic and stone tiles are easiest to install yourself, while terrazzo or concrete must be poured and require a professional installation. Drawbacks to hard surface floors include being slippery and hard underfoot. Area rugs with non-slip backings can minimize both problems. Hard surface floors can be damaged by hard heavy items like a big metal dog crate. Tiles can be replaced, so it is essential to buy extras for repairs. Chips and cracks can be repaired in concrete or terrazzo.

Softer and less slippery flooring options include PVC-free resilient floors such as linoleum or cork. Cork and linoleum are easy to maintain and fairly durable. Properly cared for they can last for decades. Both are environmentally friendly because they are made from renewable natural resources. Linoleum was the precursor to vinyl and people still mistakenly refer to vinyl flooring as linoleum. It is made from natural ingredients, one of which is linseed oil, a natural antimicrobial agent. Cork flooring is made from the outer bark of a cork oak tree that is specific to the Mediterranean region. Both can be purchased in sheets, tiles and planks. While professional installation is recommended for sheet goods, other forms can be installed DIY. Cork can be bought unfinished or prefinished in a variety of colors and textures. Linoleum or cork should not be used in basements or anywhere with constant moisture.

Recommended choices for kitchen wall finishes include ceramic or stone tile or painted drywall. For cleaning and ease of maintenance choose eggshell or satin finishes for kitchen wall paints. See more on paints in Chapter 6.

Countertops are made from a variety of materials including high pressure laminate (aka laminate), solid surfacing, stone, engineered quartz (aka quartz composite), ceramic tile, concrete, linoleum, stainless steel, glass and wood. With so many choices it isn't always easy to make a selection. If you have a large dog that likes to counter surf you will need something that resists scratches. At the other end of the spectrum, placing your small dog on the kitchen counter after a bath may result in similar damage from nails. Understanding the capabilities and limitations of these materials will prevent

Teddy shows off a durable porcelain tile floor.

most surprises and save you money. The main criteria for dog owners when selecting a countertop are cost, durability, ease of maintenance and sustainability. Recycled glass, engineered quartz, granite or quartz stone, high pressure laminates, solid surfacing and concrete can all fit this bill. Refer to Recommended Countertops table for details on material properties and composition.

Countertop surfaces run the gamut from economical laminates to outrageously expensive stone. Generally laminates are the least expensive, stone or stainless steel the most expensive, with everything else somewhere in between. Due to weight and material constraints, professional installation is recommended for most countertops.

Even if you have only one dog, you probably have better things to do than worry about maintaining your kitchen countertops. Wood, stone and concrete countertops must be sealed after installation and also require periodic resealing and/or refinishing. The timeframe varies by use and material. For example, granite should be resealed once or twice a year, while a penetrating sealer on concrete may need a coating of wax every eight weeks. Non-porous materials such as laminates, engineered quartz or recycled glass composites are easiest to maintain. They have the highest resistance to water and stains and don't require resealing or refinishing. Surfaces such as wood and stone are porous or easily abraded. Countertops can be cleaned daily with a mild soap but may not tolerate

RECOMMENDED COUNTERTOPS

TYPE	ENGINEERED QUARTZ	GRANITE	HIGH PRESSURE LAMINATE	SOLID SURFACING	RECYCLED GLASS	CONCRETE
MATERIAL COMPOSITION	90% Quartz	100% Granite	Layers of paper with a top layer of plastic	Polymers, pigments and ground stone	Recycled Glass chips, Cement	Portland Cement and Variable Additives
BRANDS	Cambria, Silestone		See Resources	Corian, Avonite	Enviroslab, Icestone, Vetrazzo	
THICKNESS	¾" to 1 ¼"	¾" to 1 ¼"	1/16"	Varies by manufacturer, ¼" to ¾"	Varies by manufacturer, 1" typical	2 ½" typical
COST	$$$	$$	$	$$	$$	$ to $$$ (can be DIY)
SCRATCH RESISTANCE	Very Good	Good	Fair	Fair	Very Good	Fair to Good**
STAIN RESISTANCE*	Very Good	Good*	Very Good	Fair to Good	Very Good	Fair to Very Good***
WATER RESISTANCE	Very Good	Good	Good	Very Good	Very Good	Good***
IMPACT RESISTANCE	Fair	Fair	Good	Good	Good	Fair
DURABILITY/ LIFESPAN	Very Good	Very Good	Good	Good	Very Good	Very Good
MAINTENANCE	Easy	Fair	Easy	Easy	Easy	Fair
EASILY REPAIRED	No	No	No	Yes		Yes
REQUIRES SEALING	No	Yes, 6 months to one year	No	No	No	Yes, frequency depends on type of sealer
SUSTAINABLE QUALITIES**** PROS	Long life, durable	Long life, durable, recyclable	Minimal materials used	Possible reuse	Long life, possible reuse	Long life, possibly recycled
SUSTAINABLE QUALITIES CONS	Made with epoxy binders	Quarried may contain high levels of radon	Can't be recycled or reused. Made with plastic	Made with plastic polymers	Made with chemical binders	High embodied energy to make
OTHER (WEIGHT)	¾" thick is 5-6 lbs/SF	¾" thick is 13 lbs/SF			1" thick is 14.5 lbs/SF	2-1" thick is 30 lbs/SF

* Must be properly sealed and maintained.
** Penetrating sealer better than topical sealer for this attribute.
*** Topical sealer better than penetrating sealer for this attribute.
**** Most of these materials have the possibility to be recycled through reuse; the reality is that most are thrown out when no longer desired.

stronger disinfectants or abrasive cleaners. If you are unsure about acceptable cleaning products for your countertop, consult the manufacturer's website. Liquid spills, including water, should be cleaned up as soon as possible on any type of countertop to prevent staining. Surfaces with seams, like laminates, or that are porous, like wood are vulnerable to water damage.

Countertops are found in countless choices of color, texture and finish. Viewing a large sample is essential for patterned material that repeats across several feet. Since stone countertops are sold mostly as slabs a small sample is not necessarily representative of the actual slab you might get. Therefore it is always wise to view your final slab selection at the stone dealer or fabricator before signing off on it.

Chlorine bleach products can also cause problems for dogs and humans with respiratory conditions. It's not right for all countertop surfaces, either. Ammonia, alcohol or hydrogen peroxide based disinfectants may be a better option. Homemade remedies, such as vinegar and water may effectively kill some, but not all, bacteria.

In truth, there are very few environmentally perfect countertops. A kitchen renovation, while the most expensive, is cited as the one job that will give a homeowner the highest return for their dollars. Because of this and the fact that kitchens have become status symbols they are the most frequently renovated room in homes. During renovations countertops are often pulled out and thrown away. Furnishings are replaced for aesthetic reasons alone even if there is still more functional life left in the materials. Be kind to the environment and select your countertop wisely. Look for materials that are durable and easily maintained. Avoid trendy colors and finishes in favor of recycled materials or those that can be recycled or reused. Post-consumer recycled content is preferred to post-industrial and the higher the content the better. Good choices include concrete, concrete composites, stone and stone composites, recycled paper and recycled glass composites. For instance, recycled glass countertops are composed of nearly 90% post consumer recycled material. Stone is retrieved by quarrying which is not an environmentally friendly method. Stone however, has a high potential to be reused or recycled. Solid wood countertops may seem like a great environmental choice. They have low VOCs, are a renewable resource, recyclable and biodegradable. But the maintenance required to keep them looking good is a major drawback. Even a proper hard finish must be reapplied on a regular basis. Wood surfaces are prone to water damage, mold, stains and scratches. Despite expert advice to the contrary, it is very difficult

to sand and repair stains in wood without it being noticeable. Innovative countertop materials include those made from recycled paper. One manufacturer claims that their material has been tested under water for three months with no visible damage. Be wary of products with antibacterial chemical additives. These may do more harm than good by fostering chemical resistant bacteria.

SINKS

Sinks are made from stainless steel, porcelain on steel, cast iron, copper, brass, stone, glass, composite resins, concrete and ceramic. All of these materials are fairly stain resistant. Stone composites made by combining resins with ground quartz or granite are the most durable. Other durable choices include stainless steel and concrete.

> A stainless steel sink with a heavier gauge will better resist dings and scratches from dog nails. The lower the gauge number, the heavier the material. The chrome and nickel content are also good indicators of quality.
>
> A sink made from 18% chrome and 10% nickel would be indicated as 18/10 stainless steel. The higher the percentage of nickel the more rust and corrosion resistant it will be. 18/10 is best but 18/8 is also very good.

Sink styles include rimmed, under mounted, and apron. Rimmed styles are common but not the best choice for dog owners. They have a raised rim that sits on top of the countertop surface which makes it more difficult for water to drain back into the sink. Food and grime will collect around the rim edge. Under mounted sinks sit below the surface and create a flush continuous look. Because they lack a rim they are easier to keep clean and water can be drained back into the sink making this a top choice for anyone who bathes dogs in their kitchen sink. These can't be used with laminate countertops. Apron style sinks, sometimes called farmhouse style, sit within the countertop; the rim and front edge are both visible. These are often oversized, an advantage if you bathe your dogs in the kitchen sink. For more info on bathing dogs see Chapters 8 and 9.

> Stone countertops have long been a status symbol in modern kitchens because of their beauty, durability and long lifespan. Stone consists of different minerals, such as quartz, calcite or talc. Because of its hardness, stone with high concentrations of quartz, such as granite, quartz and soapstone are the most durable and stain resistant.
>
> Stone containing calcite, such as marble, limestone or travertine are softer and more vulnerable to staining and scratching. Generally speaking a more visually active surface is more prone to breakage. For durability select stone that has an even consistency with minimal variation and veining.

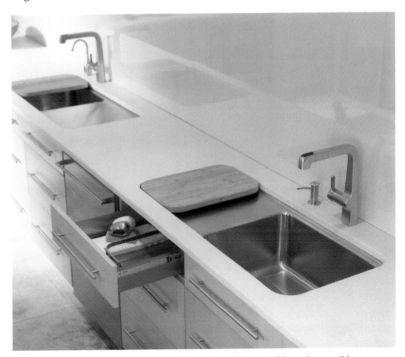

Drawers provide more storage space while making objects visible and accessible.
Courtesy of Kohler: www.kohler.com

Single, double or triple basins can make life far easier or more complicated for dog owners. If you need multiple compartments to disinfect dishes or equipment or give your dog leads a nice soak, a divider can be a godsend. If you need to bathe a dog any larger than a Chihuahua it will be a nightmare. One solution is to purchase a sink with a low divider between the two basins. (see photos)

If you use your sink for dog washing, size and depth are critical. The sink should be at least four inches longer than your dog measured from chest to rump, and at least chest deep.

Deeper bowls are more expensive, but they have important advantages. Keeping the dog in the sink is easier, safer and allows space for a taller faucet, which makes rinsing more efficient, especially if you bathe drop coated dogs with long flowing fur like Yorkies or Maltese. With high faucets, a deep bowl is essential to prevent splashing, overflow and a mess when your wet dog shakes.

FAUCETS

The two basic types of kitchen faucets are wall mounted or sink mounted. They can also be either a single-handle style or a widespread kitchen style with two handles. For most dog owners, anything that allows for single handed or hands free operation is an advantage.

Two types of hands free faucets have been used in hospitals for many years and are now available for home use. Both can be used with some existing faucets. They help to prevent contamination from touching the faucet with dirty hands, making them useful for raw food preparation areas. One type is operated with a foot pedal and the other has a motion sensor activator. The foot pedal can be used for bathing dogs, but motion activated faucets would be constantly activated whenever the dog moved, making them a poor choice if you bathe your dog in the sink.

A goose neck style faucet that is tall or swings out of the way also increases sink space for dog washing. Not every faucet has a retractable sprayer attachment, which many dog owners find indispensable. There are two basic types of sprayers, a separate sprayer unit or an integrated faucet sprayer. Integrated sprayers are the most convenient and efficient for dog washing. Sinks have different hole configurations so make sure your sink and faucet needs are compatible.

TOP Self-rimming double bowl enamel on cast iron sink with pull out sprayer.
Courtesy of Kohler: www.kohler.com
BOTTOM Undermounted quartz composite sink with separate sprayer.
Courtesy of Elkay: www.elkayusa.com

KITCHEN STORAGE

Many owners fight a losing battle with their dogs over kitchen storage space. Dogs often view the refrigerator or pantry as "the magic box" and many of them can outwit almost anything designed to keep them out.

Cabinets usually define the character of a kitchen. Unfortunately because of what they hold, many dogs are also quite fond of them. Choosing the right materials and design elements prevent many dog related complications. Cabinets are made from solid wood, wood composites with veneers of wood, laminate or melamine, metal, plastic and even concrete. Dog owners should examine individual design features to determine whether a cabinet will meet their potential needs.

Cabinet surfaces, especially the base or lower cabinets typically endure the most abuse from dogs.

- Solid wood is a good choice because it can be refinished, but serious chewing damage may necessitate replacement.
- Dog damage on painted wood cabinets can usually be patched and repainted.
- Veneers can sometimes be replaced but this requires skilled workmanship.
- Metal is the most durable, but it can be scratched, dinged or rust.

For added protection from chewing and scratching, consider covering your cabinet doors with a clear plastic, such as acrylic or polycarbonate with a scratch resistant finish. Depending upon the finish of the cabinet doors you might be able to adhere it with double stick masking tape or attach it with screws. Double stick tape may damage the finish and screw holes will need to be repaired if you remove the plastic but this is still preferable to replacing the entire unit.

The basic cabinet door styles are flush or frame and panel. The doors are further defined by the manner in which they are installed in the cabinet frame. Full inset doors fit within the cabinet frame on all four sides. Partial inset doors fit on one or more sides of the four sides of the frame. Inset doors are much more difficult for dogs to open which makes them preferable to overlay doors that sit in front of the frame of the cabinet on all sides of the door opening. Inset doors are more expensive because they are better constructed and require a more accurate fit. Sliding doors are another, less expensive, alternative. They are difficult for dogs to open and a hook and eye door catch can be added for extra security. However, they do limit access to the cabinet.

Door and drawer pulls are usually considered minor accents to kitchen design but they can cause major problems for dog owners. Puppies and dogs can get collars, jaws or feet caught on or in open ended or ring door pulls. The biggest problem results from dogs grabbing and chewing them. They are at eye level, providing constant temptation for many dogs.

THE KITCHEN SINK

If you are looking for a kitchen sink to wash your small to medium sized dog one of these styles might be best for you. Large single bowl sinks are adequate for medium sized dogs. If you have your heart set on a double bowl sink suitable for dog bathing consider one of the low divide styles on the market today, such as Kohler's Smart Divide® double bowl sink. Select stainless steel or quartz composite finishes for durability.

Stainless steel apron sink with gooseneck pull out sprayer faucet.
Courtesy of Kohler: www.kohler.com

The Smart Divide® sink has a double bowl with a low center divide.
Courtesy of Kohler: www.kohler.com

ABOVE AND LEFT Example of partial inset doors: left image shows sliding door, middle shows both sliding and hinged door, right shows hinged door closed. Note that the bottom of the frame sits under the door so a dog cannot grasp the door with paws or teeth. Additionally, no food is stored in these lower cabinets. Instead, a pantry serves that purpose.

Integrated drawer pulls. *Courtesy of Kohler: www.kohler.com*

Custom made 1/2" diameter door pulls could foil some dogs.

Recessed drawer pulls. *Courtesy of Kohler: www.kohler.com*

If your dog is a safecracker, childproof locks may prevent access to cabinets. However, these often become a nuisance for homeowners and some clever canines can figure them out. If your dog is the "problem solving type" this approach may cause more complications than it resolves.

DINING AREAS

Dining areas are a major source of interest for dogs. Dogs that are fed directly from the table can quickly become a nuisance during mealtime and this behavior often intensifies when company is watching. This is an instinctive canine survival strategy where more humans translate into more opportunities for food.

Dining tables range between 28″ and 30″ high which puts them in reach of nearly every size dog. A Great Dane can rest his head on the table top. A lively Fox Terrier could easily get on the table by climbing chairs or jumping. Bistro style tables that are 42″ to 44″ high may help in these situations. Dogs are more likely to jump onto table tops by the presence of food or food scented objects like napkins, tablecloths or dishes, but simple curiosity can be an equally powerful lure. Dogs can scratch the finish on a wood table. Worse yet, some learn to pull down tablecloths or placemats along with anything sitting on top of them. Supervise your dog in the dining room or keep your tables clear of tableware, candlesticks, and flower arrangements.

For environmental reasons, avoid vinyl (PVC) tablecloths and instead choose polyethylene, or water resistant fabrics such as Crypton® or Sunbrella®. (See Chapter 6 for more about fabrics.) Folding table pads can be placed under a tablecloth for additional protection. They usually have a soft side on the bottom and a plastic top. Make your own protector by cutting a sheet of cork or Homasote® to fit your table. Fabric table protectors can be custom made to fit your dining table and more dog resistant variations include quilted pads with drawstring or elastic to hold them in place. If you are handy with a sewing machine you can make fitted covers yourself.

Dog friendly dining tables should be stable, and sturdy enough to withstand a blow from a large dog and resist tipping if a dog jumps on an edge or the top. Tabletops with sharp

U shaped door pulls also cause problems, particularly if you hang towels from them. Puppies (and many adult dogs), tug on the towel, discover they can open the door or drawer and gain access to the contents. Once they learn this maneuver, it can be impossible to keep them out. There are design solutions for these problems.

- Finger pulls cut or integrated into the drawer or door are a good alternative to projecting door or drawer pulls.
- Many dogs have an aversion to grabbing metal surfaces. Switching to metal door pulls may be the answer—so long as you won't be tempted to hang towels from them.
- Select door pulls that are too large or small for the dog to grip, depending on the size of the dog. For example small dogs will not be able to get a tight grip on a big door pull while a very small door pull, less than ½" in diameter, is difficult for a larger dog to grasp in its mouth.

Drawers are a better storage solution than shelves because the contents are more immediately visible which improves efficiency and overall storage capacity. It's important to select full-extension drawer glides that optimize storage and access to your items. Self-closing and soft-close drawer glides have a slower release which can be more difficult for dogs to open. These types of glides combined with the right drawer pull offers the best safeguard.

edges or glass tops can pose a danger to both dogs and small children. Circular tables alleviate the danger of sharp corners. Pedestal bases should be broad, heavy and securely attached to the top. Table legs should be sturdy enough to absorb the force and weight of a large dog. Don't hesitate to test these features in the furniture store with your own body.

Hard surface dining chairs are preferable to designs with slipcovers or cushions. Dogs are attracted to any surface with a human scent which makes cushions a target for chewing. Many dogs love nibbling slipcovers and edges of cushions. Along with household damage, a dog can become ill from ingesting the stuffing. Dining chairs with cushions should have removable and washable covers.

Wood chairs are a traditional canine chewing favorite and countless dining room chairs succumb to this fate. However, many dogs dislike chewing metal or plastic chair legs. Metal legs hold up fairly well to chewing, although teeth marks and scratches may be visible. Scratches tend to be less noticeable on finishes with lower luster or shine, making them a better choice than high gloss finishes.

FEEDING

Convenience and finishes that are usually capable of withstanding spillage make the kitchen the ideal place to feed your dog. Dogs are territorial and they appreciate a consistent routine, so it's important to feed your dog in one spot, with minimal distractions. Don't place his dish in front of doors, cabinets, appliances or next to the phone. Feeding him in a crate is the easiest solution in a busy kitchen.

A plastic boot tray or one made specifically for pet dishes can be used to protect a non-moisture resistant floor. Rimless plastic mats won't prevent liquids from seeping underneath and permanently staining the floor. Other options include textile mats with a rubber backing or carpet entry mats that can be easily washed and dried.

Canine diets vary widely from raw game to plain old kibble. No matter what you feed your dog, it must be stored safely and inaccessible to your dog until it is consumed. Dogs are hard-wired to raid the food supply and given the chance, many dogs will eat themselves sick or worse.

An energy-saving freezer unit is a good investment if you feed a diet of primarily meat. This allows you to purchase up to a six month supply, divide it into daily or weekly portions and thaw as needed. Storing a hundred pounds of kibble is more complicated. Kibble has a shelf life of three months, but it begins to lose nutritional value as soon as the package is opened. It should be stored in airtight containers to prevent moisture and air from contacting the food. If removed from the bag, store kibble in food grade containers of stainless steel, glass or food grade plastic. Food grade plastics include polycarbonate, polyethylene and polyester. Regular plastics may contain harmful chemicals which can break down over time and contaminate the food. Plastic garbage bags are not food grade. Never store food in containers that originally contained chemicals, paints or other non-foods.

If you make your own dog food, feed multiple dogs or serve a raw diet, a separate canine feeding station is an ideal solution.

LEFT These plastic chairs were substituted for antique wood chairs after a new puppy began chewing the legs. The puppy left the plastic alone.

RIGHT Soft table edges eliminate hazards.

Any horizontal surface near a sink can work as long as it's large enough to accommodate all of the dishes for simultaneous preparation. Handy storage space, drawers or doors, can be an even more important convenience. It should be large enough to accommodate all your dishes, food, vitamins, supplements, measuring scoops, etc. Homemade dog food has many nutritional advantages but it can be time consuming and often impossible to disguise the aromas of simmering tripe or liver!

Homes with multiple dogs with different feeding needs:

- Tape individual feeding instructions somewhere noticeable, especially if you are not the only person in charge of this chore.
- If serving kibble purchase separate measuring cups indicating the serving size for one meal.
- Scoops can be color coded to differentiate dogs.

Wall mounted metal gates keep dogs in or out of spaces.

The only way to adequately remove odors is with direct ventilation outdoors using either an operable window or an efficient extracting exhaust fan. Many home kitchen fans simply re-circulate the air through a filter and this will not remove odors. An activated carbon or charcoal filter can help in these fans. Enzymatic cleaners, such as Nature's Miracle, are good at removing odors at the source of a spill or stain. To be effective they must be left to air dry at the location of the spill.

FOOD HANDLING

Restaurant sanitary codes provide an excellent lesson in safe food handling. Because of the ever-present risk of bacterial contamination raw meat must be kept separate from other food. Store it in a specific refrigerator bin used only for dog food. If multiple people use the refrigerator label the bin and the food. If you have multiple dogs or a large dog you might consider a separate refrigerator and/or freezer. Some newer smaller compartment drawer designs, based on restaurant kitchen equipment are perfect for this.

Raw food should be consumed in dishes on floors that are smooth, scratch resistant, easily cleaned and disinfected such as concrete, linoleum, or ceramic tile. Walls near the feeding area should also be smooth and easy to clean. Concrete, ceramic tile or fiber reinforced plastic (FRP) are all excellent wall choices. FRP is commonly used for dairy production areas and restaurant kitchen walls. Sodium hypochlorite bleach, like Clorox®, is considered the best disinfectant for killing Salmonella and e.coli. If you use these solutions on floors where your dogs eat, rinse thoroughly after each washing or consider newer disinfectants made from bleach alternatives such as hydrogen peroxide.

KITCHEN SAFETY

Kitchens are full of canine temptations but it's easy to prevent problems. For safety, train or restrain your dog to keep him outside the kitchen work zone. Gates are a helpful management tool. Placing dog beds and crates outside work areas helps too.

Dogs can be injured by hot food falling from the stove and will not hesitate to poke their paws or noses into ovens or dishwashers looking for food. Never leave food on the range top, whether it's on or off. Ovens with front controls can be accidentally turned on by a jumping dog. Older gas ranges without electric starts are equally dangerous because larger dogs can still turn on the gas. A stove guard can be placed on the front of your stove to keep paws and noses safe.

Many dogs curl up in front of the dishwasher to enjoy the warmth of the dry cycle. Others hover nearby waiting to lick dirty dishes. Most dishwashing detergent is caustic. And dogs have been known to get collars hooked in racks, pulling the entire contents out in a panic. They can also be accidentally cut by sharp utensils, or have an ear, tail or foot closed in the door. It's always better to be proactive rather than reactive. Discourage your dog from hanging out in front of the dishwasher. Body block your dog while you load the dishes or train him to sit while you work.

Dogs learn how to open the refrigerator through trial and error experiments by pulling on dishtowels or fiddling with door handles. Once they figure it out, they never forget how to do it. In extreme situations, a chain and padlock wrapped around the entire refrigerator and through the door handle has been used successfully. Less drastic solutions include purchasing a new refrigerator with a totally unfamiliar door unit and training your dog to stay away from the work zone. Refrigerators with drawers instead of doors are more difficult for a dog to open. Freestanding dog gates, such as ex-pens, can be placed around the refrigerator (not very convenient for the humans, but it does work).

Large dogs are the usual suspects in counter surfing crimes but many small dogs learn to do it by climbing from one surface to another. This adds another element of danger. Chairs with casters are especially dangerous, because the dog can lose his balance and fall. They can also get feet or jaws caught in decorative iron table legs or accidentally collapse

Refrigerator with freezer drawer below may be more dog proof!

TOP Dog proof garbage cans are essential in a dog-friendly home. This sturdy metal garbage can has a locking mechanism. *Courtesy of Doggy+Safe®: www.doggy-safe.com*

ABOVE A simple indoor/outdoor worm compost unit that accommodates dog waste too. *Courtesy of Tumbleweed Sales Pty. Ltd.: www.tumbleweed.com.au*

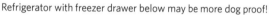

step ladders on top of themselves during climbing maneuvers. Your best option is never to leave food on the countertops unattended.

Dogs have been tempted to lick or chew sharp knives and other utensils. These should be stored in a drawer rather than in a storage container on top of the counter.

Cleaning supplies are customarily stored under the kitchen sink but this is not recommended for dog owners. Placing them in a higher location or a closet with a door prevents any possibility of your dog getting into them.

GARBAGE AND COMPOSTING

If your dog is addicted to dumpster diving simply hiding the garbage rarely solves the problem. Dogs can always find it. They can also open most trashcan lids, including the foot pedal type. Stainless steel rat proof trash receptacles will foil many dogs but these tend to be small, and comparatively

expensive. Bear proof trash containers also work but most homeowners feel they are human-proof as well. Dog proof garbage cans are usually made from stainless steel, with a foot pedal, lid and a locking mechanism on the lid. Some locks have a hole for a padlock (which should tell you something). They work for most dogs but also include warnings that they may not thwart creative, persistent dogs. They typically cost more, about $100. Considering the cost of a trip to the emergency vet and potential surgery from a blockage, the cost is worth it. A more economical solution might be to add a locking mechanism to a less expensive can.

Hanging a large bell on the side of the trashcan or setting a couple of metal dishes on top can startle your dog and ruin the sneak attack. The safest, most effective solution is to keep your trash inside a latched cabinet, special garbage drawer unit, locked closet with a passage door or dispose of it before you leave the house.

ABOVE This stylish kitchen was designed with 2 dogs and 1 cat in mind and includes an automatic waterer, pet food prep area and a door directly outdoors. *Courtesy of The Livable Home Store: www.thelivablehomestore.com*

RIGHT This compost unit can be used indoors and will compost dog waste. *Courtesy of Nature Mill: www.naturemill.com*

As part of today's efforts to live more gently on the planet many families have begun to compost food waste. This is often done with a simple bin or bucket kept in the kitchen. Compost waste is a source of temptation for dogs and can be a source of toxic mold that can cause severe gastric upset or worse. Compost waste should always be kept in a sealed container within a cabinet or behind closed doors, never on the countertop. Several companies make indoor composting units that lock.

If your dog habitually gets into trouble in the kitchen, he should always be crated or confined to another room when unsupervised.

See Resources for products and more information.

Living Rooms, Offices and Libraries

The living room evokes a peaceful scenario with you reading a book on the sofa, a fire in the hearth and your faithful companion curled up beside you. Or maybe you see yourself working at your computer with your dog contently lying at your feet. In reality sharing your living room, den or office with your dog will require special considerations to protect your furnishings and your dog. Furniture in these rooms is likely to be scratched, chewed, or soiled if your dog has access to them. Durability is a necessity that cannot be understated. While some furniture is more resilient no piece is entirely dog proof and no fabric is resistant to a dog's teeth, not even Kevlar®.

Fixed lighting and no table lamps

Plants and art objects placed high

Fireplace with glass doors and raised hearth

Distressed furniture

Swivel chairs

Hardwood floors with modular carpet

Taut back sofa, micro-suede fabric

You don't have to give up comfort or style when creating a living room for you and your dog. Dog-friendly features for this particular household include: distressed furniture that hides dog damage, swivel chairs to dissuade large dogs, plants and artwork out of reach and a taut back sofa that prevents chewing and digging.

Hardwood or ceramic tile in combination with area rugs can be an excellent dog friendly flooring solution. Mitch Frankenberg, owner of the Paw House Inn in West Rutland, Vermont, believes that the best flooring solution is hard wood floors in combination with strategically placed rugs in circulation and high traffic areas.

The Paw House Inn caters to dogs and their owners exclusively, so Mitch has had experience with a wide variety of dogs and people on a daily basis. Part of his overall strategy to cut maintenance and preserve his floors requires guests to remove their shoes before entering the living spaces.

When choosing flooring, important factors include budget, lifestyle, frequency of maintenance, heating systems and the makeup of your dog population. If you and your Labrador Retriever Greta lead a very active life and spend a lot of time outdoors durable hard surface finishes like wood, ceramic tile or concrete are more sensible choices. On the other hand, if you have one small sedentary dog, such as your Pekingese Mitzi, carpet might be fine. Dogs that are not allowed on furniture, large, heavy boned dogs or those with joint problems may require soft flooring to lie on. Dogs with mobility problems, such as those missing limbs and or mobility carts, will need even, stable, surface textures that do not change in height. (For more on dogs with special needs see Chapter 11.) The best flooring choices for a dog-friendly home include: porcelain ceramic tile, solid wood, cork, linoleum, stone and concrete. Area rugs with non-slip backings or modular carpet tiles can add softness and slip resistance.

All hardwood floors are durable, attractive and fairly easy to maintain. Solid hardwood and bamboo are both good wood floor options for dog owners. While wood itself does not produce VOCs, many finishes do, so prefinished floors are preferable. Solid wood floors are also better from an environmental standpoint because they can be refinished, while engineered or laminated floors cannot. Select wood or bamboo from Forest Stewardship Council (FSC) certified suppliers. Reclaimed or recycled wood are also good options. Reclaimed wood comes from trees that were lost in lakes or rivers during logging operations over 100 years ago; recycled wood is reused from bridges and wood buildings. Select those with a rougher finish that has the advantage of providing excellent camouflage for dog damage. Avoid using dark stains on lighter colored wood floors because scratches will be more evident as the stain layer is worn off revealing the lighter color of the wood beneath it. Porcelain ceramic tile and concrete are also good choices although concrete is porous, and must be finished and sealed.

Dogs and rugs are not traditionally considered to be compatible but in reality area rugs and modular carpet tiles can be dog-friendly. Area rugs, such as wool Oriental rugs show very little dirt and can be periodically removed for cleaning.

Indoor/outdoor rugs that resemble jute or other natural fibers work very well, making them both functional and good looking. These rugs are made of 100% polyethylene and can be washed with a hose outdoors. They dry very quickly, making them a better choice than most synthetic rugs.

Carpet modules are typically 20″ x 20″ and are fastened to the floor or to each other with adhesive tabs. They are easy to install and can be used as area rugs or wall to wall. Sections can be removed and washed in a sink and individually replaced if necessary. From an environmental standpoint they also make a lot of sense. The smaller modular size minimizes waste and many carpet modules can be recycled.

Avoid PVC (aka vinyl), carpet with chemical finishes and even some natural products. Natural materials like cotton, jute or sisal may seem environmentally friendly. This may or may not be true depending on where they came from, how they were grown and how they are processed. Cotton is typically grown using chemical fertilizers and pesticides. Chemical residue will remain on these products even after they reach your home. In order to be dyed evenly cotton is first bleached with chlorine bleach, which adds more chemicals to the finished product. If you choose cotton, look for certified organic cotton.

Also keep in mind that naturally dyed fibers such as jute and sisal may not be colorfast. Most natural fibers readily accept dye, partly because most of them are plant based and plants readily absorb water. They can release those dyes just as readily. So, if your dog dumps his water dish or urinates on a naturally dyed jute carpet, the dye will likely run, possibly staining the floor underneath. Synthetic material such as polylactic acid (PLA) which is commonly made from corn also seems to be an environmentally responsible choice. PLA, which is considered a plastic, has applications for carpet, upholstery fabric and filler for cushions or pillows. While PLA is biodegradable it must be composted using industrial standard systems that run at high temperatures. So while the quantity of environmentally friendly products is much better today, the selection process is not always straightforward.

Smooth wall surfaces are easier to keep clean so painted walls or finished paneling are the best choices for dog owners. Select washable matte and eggshell latex paint finishes for walls and semi-gloss finishes for trim. Avoid finishes that can't be cleaned easily such as wallpaper. It's almost impossible to clean dog urine off of wallpaper without destroying the paper. If you want wallpaper limit its application to the top half of the walls and use paint or a hard surface on the bottom half. A trim piece could be used to divide the two sections.

ENVIRONMENTALLY FRIENDLY PAINT OPTIONS
Although all paint must meet a minimum VOC standard, it is generally known that those with no or very low VOCs are the best choice. Select flat paint with VOCs less than 50 grams per liter and non-flat paint with less than 150 grams per liter. The most commonly used paint is latex but there are other more natural choices that include clay, lime and milk paints.

RECOMMENDED DOG-FRIENDLY FLOORING

TYPE	SOLID WOOD AND BAMBOO	PORCELAIN CERAMIC TILE	RECYCLED GLASS TILE	CONCRETE	CORK	MODULAR CARPET	LINOLEUM
COST	$$	$ to $$	$$	$ to $$	$$	$ to $$	$
LIFESPAN	50+	50+	Unknown	50+	50+	10+	50+
INSTALLATION**	Professional or DIY	Professional or DIY	Professional or DIY	Professional	Professional or DIY	DIY	Professional or DIY
SCRATCH RESISTANCE	Fair	Very Good	Very Good	Good	Good	Very Good	Good
STAIN RESISTANCE*	Fair to Good	Very Good	Very Good	Fair to Good	Fair to Good	Fair to Good	Fair to Good
SLIPPERY FOR SOME DOGS	Yes	Yes	Yes	Yes	No	No	When wet
MAINTENANCE	Easy	Easy	Easy	Easy	Fair	Fair (some can be washed)	Easy
REPAIRED	Yes	Tiles can be replaced	Tiles can be replaced	Yes	Tiles or planks can be replaced	Tiles can be replaced	Tiles or planks can be replaced
REQUIRES PERIODIC REFINISHING	Yes	No	No	Yes	Yes	No	No
SUSTAINABLE QUALITIES PROS	No VOCs*** Can be refinished Renewable Biodegradable Recyclable	No VOCs Durable Long Life Modular size	No VOCs Durable Long Life Modular size Recycled content	Durable Long Life No underlayment required Can be recycled	No VOCs*** Long Life Renewable Biodegradable	Modular size Recycled content available Some can be reused or recycled	Low VOCs Biodegradable Natural
SUSTAINABLE QUALITIES CONS	Finishes may emit VOCs for awhile Concerns about sources	High embodied energy	High embodied energy Some tiles made with chemical additives (epoxy)	High embodied energy	Formaldehyde binders in some Concerns about harvesting	VOCs Made from synthetic polymers Not biodegradable	Strong odor initially
OTHER	Select FSC, Recycled or Reclaimed and Prefinished	Buy extra for replacement	Buy extra for replacement			Buy extra for replacement	

* This will depend on the finish on the material
** All of these can be installed by a highly skilled individual, professional is recommended for all but modular carpet.
*** The materials themselves contain no VOCs but finishes may off-gas.

Natural paints use linseed and soy oils as binders and plant derived compounds as pigments. Milk paint is perhaps the least toxic of all paint types. The most common form of milk paint is a powder that is mixed with water. Milk paint is also sold pre-mixed in a can and preservatives are added to maintain shelf life, negating some of its natural qualities. Milk paint is very durable and works best on raw surfaces such as bare wood floors.

SELECTING FURNITURE

The basic furniture categories are: soft surface pieces such as upholstered sofas and hard surface pieces such as cabinets, tables and storage units.

Here are a few tips for choosing dog friendly furniture:

- Look for upholstered furniture made from durable and cleanable fabrics such as twill, microfibers, non-PVC faux leather, leather or outdoor fabric.
- Upholstered pieces with a taut back are preferable to loose cushions or pillows.
- Chairs that swivel or are on casters can move and deter large dogs from getting on them, but their unsteadiness can pose a hazard to all dogs.

Although you generally get what you pay for in terms of quality this may not always translate to durability or easy maintenance when it comes to furniture. Upholstery fabrics are a good example; handmade designer fabrics can be very beautiful, but not durable. For dog owners, removable and washable upholstery fabric is an absolute necessity. Something as simple as being able to remove and wash cushion upholstery can greatly enhance the lifespan of a sofa or chair. Select colorfast washable fabrics or you may end up with washed cushion covers that no longer match the rest of the sofa. Dogs will scratch or chew hard surface furniture but some materials are more impervious to damage. From a canine point of view metal, plastic and glass have far less appeal than wood and wicker. Aversive sprays and appropriate chew toys can provide a temporary fix to divert puppies from chomping the chair legs. Covering furniture is another solution. Wood legs can be covered with plastic or metal pipe—buy the appropriate diameter, cut it to length and slide it over the leg. For chair legs you will need to drill holes in the pipe and secure it with wire or tape. It pays to select furniture that is repairable or comes with replaceable parts. Certain materials are easier to fix than others are. Wood parts, even veneers, can usually be reproduced and replaced. On the other hand, a broken leg on a solid plastic chair may not be as easy to repair.

Accidents will always happen, and life will be much less complicated if you can easily clean canine bodily fluids from furniture surfaces. Upholstered furniture can be protected from dirty paws with slipcovers or decorative throws. If you have a problem with territorial marking you can apply a "pee skirt" around the furniture. Buy a roll of sheet plastic 4ml thick minimum and cut it to just below seat height and the length of your chair or sofa and wrap it around it. Secure it in place with clips or Velcro.

Antiques experts often use the word "patina" as a desirable quality in old furniture. Technically patina refers to a film, coloring, or encrustation on the surface of an old object, but antique dealers use it to define the wear and tear of use, including abuse by dogs, over time which often makes a piece of furniture more valuable.

The two basic types of wood finishes are topical and penetrating. Topical finishes sit on the surface of wood and therefore show scratches more easily. They include lacquer, polyurethane, shellac, wax and varnish. Hard finishes protect wood from stains and deeper

The simple elegance of this living/dining room is a good example of a dog-friendly space. The furnishings are minimal with plenty of room for the dogs to move around or relax. The sofa and chairs are covered with durable stain resistant Crypton upholstery fabrics. The floors are white oak with a commercial grade matte finish. The walls are painted with an eggshell finish low VOC paint.

Courtesy of The Liveable Home: www.theliveablehomestore.com

scratches better than low luster finishes. However, scratches are much more visible on hard, glossy finishes, such as lacquer. Therefore hard finishes can be difficult to maintain in prime condition if you have dogs.

Penetrating finishes, on the other hand, are absorbed into the wood, which makes them more durable and easier to repair and a better choice for dog owners. They create a layer of color in the wood itself which makes them more difficult to remove. Examples of penetrating finishes include oils, such as linseed oil, paint such as milk paint, and stains, either oil or water-based.

Be prepared before shopping for furniture. Measure the existing space and don't forget to measure the ceiling height if you are looking for vertical pieces. Measure other furniture in the space so that you can be sure the piece will fit in both size and proportion. Draw a floor plan.

Bring a measuring tape, pertinent color swatches of paint, fabrics, etc. and sample photos to show designers and salespeople. Be prepared to discuss your budget and buy the best that you can afford.

UPHOLSTERY

Every dog loves to curl up in a comfy chair. Many dogs also love gnawing on their favorite chair, digging in the cushions and leaving muddy footprints, hair, and oily coat residue in their wake. Tight or taut-backed sofas or chairs are less of a temptation to dogs than loose-back cushions or pillows which are very inviting for tugging, digging and nibbling. Skirts around the bottom of chairs and sofas are also more vulnerable to chewing and territorial marking.

Dogs are more inclined to "jump" on furniture rather than carefully sit on it. Since dogs go through frequent sleep/waking cycles and will wake at the drop of a feather they often jump on and off the sofa in a constant cycle throughout the day. When choosing fabrics dog owners should look for abrasion resistance, elastic recovery, dimensional stability, seam breaking strength and colorfastness. Fabrics intended for commercial applications are tested for many of these qualities and are more durable and stain resistant. They must meet more rigid performance and fire safety standards

Abrasion resistance refers to the ability of fabric to withstand rubbing forces and friction. This aspect is important because it directly relates to the lifespan of fabric and how well it will wear over time. Two tests widely used to measure abrasion resistance are the Wyzenbeek test (aka Double Rub Test) and the Martindale test. Fabrics are classified as heavy duty if it completes 30,000 or more cycles for the Wyzenbeek test and 40,000 or more for the Martindale test. Look for this on an upholstery fabric label.

- Simple weaves, such as plain weave or twill, are flat, even in height and tightly woven, making them more abrasion resistant.
- Nylon, polyester and polypropylene, all synthetic fibers, are strong and abrasion resistant.
- Most microfibers are strong and abrasion resistant.
- Most natural fibers are less abrasion resistant.

Dimensional stability refers to a fabrics ability to maintain its shape over time and with use. Elastic recovery refers to a fabric's ability to stretch and return back to its original shape. These qualities are important if your Bull Mastiff Buster frequently jumps on and off the sofa.

- Except for wool most natural fibers do not have good elastic recovery.
- Nylon and polyester both have good dimensional stability.
- Upholstery construction such as tufting, channels and quilting can all improve the dimensional stability of an upholstery textile.

Colorfastness and crocking (color transfer due to rubbing or washing) is another important consideration if the fabric will need to be washed frequently, or when a wet dog might jump on the fabric. Select fabrics with dyes that won't bleed or fade. Although natural dyes are an attractive "green" solution, natural dyes may not be colorfast. If the only alternative is to live with or even worse, throw away a damaged upholstered chair, natural dyes may offer no advantage.

Upholstery fabric choices include non-woven and woven. The best non-woven choices include leather, faux leather and suede and other microfibers made from nylon, polyester or polyurethane. These products have very high abrasion resistance and are scratch, nick and blemish resistant making them an excellent choice for homes with dogs. Woven upholstery fabric has a flat or pile weave. Flat weaves create smooth, even, thin types of fabric such as twill and plain weave. Twill and tightly woven plain weave fabrics are among the top choices for homes with dogs. Both can be woven into thousands of patterns and types of fabric.

Pile weaves like corduroy and velvet are made of raised loops, which may be cut or left looped. They are thick, textured, and feel softer. If these are tightly woven they are also abrasion resistant making them good upholstery choices. Cut pile weaves wear better on upholstery. Loop pile weaves may become and remain crushed. Tiny dogs can also ruin this type of fabric by catching a tooth or nail tip in a loop.

Construction technique alone is not enough to judge a fabric. Other important considerations include:

- Yarn Count: when assessing two fabrics with similar construction higher yarn count (yarns per inch in one direction) indicates superior strength.
- Weave tightness: upholstery fabrics, in particular, require a rather tight weave, because loose yarns can catch and snag on anything from a pencil to a dog's toenail.

- Weave balance: this means that the yarns used in both directions (warp and weft) are of equal dimensions and strength. Fabrics with balanced weaves wear better than those with heavy yarns in one direction and thin ones in the other direction.
- Yarn twist: higher yarn twist can increase the strength of a yarn.
- Plying, which is the twisting of two or more yarns together, can also increase strength.

Finally, fiber content can be critical to the overall performance of fabric. Fibers are classified as either natural or man-made synthetic. Natural fibers are further categorized as plant such as cotton or animal such as wool. Man-made synthetic fibers are classified as plant such as rayon or chemically made polymers such as nylon.

As we learned with natural carpets, absorbency is an important factor and textile fibers that easily absorb a dye just as easily release that dye when washed. This property has advantages and disadvantages. Fibers that easily absorb an unwanted stain just as easily release that stain when wet. On the other hand, the dye is more likely to fade over time.

Good upholstery fabric fiber choices:

- nylon is known for its strength, resilience, abrasion resistance, easy care, and maintenance
- polyester is somewhat stain and abrasion resistant, resilient, and colorfast
- wool is inherently resilient and flame resistant
- micro-fibers are strong, durable and repel moisture

Traditionally, manufacturing textiles has not been a sustainable process, as it consumes large quantities of energy, water, and chemicals. Furthermore, most fibers and fabrics are traditionally bleached with chlorine bleach before dying; further polluting air, water, and ground.

SELECTING SUSTAINABLE FABRICS

Hybrid fabrics with mixed fiber content like nylon and wool, can't be recycled or composted

SELECT
- certified organically grown natural fibers
- natural dyes or un-dyed fabrics
- 40 to 100 % post-consumer recycled content

AVOID
- chemical finishes or additives
- chemical enhancements

Chemicals are added to textiles to improve specific qualities and performance. These include qualities such as fire resistance, stain resistance, microbial resistance, durability, and strength. While many of these chemical additives are proven to be effective for their purpose, some are controversial because their long term effects on humans and animals are unknown. Two categories seem to be most problematic: fire retardants and stain/water resistance. A third type, antimicrobial finishes, may not even be necessary.

Residential upholstery fabrics do not have to adhere to fire safety standards expected of commercial fabrics. While wool is inherently flame resistant, others must be chemically treated at the fiber or fabric production stage. Fire retardants have helped diminish fire spread but they have been implicated for potentially causing health problems. Brominated flame retardants are most problematic. The fire retardant chemical compound polybrominated dephenyl ethers (PBDEs) was removed from the US market in 2005. However, it can still be found in older furniture components, such as fabrics and cushions. Safer substitutes for PBDEs include phosphate flame retardants and flame resistant barriers.

Soil, stain and resistant finishes are made from chemicals known as fluoropolymers which utilize perfluorinated compounds (PFCs). While all fabrics with stain and water resistance contain PFCs it is important to note that presently some, such as PFOS and PFOA are considered more hazardous than others. Nanotechnology has been used to create a precise chemical formula that allows fluorocarbons to be used sparingly, but it does not completely eliminate the hazard. Studies of these chemicals show links to some cancers and thyroid diseases, and the EPA considers PFOA and PFOS a carcinogen in animals. Currently PFCs are the best technique to waterproof textiles. Look for products that do not contain PFOA or PFOS. Many fabric manufacturers are aware of the problems and are working to create safer alternatives. This info can't always be found on labels, be sure to ask when you are looking for furniture.

Because upholstery fabric is such a visible aspect of your home it's easy to overlook what lies beneath it. These hidden elements are far more important to the overall life of your sofa or chair. Construction techniques have not changed a lot in the last 100 or so years, but some of the materials have. Here is an overview of what to look for in construction.

- Wood frames are still common in high quality furniture today. Kiln-dried hardwood or engineered wood frames are dimensionally stable and are equally viable.
- Plastic and rigid foams are used widely in the frames of low cost upholstered furniture. They greatly reduce the weight of furniture, making pieces easier to move. This also means that they are easily moved or tipped over if jumped upon by a dog.
- Cushions are stuffed primarily with polyurethane foam. These soft pads can vary in density, but generally higher density equals firmer and more durable cushioning.

- Seam breaking or seam slippage strength is another important upholstery construction quality. Upholstery fabrics are sewn together to create cushions and other covered parts. When your dog runs back and forth on the sofa to bark at a chipmunk outdoors cushion seams are subjected to a great amount of stress. If the fabric is not strong the seams may rip it apart.

- The construction technique used on cushions does make a difference in terms of durability and lifespan. Cushion designs include boxed, welted and knife-edged. Boxed and welted cushions are preferable in homes with dogs because they can withstand more pressure. Boxed cushions are made with top and bottom panels with a strip of fabric wrapped around the front, sides and back. Welted cushions are box cushions with a fabric cord sewn into the seam. A knife-edged cushion has a top and bottom panel sewn directly to each other. This single seam is more vulnerable to pressure from lively dogs.

WINDOWS AND WINDOW TREATMENTS

Large expanses of glass are beautiful but they can pose as hazards for dogs. The most common injury results from your dog running into a sliding glass door because he fails to recognize the difference between a closed and open door. Crashes like this can also happen in multiple dog homes if dogs are playing or chasing each other near the door. Or a bossy dog may force another dog into a window. Puppies and visually impaired dogs benefit from window treatments or visual clues like plastic film, tape or decals placed on the glass at the dog's eye level.

Safe window treatments should never be overlooked in homes with dogs. Loose cords used to operate some drapes, blinds and shades are a common safety problem. Dogs (and children) can become entangled in cords and in this situation dogs often panic and make the situation worse resulting in serious injury or strangulation. Separated cords are now mandated for child safety, but these can also entrap a dog. Looped cords

SAFER WINDOW TREATMENTS
Proper selection of window treatments can prevent safety problems and barrier frustration. Roller shades may be the best choice for both problems. The biggest safety problem is loose cords that can strangle a dog.

TOP LEFT Drapery ring clips turn any fabric into instant drapery. The absence of cords makes this style safer.
TOP RIGHT This device automatically and safely retracts the blind cord up and out of the way. *Courtesy of Kidco: www.kidco.com*
BOTTOM LEFT Roller shades eliminate the need for cords.
BOTTOM RIGHT Roller shades with integrated chain loop pulley systems placed out of reach are effective and safe.

can be made safer with a pulley system that attaches to the wall and holds the cords taut. Cord winders can also be purchased wherever child safety products are sold.

Cordless window treatments include cordless drapes, roller shades or shutters. Roller shades come in many choices including: fabric, solar shades and natural materials like grass, reed and wood. Solar shades have a fairly open view and block some light. When they are closed during the day they cut the glare and heat transmission. They may deter your dog from barking at outdoor activity.

ARTWORK, ANTIQUES AND BOOKS

Common sense will dictate where to place artwork in a home with dogs in mind. Certainly items hung from the wall should not be problematic unless they have loose items hanging low enough to tempt your dog. Three dimensional works, such as sculpture, antiques or craft items should be placed in a secure location where they can't be chewed, scratched, urinated on or toppled onto your dog.

Valuable items should never be left within a dog's reach. Do not assume that an older, well trained dog is immune to this temptation. The fact that you have recently handled an item makes it more enticing. If you put temptation in his way, you can only blame yourself for the results. Store valuable artwork and books out of canine reach. Dogs are attracted to materials in paints and book bindings such as linseed oil or glue. Storage units with doors are recommended but anything especially valuable should be placed on upper shelves, preferably in a dog free room.

ELECTRONICS

New technology is rapidly replacing the need for large, bulky electronic equipment with endless masses of wires. At the same time, we find ourselves increasingly unable to cope without constant access to technology. Whether you like it or not, new technology is increasingly dog friendly. These items are now much smaller, sleeker and often can be easily hung from a wall or hidden in a cabinet placed in one room without any need of wires or electrical hookup.

PLANTS

Dog lovers tend to be nature lovers and plants can contribute to the aesthetic and psychological enhancement of a space. Dogs love them too, but for very different reasons. They will invariably dig in the dirt, urinate on the pot or most worrisome, try to eat the leaves. Many indoor plants can be toxic or irritating to dogs. The best solution is to put any houseplants out of canine reach. Be sure that they can't climb on something else to reach them. Hanging plants, plant shelves, plant stands and countertops are all potential solutions. Prune branches and leaves that are within your dog's reach. Place a layer of large rocks or decorative stones over the soil to discourage digging.

LIVING SPACES SAFETY
FIREPLACES

Nothing completes the picture of family contentedness like a sleeping dog curled up by the fire. However, fireplaces and woodstoves are potential hazards and numerous dogs are injured this way every year. By law, fireplaces are required to have a fire screen. Better still, dog-friendly homes should have

A well designed metal fence can keep children and dogs safe from a roaring fire. *Courtesy of Kidco: www.kidco.com*

Hearth "bumpers" can protect babies and puppies from sharp edges. *Courtesy of Kidco: www.kidco.com*

the additional protection of glass doors. Dogs love to chew on wood and kindling and logs should be stored out of your dog's reach. Many dogs also love to eat the charcoal leftover from firewood. When cleaning your fireplace or woodstove, charred wood and ashes should be disposed of in a dog proof receptacle. Although it's usually not harmful, dogs can create quite a mess with this debris.

Freestanding protective fireplace gates are another valuable safety feature to keep your dog away from the dangers of fireplaces and woodstoves. Fireplace gates are available from child safety product retailers. Raised hearths made of hard surface fire resistant materials like stone, concrete, tile or brick present another hazard for dogs. Dogs can be protected from sharp edges by hearth bumpers. They are typically installed with self-adhesive Velcro® strips along the hearth edge.

SAFETY TIPS

- Living with dogs may require some compromise of expectations and lifestyle. You cannot expect to let a puppy or young dog run unsupervised in your home without incurring damage to furniture or belongings. All puppies experience a chewing stage, but for some dogs this can last until three years of age or beyond. Plan to dog proof all parts of your home that will be shared with your dogs. Home damage can be avoided by confining your dog when he is unsupervised, monitoring him when he is loose and keeping things out of his reach. If you have expensive, irreplaceable possessions put them away until your dog is old enough to be trusted. It's best to roll up the Oriental rug and store it away until your puppy is housetrained and stops chewing.
- Candles are popular for creating mood lighting but they can pose a danger if left unattended. Artificial candles made with LED lights are a better alternative in a dog-friendly home.
- Home offices and libraries tend to have a lot of small "stuff" lying around that dogs may ingest without being noticed. Tacks, staples, rubber bands, and paper clips are all the perfect size to fit in a dog's mouth. Closed storage and closing the door to these spaces are the best solutions.
- Tall freestanding pieces of furniture such as bookcases should be fastened to the wall with furniture brackets. A climbing or jumping dog can topple an unstable piece of furniture causing serious injury.
- Furniture with sharp edges and corners, especially at the dog's eye level, can pose a hazard especially for visually impaired or elderly dogs.
- Glass tabletops should be avoided. Dogs crawl under glass topped coffee tables and displace it or bump into it.

See Resources for products and more information.

CHAPTER 7

Bedrooms

Fixed lighting and
no table lamps

Roller
shades

Art objects displayed
out of reach

Simple side tables
with drawers

Two twin size quilts
on a king size bed

Low bed for
easy access

Modular carpet tiles and
hard surface flooring

The best dog-friendly bedrooms include specific places for dogs to sleep and minimize the quantity of furniture. This bedroom is used by 3 dogs and their human parents. One dog sleeps on the bed, one in a crate and one on a bed on the floor. All clothing is stored in a large walk-in closet. Two twin size quilts make it easier to share this bed with a large dog.

In our bedrooms we go to great lengths to create a quiet, peaceful environment that will ensure a restful night. Canine sleeping arrangements can have a major impact on our ability to achieve a restful state. As we learned in Chapter 2 dogs spend a good deal of time sleeping or reclining. Bedrooms are the most suitable place for nighttime sleeping for you and your dog. To achieve the best balance for both of you it's wise to keep the bedroom design simple. Minimize furnishings and finishes and select easily cleaned flooring such as wood, ceramic tile, cork, concrete, or linoleum topped with area rugs. If you are like many humans and enjoy the feel of carpet beneath your feet, especially on a cold morning, then select modular carpet that can easily be removed and cleaned. The walls should be simple as well. Stick with painted walls or smooth finished paneling. Stay away from surfaces that are easily soiled and difficult to clean such as wallpaper.

Whether or not they are invited, it's hard to keep your dog off of your bed. Dogs view a bed as a fun place to frolic and the result can be chewing, digging or scent marking. If your dog sleeps in bed with you plan to wash your bed linens, pillows and dogs more frequently, as often as once or twice a week. Needless to say, avoid fabrics that must be dry cleaned. Moisture controlling covers or fitted mattress pads can be used to prevent odors and leakage into the mattress and will prolong the lifespan of your mattress. While most waterproof covers are made with vinyl there are good alternatives that are made with a polyurethane barrier that is both waterproof and breathable. Some have the added benefit of acting as a dust mite and allergen barrier. If you are handy with a sewing machine, consider making your own covers or fitted mattress pads with fabrics utilizing new technology for moisture control such as Crypton® or Nano-Pel™. Waterproof dog blankets or coverlets can provide a clean layer between you and your

Does your large dog share a bed with you and your partner? If yes, consider buying two twin size covers rather than one large one. That way, the dog can move around during the night, sleep in between or sleep under the covers without disturbing you by stealing the covers.

dog if you want your dog on the bed but not under the covers. Like us, dogs have all kinds of sleeping styles. Some spread out, some curl up, some burrow, and some are very territorial. Make sure your bed is large enough to ensure that everyone gets a good night's sleep. It should not be too high off the floor, especially if your dogs are small, old or have mobility problems. Jumping or falling off a high bed to a hard floor can result in serious injury.

Most dogs nest which means wadding up all the bedding into a very messy pile. You can prevent this by giving the dog a small throw or a donut type bed for this purpose. Sleeping with multiple dogs is more complicated because most dogs are regimented about where they sleep. Giving each dog a throw or pillow to designate territory on the bed often helps to keep things calm. These small blankets can also be laundered easily and frequently, donut beds can be covered with removable covers or pillowcases for easy cleaning. Lots of small sheets, pillows and blankets will vastly cut down the day to day laundry experience. Rather than stripping the bed, this allows you to wash it in parts.

If you like having your dog in the bedroom but prefer not to share your bed consider adding a twin size bed or a lounge chair covered with a sheet for your dog. Twin sized sheets are a very economical way to protect beds and furniture.

Zoey enjoys the soft fleece top of a waterproof blanket: an excellent way to keep your bed clean and dry. *Courtesy of Mambe Waterproof Blankets: www.mambeblankets.com*

Dog-Proof Laundry Hamper: Joey demonstrates how a metal garbage can with a tight lid might foil the most persistent dog. *Courtesy of K. Landau*

Traditional bedrooms are furnished with several conventional pieces, most of which functions as storage space. If your dog shares your bedroom, it makes sense to minimize the quantity of furniture. Dogs are tempted to steal items carrying your scent, ranging from your dirty socks on the floor to eyeglasses and prescription meds on the bedside table. Reducing clutter limits opportunities for your dog to pilfer and chew your personal items or damage valuable furniture. Rather than an assortment of side tables, cabinets, armoires, and dressers, consolidate your things in one large closet that is inaccessible to your dog. If this isn't an option, consider utilizing another room as a dressing room. Removing excess furniture has the added benefit of creating extra space in your bedroom. It becomes much easier to keep track of your things and you will have plenty of room for a crate or dog bed if needed.

DIRTY LAUNDRY

Is your dog a laundry thief? You may need to dog proof the laundry hamper. Ideas include heavy wooden chests, large foot pedal garbage cans or a traditional large metal garbage can with a tightly fitted lid.

DAYTIME SLEEPING OPTIONS

Dogs don't confine their slumbers to nighttime and usually have preferences about where they like to take their afternoon siestas. If this happens to be a totally inconvenient spot like the middle of the kitchen floor it can cause problems. The easiest solution is to use several dog beds that can be located around the home as needed. Choices range from an old rug to handmade miniature canopied beds complete with springs, platforms and frames.

Dog beds range in price from a few dollars for a simple blanket to thousands of dollars for a custom designed bed. Most of us settle for something in between, usually a large, covered cushion with a soft filled insert. A recent study indicated that most dogs prefer beds that are suitable for "nesting". These include donut styles and beds with bolsters. Every dog however, is different and suitability is dependent on size and physical abilities.

From a practical perspective look for something with a removable, machine washable cover. The fabric should be durable, such as twill, plain weave, or microfibers such as ultra suede or faux leather. Nylon is one of the strongest fibers, but cotton also works as long as the weave structure is durable such as twill. Most synthetic fabrics, such as nylon, and natural fibers, such as cotton, are machine washable and they can all be dried on a low setting. Fleece, fake fur and fake sheepskin can be machine washed but should be air dried for a longer life. Fleece and other synthetic furs can melt at high temperatures.

The yarns of woven fabric should be tight and close, with no loose ends that catch nails or encourage chewing. Fake fur or sheepskin is visually and tactilely appealing but not suitable for puppies or destructive dogs that may chew on or dig at these fabrics.

Several manufacturers sell "indestructible" dog beds or bed covers. These are mostly made from ballistic nylon used for luggage. While they may deter some mild chewers they are no match for a hardcore chewing machine. In reality they are only somewhat less destructible than other beds.

Moisture and stain resistance is another consideration. Several dog bed manufacturers use water and stain resistant fabrics with Crypton® fabric treatment. Sunbrella® is an acrylic fiber that is suitable for outdoor use. Although it is not waterproof it dries rapidly and is not affected by UV light. Fabrics made with Crypton® or Sunbrella® are readily available for anyone handy with a sewing machine.

A borax solution of ½ cup borax per gallon of water is a safer chlorine-free alternative for deep cleaning your dog bed. White vinegar or hydrogen peroxide may also help to kill some germs as well. Enzyme based cleaners, such as Nature's Miracle®, can help eliminate odors in pet beds.

Dog beds can be filled with polyurethane or polyester foam, memory foam, latex foam, and fiber fill. Memory foam and latex foam top the list for comfort and are the most expensive. Memory foam is made from polyurethane and molds to body contours. It is firmer in cool temperatures and softer when it is warm. Memory foam beds for dogs are stuffed with either solid blocks or chopped pieces. Latex foam is a natural material collected from rubber trees. It is naturally flame retardant, insect resistant and dust mite resistant. Synthetic foam made from polyurethane or polyester is also frequently used for bedding. The foam is made in blocks and sheets of varying densities or chopped pieces in a bed insert.

Spot cleaning is recommended first for any type of foam bed. Enzymatic cleaners or hydrogen peroxide can be poured on a specific stain to help remove it. Flush the liquid through the bed to the other side by compressing it and placing a towel under it. The bed will need to air dry before further use. Hydrogen peroxide will discolor the foam, but this has no impact on function. Dog bed inserts made from foam can be completely washed in a bathtub or outdoors by hand with a mild detergent. Be sure to rinse thoroughly and air dry.

Fiber fill can be made from a variety of materials including synthetic, natural and hybrids of both. Synthetic varieties called poly fill include polyester, and PLA (polylactic acid). PLA is manufactured from plant starch such as corn, rice or beets. Natural materials include cotton, kapok, wool, bamboo and hemp. Poly fill can be chopped into small pieces or used as one continuous sheet of varying thickness. These fillings are initially soft, but often compress with age, washing and the weight of your dog. The entire filling may compress, or individual lumps occur spaced throughout the bed. When compressed, they can be as hard as a rock. It also shifts if it is placed in a large bed or a loose cover. When choosing a dog bed filled with poly fill, look for one that has interlocking baffles or quilting to offset shifting and compression. Polyester and PLA fillings should be hand washed and air dried to prevent compression and decomposition. Cotton and kapok are machine washable but hemp filling is not. Since most dog beds eventually get wet at some point hemp is not recommended.

Hybrid fillings can be made from combinations of materials such as chopped fiber fill combined with chopped or solid high density foam. This method keeps the fiber fill from over-compressing, making the bed last longer. Most of these materials are readily available for the DIY dog owner. Hybrid fillings combine natural and synthetic materials and therefore can't easily be composted or recycled.

> Dogs are extremely attracted to soft filling materials whether it is a plush toy, cushion or their beds. Fiber fill seems to top the list but other materials can be equally as attractive to your dog. This habit has the potential to cause serious gastrointestinal obstruction so it should be a major consideration when choosing his bedding.

NOT RECOMMENDED

Polystyrene beads, cedar chips and down feathers should be avoided. Polystyrene beads although tiny, pose a choking risk if your dog chews his bed. And once these things are released, they will spread to every corner of your home! This can also ruin your washer if the bedding happens to spring a leak dur-ing routine cleaning. Cedar chips are not soft and they have a very strong smell. They can cause coat staining on white dogs and illness if ingested. Cedar chips don't launder well, so they aren't very practical for a high maintenance sleeping space. Down feathers, while luxurious, may be attractive for dogs who love to rip and shred. It also compresses easily and frequent washing destroys the down.

TEMPERATURE CONTROLLED BEDS

Heated beds can provide relief and comfort for neonatal puppies, elderly and convalescing dogs. If they utilize heating coils, similar to an electric blanket they must be placed near an electric outlet. Furthermore they should:

- never be used for dogs that might chew the cords or the pad.
- only be covered with approved fabrics and never used in conjunction with other beds.
- never be used with dogs who can't move due to paralysis or injury. Immobile dogs have been burned from heating pads.

Microwaveable discs are a good option for short term needs. They hold heat for about eight hours and can be placed inside a bed or crate.

Cooling beds are fluid filled and activated by adding water or soaking the bed and placing it in a freezer. Select beds with PVC-free covers.

DESIGNER AND CUSTOM DOG BEDS

Beds can be designed by a designer and constructed by a single furniture maker or a large manufacturing facility. The styles range from contemporary platform beds to canopy beds as well as more traditional styles with headboards. They come

STYLISH DOG BEDS

These beautiful interpretations of modern furniture are examples of how dog beds can match your own personal style.

LEFT RIGHT *Courtesy of Pre-Fab Pets: www.pre-fab-pets.com*

A line up of different styles of crates. From left to right: Soft crates, wire and plastic crates and an ex-pen.

complete with box spring and mattresses. Some are low to the ground to accommodate old, giant or small breeds.

Custom dog beds are designed and built by an independent furniture maker and fabricated out of materials such as wood or metal. Due to the unique designs and limited construction these beds tend to be very expensive. There are many talented furniture makers throughout the US, Canada and other countries some of whom specialize in furniture for pets.

COTS

Cot style beds look like an old fashioned camping cot, consisting of a metal or plastic frame with fabric stretched across it. Some fold and others remain rigid. The actual bed surface sits off of the floor which keeps the dog cooler and clean. This is a good solution for dogs that like to sleep on a porch or patio. Mobility impaired dogs may have difficulty climbing in and out of this style bed. A few cot designs are meant specifically for incontinent dogs—see Chapter 11.

CRATES

Crates have completely revised so many aspects of dog training and routine care it's hard to imagine how we managed without them. A crate serves as a housetraining aid, safe temporary confinement, as a permanent sleeping space, and a travel box.

- A crate is a safe way to keep your dog out of harm's way when workers are in your house.
- Many dogs seek out their crates when they are tired or stressed.
- They are a good way to monitor an ill or convalescing dog.
- Crates are particularly helpful in a multiple dog home.
- Crates are indispensible in the car, protecting you and your dog from injury. It also prevents him from bolting out of a door or window.

Numerous accessories are available that can be clipped onto your dog's crate. Fans, lights, water and feeding bowls can all enhance your dog's crate experience.

Crates are indispensable but few crate designs can be called innovative or aesthetically appealing. When selecting a crate, your priorities should be safety, comfort and durability rather than beauty. Ugly crates can be disguised by fabric covers, wood structures, wicker, or hidden under a counter. Your dog's crate should be big enough for him to stand comfortably erect and turn around easily. Obviously, a puppy's crate must be upgraded as he grows. You don't want a crate so large that the puppy will create spaces within it to sleep, eat and eliminate. Models with removable dividers that allow expansion as a puppy grows are recommended.

Hard sided crates can be made from wire, plastic, aluminum, and combinations of plastic and wire or wood and wire. Most are collapsible but the process is not always simple or convenient. Wire crates are made from welded steel wire. Many designs fold for transport. They are a good choice for breeds that need good ventilation or tend to chew through softer materials. A metal or plastic tray serves as the bottom and slides out for cleaning. They can be heavy and awkward to move. Larger sizes may not fit in your car and they aren't airline approved. Price variations are based on design features. Wire crates are fairly sturdy but they vary in quality and determined dogs can escape from flimsy crates. Choose a model made with heavier gauge closely spaced wire. When evaluating wire gauge, the smaller the number the stronger the wire. Some designs are coated with epoxy to prevent rusting but periodic repainting will prolong the lifespan of most wire crates.

Because they are so useful, many owners have more than one type of crate such as a metal or plastic crate for home and a soft sided mesh crate for travel. Crates can be a nuisance to move around, so having more than one can be very helpful if you can afford it and have adequate space. Place one in the bedroom, a second one wherever you spend most of your time with your dog during the day, and keep a third one in your car.

Leggy or long muzzled breeds can reach through the openings with nose, tongue, teeth and paws to pull items into the crate or get a jaw or leg stuck between the bars of some models. Dogs can also injure themselves or get their fur caught on door latches. If your dog is adept at opening latches additional locks can secure the latch. Leash clips work well as locks.

Plastic kennels are made from durable plastics such as ABS and polypropylene. They vary in durability. Crates made of thin plastic are comfortable to carry but they are likely to fall apart in a short time. Thicker plastic models with substantial heft provide better protection. If you plan to fly look for airline approved models with reinforced sidewalls for protection against impact. These crates are bulky and cumbersome to move more than a short distance. They can be dismantled but they do not fold and may not fit easily into some cars. Some models have casters that can be snapped into place easily for

CRATE DAMAGE

Dog crates are not invincible! The wire crate shown at top was destroyed when a young Border Collie rescue pulled a full size quilt through the crate rungs. He was able to then squeeze through the opening he created. In the middle he is shown with his prize. Immediately above is "maximum security" that his owner created to fit over a new crate. *Photos courtesy of J. Sahrle*

transport. They are the best choice for small, delicate breeds that need protection from cold, but they also heat up more quickly than wire crates. Take precautions using these crates outdoors or in a car during warm weather especially for dogs that are most susceptible to heat.

Folding crates are not acceptable for airline travel but they are convenient for car travel. Choices besides folding wire crates include plastic crates, and soft sided "tent" style crates. Folding wire or plastic crates are fairly heavy but provide more durability and security than their soft sided counterparts. One company makes a combination wire and plastic folding crate. Soft sided nylon mesh tent crates are convenient, lightweight, portable, collapsible and set up quickly. They are less secure than wire or plastic so they are not suitable for puppies or dogs that are left at home all day alone. Dogs need to be acclimated regardless of whether they are crate trained already. Even a small dog can tear through the mesh or open the zipper. Your dog should never be left in a vulnerable situation in one of these crates. Dogs have also been known to rip through tents to attack the dog inside. Avoid models made with PVC because it will give off an unpleasant chlorine odor that will be more concentrated for your dog, confined in his crate.

If you are not crazy about the idea of dog crates all over your home, it is possible to find some that combine function, durability and beauty. Several companies manufacture models that use more attractive materials like wood, faux wicker and rattan to cover the less appealing aspects of crates. It's also possible to find crates made from wood or metal that double as a piece of furniture – typically as an end table next to a sofa. Obviously these are not portable but can be very handy for home use. Wood, wicker or rattan should not be used with dogs that are likely to chew.

CRATE COVERS

Crate covers effectively disguise a dog crate in the corner of your living room. They can be found in a wide range of fabrics and colors, to fit most standard size crates with zippers or Velcro® tabs to hold them in place. A blanket or rug draped over the crate will also do the job at a much lower price. However, many dogs love pulling them through the bars to chew and shred them at a leisurely pace. Dogs can ingest pieces or be injured if a foot or mouth becomes entwined in the resulting mess. To prevent this add a piece of plywood or solid material on top of the crate that overhangs the crate by several inches all the way around it. This will serve to keep the draping fabric away from the sides of the crate and out of the dog's reach. Cold sensitive dogs will appreciate the added protection of a crate cover when traveling or during cold or windy conditions. Occasionally dogs will also try to grab padding placed under the crate to protect the floor. The pad should be made of a rigid material with no edges extending beyond the bottom of the crate.

Visibility can have a big impact on a dog's behavior in the crate. Enclosed crates provide more visual security and some

DOG CRATES AS FURNITURE

Designer dog crates do double duty as furniture. There are many styles designed to blend in with your home decor. Be sure to choose according to your dog first. They may not all be suitable for use while you are away from home. If your dog likes to chew wood, a solid wood crate may not work unless a wire crate can be inserted inside of it.

dogs find it stressful to be confined in a wire crate. This visible exposure makes them feel vulnerable to other dogs even though they are actually safer inside. Vulnerable dogs may whine, cry, dig or bark. Crate covers are a handy way to quiet down a noisy dog that refuses to settle down.

CRATE PADS

Most crate pads are downsized versions of dog beds made to fit standard size crates. If your dog or puppy chews everything placed in his crate it is safer to do without a pad temporarily. Shredding can become habitual and the earlier you eliminate the source the sooner the dog might learn to stop.

CRATE ALTERNATIVES

Not everyone wants a crate in their home and a few dogs never adjust to crate confinement but there are occasions when you will need to confine your dog. Ex-pens or playpens may be a good solution. An ex-pen, short for exercise pen, is a small fence-like enclosure without a top or bottom. They can be made from wire, plastic or wood, and folded for transport or storage. Some styles are made from plastic coated wire, which will help to minimize rusting, corrosion and scratched floors. Toy dog size pens (18–24 inches high) do not need doors unless they are accessorized with floors or tops. Floors are usually epoxy coated racks that can be attached at adjustable heights off the floor. This protects flooring and makes it easier to reach inside for very small dogs. Pens for larger dogs are manufactured in sizes up to 48 inches high, with doors. Ex-pens come with six to twelve panels. Panels are usually easy to add or remove to customize the size. Larger sizes can be quite heavy. For portability, an economical, lightweight model may be more suitable. Optional clip-on top panels can also be purchased for dogs prone to jumping and climbing. A sheet or sunshade may also serve this purpose.

Ex-pens can be very useful for housebreaking puppies. Many dog owners attach a wire crate to an ex-pen or place it inside of the ex-pen. They then place a large piece of plastic under the entire arrangement. Puppies use the crate for sleeping and can use the ex-pen for eliminating or just moving around.

Heavy or rambunctious dogs can tip exercise pens by jumping and lunging against the side. Outdoors the ex-pen can be held in place with tent stakes. It is best to monitor your dog's behavior before leaving him confined to a pen and never leave him alone if you suspect that he may attempt to dig underneath, climb over, or topple the pen and escape.

A baby playpen, or play yard can make a good playpen for a very young puppy or a toy size dog. They have the advantage of being lightweight, portable and collapsible for storage. Some models are relatively easy to clean. The sides and floor should be regularly wiped down with a damp sponge and disinfected. Stay away from styles with a floor made from absorbent material that can be very difficult to clean and deodorize.

See Resources for products and more information.

CLOCKWISE FROM TOP OF OPPOSITE Green crate by Denhaus, Wicker crate by Midwest Homes for Pets, Wood and Wire crate by Midwest Homes for Pets, Wood crate by Denhaus and Silver crate by Denhaus
Courtesy of Denhaus: www.denhaus.com
and Midwest Homes for Pets: www.midwesthomes4pets.com

CHAPTER 8

Bathrooms

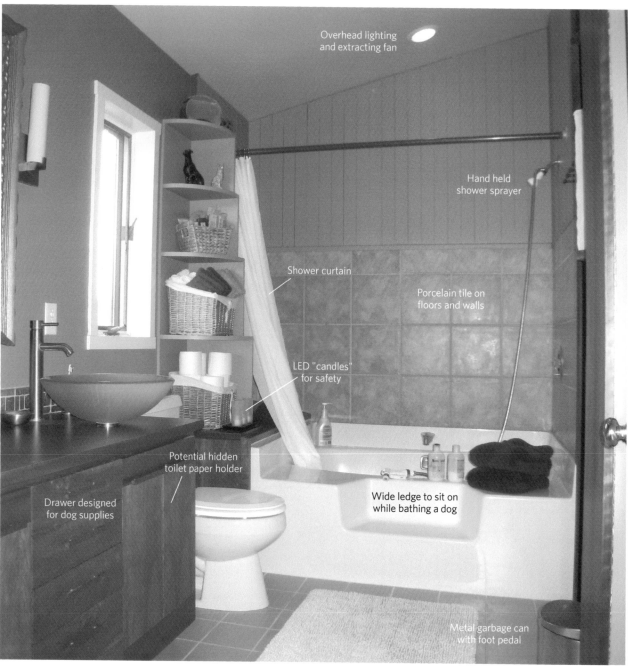

Overhead lighting
and extracting fan

Hand held
shower sprayer

Shower curtain

Porcelain tile on
floors and walls

LED "candles"
for safety

Potential hidden
toilet paper holder

Wide ledge to sit on
while bathing a dog

Drawer designed
for dog supplies

Metal garbage can
with foot pedal

This mid-sized bathroom is simple with plenty of storage and easily cleaned surfaces. The deep bathtub is used for both humans and dogs.

When bathing a dog a shower curtain is easier to use than a fixed glass door.

Bathroom design has become an art form combining elegance and practicality. Today, dogs should be a part of this equation. Dogs gravitate to the bathroom for a variety of reasons. They are attracted by a myriad of human scents and the possible entertainment found within. Drinking from the toilet is the classic canine bathroom faux pas. An equally popular activity is unraveling or shredding rolls of toilet paper. The common sense solution to these problems is to keep your dog out of the bathroom. This is not always easy, especially in a busy home with kids. If your bathroom also doubles as your dog grooming area, modifications for safety and convenience are essential.

Slippery floors and surfaces are a major hazard to both dogs and humans. Getting a secure grip on a wet, soapy dog is challenging. Normally calm dogs can attempt daredevil maneuvers when trying to evade a bath. It's not that unusual for both dog and owner to sustain injuries in situations like this. During bath time it is important to plan ahead and have control over your supplies and your dog. Limit your dog's accessibility to everything by using closed storage cabinets with doors and drawers. Dogs can and will eat bars of soap. The best solution for a dog with this propensity is to purchase a refillable soap dispenser that can be attached to a wall. Commercial varieties are most durable.

Tips for keeping the bathroom safe include keeping:

- the bathroom door closed
- the toilet covered or use a childproof toilet lock
- recessed tubs covered
- medications in a secure cabinet: human drugs are the leading cause of canine poisoning emergencies
- human medications and dog medications separated to prevent accidental use of the wrong medication
- razors and toiletries out of reach of your dogs
- secure garbage cans for disposal of tampons, sanitary napkins, diapers and bandages
- an eye on your dog when your tub or sink is full of water

From a maintenance perspective, in contrast to many rooms, the typical bathroom floor is an ideal surface for dogs. Porcelain ceramic tile is the top choice because it is durable, easily cleaned, and stain and odor resistant. It's also a good choice for dog bathing or puppy raising and paper training. A less expensive alternative would be linoleum. For non-slip ideas refer to Chapter 3.

If you plan on bathing your dog in the bathroom install ceramic tile three to four feet in height on the walls. Regardless of the size of your dog, do not underestimate the amount of water that will end up on the walls. Durability is not as important on walls as it is on floors so any type of stone or ceramic wall or floor tile will do the job. Semi-gloss, eggshell or washable matte paint finishes are also suitable.

Good bathroom lighting is essential if you plan to use the bathroom for fine grooming chores such as close scissoring or nail trimming. The light should be bright and evenly distribut-ed over the work area with no glare. Side lighting is preferable to overhead lights which will be obscured whenever you lean over the dog for close work.

PLUMBING FIXTURES

If you prefer to groom your small dog in the bathroom you will be delighted to learn that the ubiquitous tiny, shallow bathroom sink is a thing of the past. Today sinks are available in any shape imaginable and are made from a variety of materials with the most common being ceramic, glass and metal. They can also be made from the same materials used for the vanity or countertop surface which would include stone, stone composites, concrete and solid surface resins.

Sink configurations include: under counter mounted, surface mounted with a lip, vessels, wall mounted, or pedestal. Some sinks require a vanity or cabinet, wall mounted and pedestal sinks do not. These design features can make a big difference if you use your bathroom sink for bathing or spot cleaning your dogs. If you plan on using a bathroom sink to bathe your dog select a:

- faucet that is tall enough to fit over your dog and swings out of the way (i.e. kitchen faucet)
- deep sink large enough for your dog (i.e. kitchen sink)
- sink/vanity height optimal for your physical comfort
- durable sink, quartz composite or stainless steel are best

Drinking from the toilet is not only a nasty habit; dogs can be poisoned by cleaning chemicals in the water. Keeping the lid closed and providing a dish of fresh water in the bathroom discourages most habitual toilet hounds. If these measures fail, toilet lid locks are available from child safety supply retailers. A separate enclosed space for just the toilet also prevents toilet paper thievery.

ANTIFREEZE

Winterizing a seasonal use home usually includes adding anti-freeze to the water in the toilet. Use a safer type of antifreeze made with propylene glycol.

TOILET PAPER

Dogs love to shred toilet paper. This hobby seems to be popular with every breed so don't assume that your puppy will simply outgrow the habit. It is self rewarding and most dogs will continue to do it unless otherwise trained or hampered. The obvious solution is to "close your bathroom door." Yes that does work, but when your grandmother visits how often would you need to remind her to close the door? There are a few other solutions that may work. The emphasis is on may because some determined dogs can foil any solution if they really want something. Dogs are opportunists. They do not forget their favorite pastimes and will patiently wait weeks or months until someone forgets to close the door.

TOP LEFT This clever design features a door that closes when not in use. The unit can be painted to match the wall color. *Courtesy of Hidden TP Holder www.hiddentoiletpaper.com*

BOTTOM LEFT A stylish covered toilet paper holder. *Courtesy of Blomus www.blomus.com*

ABOVE DIY solution using an existing box. Two rubber feet were added to prop open the lid just enough for the paper to move smoothly.

Fully enclosed commercial toilet paper dispensers will foil most dogs because it's difficult to grasp the edge of one sheet without an opposable thumb, although persistent tongues might prevail. One hidden design called Hidden TP fits into the wall and has a door that swings down with the bar and paper roll in it. A few manufacturers make toilet paper holders with flaps that cover over the toilet paper. Other possible solutions include toilet paper storage canisters and small cabinets.

DO-IT-YOURSELF IDEAS

- Purchase a small cabinet or hinged box with interior minimum measurements of 5" deep x 5" high x 8" long and repurpose it by adding a toilet paper holder inside. This can be fixed to a wall or cabinet.
- Install a small door or drawer in a cabinet next to the toilet. Add an inexpensive toilet paper holder inside. The toilet paper will only be accessible when the drawer or door is opened.
- If your dog loves to grab the paper and run, try the TP Saver or a toilet paper holder with a flat bar instead of a cylinder. It's difficult to unroll the roll—which can be equally frustrating for humans!

BATHING OPTIONS

If you only have one or two small to medium sized dogs, they can be bathed in the bathtub or sink. Neither arrangement is ideal but there are ways to make the job easier. A standard bathtub or shower can be improved for dog bathing by adding a handheld shower wand. It should be long enough to reach the bottom of your dog and the shower. Measure before buying but six feet is probably sufficient. Handheld wands with an on/off or trigger switch is best. Select one with an overflow device to maintain an even water temperature.

Handheld showers for dog bathing are designed to either hook up to your existing shower, washing machine valves or sinks. Determine what type of hookup you need prior to purchase, they are not interchangeable. Choose one with a screw type or compression connection. Cheaper models with suction connections that attach to faucets do not work well or last very long.

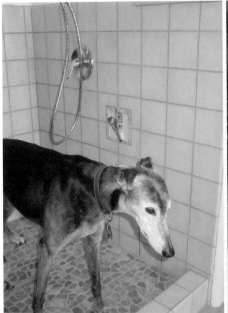

TOP LEFT AND RIGHT Dog showers don't need to be bland. These showers were designed with standard and custom made tiles. *Courtesy of Sondra Alexander: www.sondraalexander.com*

BOTTOM LEFT The Jentle Pet®, is a whirlpool tub just for dogs, with jets and a handheld sprayer. The lower front edge makes washing easier. *Courtesy of MTI Whirlpool: www.mti.whirlpool.com, (800) 783-8828*
BOTTOM RIGHT Standard equipment such as this utility basin can easily be adapted for a dog shower. *Courtesy of Kohler: www.kohler.com*

If dog bathing is a frequent chore, the tub or shower and/or the dog should be elevated to avoid the need to continually bend over. Of course, lifting a heavy dog into the tub will be equally hard on your back and a ramp may be necessary. You can also modify a plastic, wood or stainless steel table in your bath or shower to raise the dog to a convenient level. Be sure to add a non-slip surface or mat on top of the table.

Extra accessories that make baths easier for difficult dogs include:

- leash clip attached to wall
- non-slip coating in tub
- shower attachment for rinsing
- step or ramp access for big dogs

ABOVE LEFT Savvy demonstrates the custom raised dog shower made for her. The components are standard including a shower basin, handheld shower wand and wall tile. *Courtesy of J. Symmons*

ABOVE MIDDLE The manufacturer of these durable tubs offers many accessories and configurations to fit any dog owner's needs. They can be custom finished to complement your style. *Courtesy of New Breed Dog Baths: www.newbreedtubs.com*

ABOVE RIGHT Hugo shows off his outdoor shower at the dog-friendly inn where he resides. *Courtesy of The inn on First, Napa, CA: www.theinnonfirst.com*

. . . .

A handicap shower system makes an excellent dog wash. The typical size is 5′ long, 3′ wide and it has a very low lip for wheel-chair access. The shower is a long hand-held device. These shower systems often include folding seats that could be used to stand your dog on.

Customized showers lined with ceramic, stainless steel, concrete, glass or stone tile, can be built to accommodate your dog's breed and size. It should be large enough for the dog to completely turn around. Add a minimum of 6″ to the total length of your dog measured from nose to the base of the tail for both the width and length. Elevating the shower will depend on your height and whether or not your dog needs a ramp. A standard size bathtub can be elevated on a platform about a foot off the ground. Steps or a ramp can be added

A mop service basin is a type of utility sink installed at floor level. It looks like a very shallow bathtub measuring 6″ to 11″ deep. To customize a mop service basin for dog bathing the base can be raised off the floor and the walls around it finished with a water resistant material such as ceramic tile or stainless steel. This is an excellent way to create a convenient custom

ELEVATED SHOWER HEIGHT

First you will need to measure your dog's height at the shoulder. Next, while standing up bend your arm with your elbow at a right angle to the floor. Keep your forearm parallel to the floor and measure the distance from your forearm to the floor. Subtract the height of the dog plus 6″ to 9″ from the total. (6 to 9 inches is the ideal distance for bent arm activities). This will give you the optimal elevated shower height.

EXAMPLE

The distance from your elbow bent to the floor is 43″. Your dog is 24″ high at the shoulders. 43 - 24 = 19 inches. Subtracting another 6″ to 9″ for your work area will leave 13″ to 11″ which is the height you need to elevate your shower.

dog shower. Small free standing containers such as galvanized washtubs or rubber basins for watering cattle can be used to bathe tiny dogs and are also great for spot cleaning big dogs. Both are lightweight, inexpensive and portable. Laundry or utility sinks can make useful dog bathtubs for small to medium sized dogs. They are usually heavy duty, made from plastic, composites, porcelain, concrete or stainless steel and often have legs which raise them to a comfortable work height. The height can be adjusted by adding blocks under the feet. Plastic utility sinks are cheapest. Some have high backs which act as a splash guard. While single bowls would be preferred for dog washing, double bowl plastic sinks can be modified into a single sink by cutting out the middle divider using a reciprocating saw. To eliminate sharp edges sand them before using.

DOG SPECIFIC TUBS AND SPAS

There are many dog bathtubs on the market. At the lower price range are tubs made out of plastic and this is fine if you only bathe one or two dogs a couple of times a month. If you bathe multiple dogs on a daily or weekly basis it pays to consider a higher quality fiberglass or stainless steel tub. There are even whirlpool spa tubs made just for dogs.

Fiberglass models are similar to the bathtubs in most homes. The cost is generally less than stainless steel and the style is more likely to fit into your home. Stainless steel is the most durable choice but is limited to a cold, boxy style which may not be aesthetically compatible for all homes. Factors to consider while evaluating a manufactured dog bathtub include:

- Is the height adequate to accommodate both you and your dog? If not will you need to purchase additional accessories such as a table?
- How will the dog access the tub? From the side or one end? Will this require a ramp?
- Where are the plumbing features located? Are they within easy reach while you are working with a dog? The drain and faucet should be located at the same end of the tub for ease of installation.
- Ask about the quality of the faucets, hoses and other plumbing features. Heavy duty hoses and faucets will last longer. Can you upgrade these items?
- Can the tub be accessed from more than one side? A tub that can be installed with 3 sides exposed is more convenient. Rather than turning the dog around the groomer can simply move around the dog. This type does sacrifice space for convenience.
- Does the tub or shower come with a device to trap fur?

OUTDOOR BATHING

In warmer climates it's possible to minimize the mess by bathing dogs outdoors. This shower/bath could be as simple as an outdoor faucet and a hose or it could be an outdoor shower with a shower wand that you and your dog could use. Your outdoor faucet must have a hot/cold hose bib. To hook up to an outdoor hot/cold hose bib you will need a special hose connector that is used for washing machines and is called a Y-mixer hose. They are available at most hardware stores. A sprayer nozzle with adjustable settings is kinder on your dog. You will need a plumber to supply the necessary hot/cold lines and hose bibs, but the hose hookup is quite easy.

No matter where you bathe your dog after the bath you will need dog designated towels and/or a blow dryer. 100% cotton towels are the best choice because they are highly absorbent. A handheld blow dryer will suffice for a one dog home. Clips, available through grooming supply companies, can be used to clip handheld dryers to a post or shelf. However, a professional dryer is necessary for serious grooming. The qualities to look for in a blow dryer include low noise, temperature control and high velocity. New models of forced air dryers are small, powerful, and reasonably priced.

An infrared overhead heat lamp or an electric surface mounted wall space heater can take the chill out of the air after a bath. This might be especially important for toy and short haired dogs. Safety is paramount with any type of heating element. It should be rated for use outdoors or in wet conditions. Look for appliances tested by a recognized laboratory such as UL (Underwriters Laboratory), CSA (Canadian Standards Association) or ETL (Intertek). These should be installed by a professional electrician. Overheat protection and a timer are necessary features for a heat lamp. Do not purchase a wall heater with open coils. Safer designs have tubular, finned tubular or plate finned heating elements and an enclosed motor. For safety reasons portable space heaters are not recommended for this use.

CLOGGED DRAINS

Brush your dog thoroughly before bathing. Mats in the coat will congeal into a solid mass when wet. Bathing also loosens dead coat. The result can be a bathtub filled with an avalanche of dog hair and a $300 plumbing repair job. If your dog sheds heavily purchase a strainer to place over the drain before bathing. Some dog showers and baths come with small cloth strainers, but fine or short fur can slip through the drain trap. A piece of steel wool or fine meshed fabric placed over the drain is more effective. Other choices include buying a disposable hair strainer for a few dollars to expensive hair traps that can be installed in your sink, shower or tub.

Clogs in drains are best removed using mechanical rather than chemical methods. If a plunger or a hand auger fails to dislodge the clog, disconnect and clean out the trap. Place the plunger directly over the sink drain so that the rim of the plunger is in complete contact with the surface. Press firmly and straight down on the plunger handle. It may take several "plunges". You will usually see water moving down the drain and hear it in the trap if it works. A hand auger has a flexible cable that is pushed into the drain line to loosen clogs. It's a bit more complicated than a plunger so read the instructions before you try it. The trap is the U shaped section of pipe immediately below a sink. If neither the plunger or auger work and you feel that removing the trap is beyond your capabilities you may need to call a plumber.

See Chapter 9 for grooming facilities and other spaces that can accommodate a dog shower, tub or bath.

DOG TOILETS: WHERE WILL YOUR DOG ELIMINATE?

When your dog moves into your home this will immediately become a priority if your dog weighs more than ten pounds. For owners of tiny dogs or young pups that are not yet vaccinated temporary housetraining is often the best option. While it's true that whatever a dog learns first, he learns best, elimination habits remain fairly flexible until four months of age. After that, they may become reluctant to begin eliminating on an entirely different surface. So, if you plan on indoor training only, think about taking your dog outside once in awhile so they become accustomed to that occasional outdoor elimination opportunity.

It is essential to have a workable arrangement in place before you bring a new dog into your home. Consider:

■ **THE SIZE AND BREED OF THE DOG**
Small to medium sized dogs are easier to accommodate indoors.

■ **CLIMATE AND WEATHER**
Can your Chinese Crested be expected to "do his business" in a blizzard or your Bulldog take a midday walk in 90 degree weather?

■ **YOUR LIFESTYLE**
Urban, suburban or rural? Will you need to walk your dog? Do you have a fenced yard?

INDOOR DOG TOILETS

A major advantage of small dogs is their ability to adapt to small spaces, including using a small indoor toilet area. If you live in an apartment or have limited access to the outdoors, this makes a lot of sense. Mobility problems or living several stories above the ground floor can make getting your dog outside several times a day a major challenge. In some climates, outdoor exercise may be limited seasonally. In some cases, predators (animal or human) can make outdoor exercise risky. An indoor dog toilet may be the best solution if you fit into one of these categories. The choices range from paper training your dog, using a litter box or installing a real flushable toilet made for dogs.

It's a common misconception that paper training will never result in a reliably housetrained dog. Dogs can be reliably trained to eliminate in any area designated for this purpose. The key issue is to utilize scheduling, supervision, and restriction methods rather than allowing constant access to the toilet area. Provide access to the toilet area at scheduled times, supervise your dog to ensure that he completes the task at hand, and do not allow free access to your home until he is trained. In between toilet breaks, remove the paper or litter box, or bar his access to the toilet area. Leaving the soiled paper or litter in place sends the wrong message to your dog. Basically, you are telling the dog that eliminating all over this floor all day long is fine. Constant access will provide no incentive for him to learn self control. More importantly, he will have trouble distinguishing where and when this behavior is okay in the house.

The classic solution is to create newspaper layers on a moisture resistant and easily cleaned surface such as linoleum flooring or a plastic tray and removing them once a day. Put the papers down at the dog's scheduled elimination time. After the job is done, pick them up and dispose of them. Dogs can detect minute traces of odor that we don't notice so it is vital to wash this area every day. If you use a plastic tray be sure to wash both sides.

Box toilets include cat-style plastic litter boxes to sophisticated freestanding toilet systems that must be emptied on a daily basis. Plastic litter boxes are three to four inches high with an opening at one end and are filled with special dog litter. They work well for small to medium size dogs, but are not recom-

Enzymatic based products are best for eliminating odors and stains from urine and feces.

mended for short legged dogs or multiple dog homes. Many puppies will also dig or play in the litter, kick it all over the floor or ingest it.

The litter box should be wide enough for your dog to circle comfortably, approximately 1 ½ times his length. The sides should also be high enough to prevent litter from being kicked out of the box. Also keep in mind that both males and females may hike a leg to urinate. Hock high sides should effectively contain any female territorial marking, but male dogs can lift their legs to nearly the height of their abdomen.

Sophisticated litter box designs include a layer of real or synthetic grass with a removable tray below. Your dog eliminates on the grass; the urine filters to the tray. Any solid waste and urine in the tray can be flushed down the toilet. A version of this product made with synthetic grass can be washed periodically, which makes for more effective odor control and less work. The version with real grass must be watered frequently to keep it alive. It is normally replaced every six months when urine burn tends to set in. Often the real grass is only used until the dog is reliably using the box. One manufacturer sells a sun and rain cover to shield your dog for outdoor use.

These products work if your dog is:

■ small enough to effectively utilize the product
■ trained to use this toilet system

And...
■ you are prepared to keep the elimination area scrupulously clean

A portable dog potty for use on boats, patios and RVs is similar to some of the box style products and also utilizes synthetic grass, a plastic grate and a tray to hold the liquids.

If you have the space and the budget, a plumbed toilet specifically made for dogs may be the ideal solution. One manufacturer has created a large box structure slightly raised off the ground with three raised sides which the dog enters from one side only. The top surface is corrugated to prevent urine from getting on the dog's paws. It slopes towards a drain that is attached to a waste pipe in your floor. The product includes a hose and sprayer to wash down solid waste and clean the surface. A homemade version of this system can be constructed from a prefabricated shower stall. See Resources for a link to instructions.

An indoor plumbed toilet can be created by installing a floor drain in a garage or kennel area. This can be a good choice for larger dogs, disabled owners or owners contending with prolonged periods of bad weather. After the dog eliminates a hose and sprayer is used to wash everything down the drain.

Important design considerations include:

- floors sloped 1" per 3 to 4 feet of length to facilitate draining
- smooth water resistant floors and walls such as concrete or poured epoxy
- a drain plumbed to a sewer line and properly vented
- a hot and cold water line with hose bib(s)
- a garden sprayer nozzle to wash everything down the drain
- heating or insulation to prevent pipes or flooring from freezing
- ventilation
- a stainless steel post can be added for male dogs to urinate on

The cost of adding a floor drain in your garage will vary significantly depending on your location. An architect and/ or plumbing contractor should be able to help design such a feature. This is a job that will require the services of a plumber and you may need to obtain a building permit.

OUTDOOR DOG TOILETS

Most dogs use the same favorite elimination spots again and again. If you intend for your dog to eliminate in your yard it's easy to reinforce this behavior through training. This has advantages for you, your dog, and your yard.
It's easier to monitor:

- his health by keeping track of urination and bowel movements and collect samples when needed
- his elimination schedule
- your yard to keep it clean and prevent stepping in dog poop!
- And can lessen the possibility of stool eating.

The major drawback is that your dog is apt to become very set in his ways. If you plan to travel with him, board him, or leave him with a temporary caretaker he may be extremely reluctant to relieve himself in unfamiliar territory.

Since a dog's instinct is to first mark the perimeter of the territory most dogs select a spot at the edge of the yard near a fence, or even outside your yard. If your yard is not fenced your dog may end up using your neighbor's yard, a classic source of poor neighbor relations. Some dogs are rather bashful and prefer to use a more hidden area, such as tall grass, shrubs or your perennial beds. If your dog is already in the habit of fertilizing the flowers, you may need to fence off the area to stop this. As an alternative you can create a small "wild" area of low growing dog resistant plants and a wall of shrubs for canine privacy. Dog resistant plants include any hardy fast spreading low to medium height perennial. Look for plants that might be labeled as an aggressive grower for your particular region. For example, in the northeast US, groundcover plants that work well and include goutweed or thyme. It has to be a plant that you don't mind being damaged. The surrounding privacy could be any shrub or medium to tall perennial. Another benefit is that the excrement will naturally decompose rather than contributing to a garbage landfill or contaminating water supplies. Pheromone treated yard stakes can encourage your dog to urinate in a specific area.

TOP A covered dog potty with synthetic grass. Note the plexi-glass "walls" to prevent overspray. *Courtesy of Doggy Solutions: www.doggysolutions.com*
BOTTOM A simple indoor dog potty for small to medium sized dogs. *Courtesy of Wizdog: www.wizdog.com*

The logistics become more complicated for multiple dogs. Usually they prefer individual areas rather than a communal potty zone. The designated area should be large enough so that each dog feels like he has some choice of territory. Depending on the size of your dogs, this can range from three to fifty square feet per dog. Dogs in the same household often avoid using the same area, especially for bowel movements. Keeping the area clean is important for sanitation reasons. It also discourages your dogs from searching for a clean area. Consider your own reluctance to use a public bathroom that is not scrupulously clean. Whether it is indoors or outdoors, do not expect your dog to willingly eliminate in an area that is not clean and safe.

Surface materials other than grass may be a better choice for a very small yard. Dog urine will eventually kill grass, leading to erosion and drainage problems. The end result is additional housecleaning chores as dirt and mud are tracked into the house. Artificial turf, gravel, concrete, and stone may be viable alternatives. Artificial grass has come a long way since it was

WHAT DO YOU DO IF YOUR DOG HATES
GOING OUT IN THE RAIN?

ABOVE LEFT Covered area used as a doggy potty during inclement weather.
ABOVE RIGHT This light weight kennel cover could make an excellent and
economical covered dog potty. *Courtesy of Shade 'n Things: www.shadenthings.com*

first used on athletic fields. Today it looks more realistic and is designed for specific purposes, including a place for your dog to pee. Newer designs allow fluids to drain through and incorporate antimicrobial agents to reduce odors. The product is installed over concrete or crushed stone and can be further elevated with a plastic grid. It is currently installed at kennels, animal resorts, animal hospitals and dog parks throughout the country. You can use it in a small area or replace an entire yard with it. There are concerns about lead in artificial turf which is added to give turf a brighter green color. Newer laws will restrict the use of lead in turf products, but older products may still contain lead.

"Stone" is the surface of choice for many commercial kennels and animal shelters because it is more economical, durable and can be hosed and disinfected. Gravel refers to natural stone that is round and smooth. Crushed stone is manually crushed rock and because of its sharp edges it tends to remain in place better than smooth gravel. Geo-textile placed under the gravel will block light and prevent plant growth. The stone beds are between 3 to 6″ thick. If you are doing large areas this will require several tons of material and it is best to have your supplier estimate the quantity you will need. To make the best choice it is important to go to a local supplier and look at them firsthand. There are several drawbacks to using stone. It is difficult to scoop poop without picking up some of the stone. Dogs may ingest it which can lead to obstruction. In winter it attaches to wet fur and can lodge in paws causing injury. Crushed stone has sharp edges that are harsh on paws, bare feet and your flooring.

Concrete and solid stone surfaces are easy to clean and impervious to dog destruction. They can be hosed off with a sprayer nozzle and occasionally disinfected with cleaning solution. Concrete can be poured as one relatively continuous surface or utilized as individual pavers. Stone is cut into pavers of different sizes depending on the type of stone. Pavers can be placed snuggly together to create a somewhat continuous surface or spaced far apart with grass or other natural material in between. If the surface is continuous or tightly laid pavers it should have a minimum slope of one inch for every six to eight feet of length. At the edge of the surface there should be a drainage area which could consist of porous material such as gravel or it should be connected to a drain.

Wood porches and decks are not recommended as dog potty zones. Urine will permanently penetrate the surface causing the wood to decay. If your dog is confined to a wood deck add a ready-made dog potty or make your own.

It is amazing how many housetraining accidents occur during rainy or snowy weather because dogs are reluctant to use an outdoor area that is wet, icy or covered with snow. Then there is the equally annoying problem of dogs relieving themselves immediately outside the door. Consider adding a roof over your dog's daily elimination area to protect him from rain, snow and the hot sun. Your dog and house will thank you for it.

A permanent roof structure attached to your house will work best in areas with moderate to heavy rain or snow. This would

DECK DOG POTTY

Purchase a large durable plastic tray, like the ones used under washing machines to catch overflowing water. For extra large dogs two trays may be necessary. These trays come with or without a drain. A drain hole could be cut through the deck and a PVC drain pipe inserted. Dog waste can then be flushed down the drain with a hose.

You will need to periodically clean and disinfect the area under the deck or connect the drain to a sanitary sewer or septic system. Artificial turf could be used on top of the plastic tray.

be a porch with a floor of gravel, concrete, artificial turf or any cleanable material. If you have a porch you can add a ready-made or homemade dog potty. A permanent structure may require a building permit and architect.

In areas with little or no snow a less expensive alternative is an awning. Many awnings are manually or electronically retractable. Freestanding shelters, such as pavilions, gazebos or carports, constructed from a design or prefabricated kits can also work as dog potties if located relatively close to the house. The terms gazebo and pavilion are often used interchangeably but technically gazebos are elevated off of the ground and typically include a floor and railing. Freestanding shelters are most often made of wood, less frequently of stone or concrete. Temporary shelters made from canvas or plastic are not durable or permitted in all localities. Prefabricated kits can be erected by a skilled do-it-yourselfer. A ready-made or homemade dog potty is recommended in shelters with elevated floors. If the floor is at grade level cover it with artificial turf, concrete, stone or gravel.

Convincing your dog to eliminate in the right spot is only half the job. Then it's up to you to keep it clean. For methods on waste removal and disposal see Chapter 2.

See Resources for products and more information.

CHAPTER 9

Dog Rooms

Adequate
overhead
lighting

Modular carpet tiles

Space for
training
equipment

Basements are easily converted into dog rooms for training. Finishes
and materials can be simple. Storage should be accessible for humans.
This room uses modular carpet tiles which is fine for low impact training. If jumping or running will take place rubber, EVA or other sports
flooring would be more appropriate.

Breeders and professional dog trainers are very familiar with the concept of separate spaces for dogs, but dog rooms are a relatively new trend for the average dog owner. They range from a separate space to groom, train, exercise or just play with your dog and store all of the accessories associated with these activities.

Although quality time is essential to every human/canine relationship, there are many situations where a dog room comes in handy. Anyone with multiple dogs may temporarily need to separate them for a variety of reasons. You may need to isolate a sick or injured dog, confine bitches in season, or call a time out for dogs that are not getting along with each other. If a family member is allergic to dogs or objects to having them throughout the house a dog room can be a workable solution. A dog room is also a place for your dogs to stay safe and calm while you are entertaining guests who may not love dogs or while workmen are doing construction in other parts of your house.

The design of your dog room depends on several factors. Will you be modifying an existing room, building an addition or creating a separate building? In addition to canine considerations these decisions depend on budget, existing space, building codes and whether your site permits expansion. An architect, designer and/or contractor could help with these decisions. Your budget and design constraints will dictate size but never underestimate the amount of space. If it is well designed, comfortable and convenient, you will find yourself using it more and more. A room originally intended for grooming may turn into a great place to train your dog, and as a result, suddenly seem far too small. Ask yourself what will be needed in the room? Will any other activities take place here? Is this where your dog will be fed? Is this where you groom your dog or wash his bedding? Think these things over before you decide on the final size and location of the space.

The easiest option is to modify a room that your dog and family members already use such as a spare room, laundry room, mudroom, basement or a garage. Ground floor or at grade walkout basement rooms located on an exterior wall work best for outdoor access. Plumbing needs such as a sink, washing machine or dog shower can complicate additions and renovations. Additionally, when renovating an existing space preexisting flooring and wall finishes may be inadequate.

Once you have made your final space selection and determined that the project is feasible, you must address a few more important design details. Easy maintenance, adequate light, heat and ventilation are the keys to a well designed dog room. It's easy to fall into the trap of making the space feel stylistically like a kennel by filling it with kennel equipment. But it's doubtful that you or your dog will find this very satisfying. This room should be treated like any other space and meet all construction standards for the rest of your home. A comfortable space for both dogs and humans will make for a better human-dog bond.

If the space is designed for canine comfort your dogs will gravitate to it. The dog room should be large enough for human comfort as well. You may want to add a couple of comfy chairs, a radio, or home computer. A TV and DVD are handy for watching videos of you and your canine athlete in action. Make it a human-dog interactive space and everyone will win. If you can't be in the room all the time and want to monitor your dog's activities consider adding windows or openings in the wall so that he can see, smell and hear you. Dogs can also be monitored by installing a "doggycam" in the dog room, a feature that allows you to keep an eye on them via your laptop computer.

OUTDOOR ACCESS/DOGGY DOORS

Do not underestimate the value of outdoor access. Carrying your dog up and down the stairs or herding him through the house to the backyard can quickly turn from a minor to major inconvenience. Ideally your dog room should have outdoor access to a secure fenced area. You will have the luxury of simply opening the door and letting him out, or installing a dog door if so desired. A smaller fenced area within a fenced yard is a popular solution. This makes it much easier to keep track of your dog at all times. In multiple dog homes it can be further divided into areas for males, females, adults, or puppies. Exercise pens are a great way to create barrier fencing that can easily be revised as needed. For instance, to prevent fights, you may want to confine some of your dogs while others go in or out.

Dogs should be kept indoors, especially during extreme cold or hot weather and when you aren't at home. Using a dog access door (doggy door) can provide access to a garage or outdoor kennel for elimination, which is useful for individuals who work long hours away from home. Doggy doors have really evolved in the past 20 years. A major concern of a doggy door is security. Wildlife or uninvited neighborhood pets and most importantly, humans may gain access through a doggy door. Security is not a big problem for a small pet door but larger doors can allow unwanted human access. Pet door companies have solved this problem to some degree. The doors can be locked but that means that you can't expect constant free access for your dog. There are also electronically activated doors which are opened by remote control sensors on your dog's collar. Two more things can help to make the space more secure. First, make sure that the interior dog room is secure. That would require an exterior grade door between the dog room and the rest of the house, complete with deadbolts and/or locks. Secondly, pet doors should always be installed with the screws on the inside of the building—if a thief could unscrew it, access would be easier for them. Look for dog doors that have steel, not plastic, security panels. Some owners also worry about their dog being unsupervised outdoors when they are away from home. Never leave your dog in a situation where he could be stolen or become a barking nuisance to neighbors. Outdoors, a smaller kennel with a solid cover over will deter thieves. This also prevents escapes by your dog. The cover can be fencing material or a solid roof, which also provides shade and some protection in bad weather. For com-

All dog doors come with a warning about security and child safety. Small children can fit through most dog doors and the last thing you want is your toddler venturing out in the world on his own.

plete security the fence or kennel should have gates that can be locked. (See Chapter 10 for more on fencing)

Doggy doors today have improved in terms of energy efficiency and weather protection. Higher quality doors have thicker panels with better thermal qualities, weather-stripping and self-closing abilities. Specific types of doggy doors are made for installation in doors, walls, windows and screens. Wall installed dog doors can be used in nearly any type of exterior wall including stud framed, brick and concrete block.

Most dog doors require cutting a hole in a door or a wall. When selecting a dog door look for a heavy duty frame. If you are cutting a hole through a door or a wall you want something that is going to last and look good. There are even a few that come as large units that install within a sliding patio door. Most manufacturers provide detailed installation instructions, often as videos on their websites. This can be a DIY job for anyone with basic tool skills. Keep in mind that if the dog door is removed the wall or passage door will need to be repaired or replaced.

The access between the dog room and the rest of the house depends on your individual needs. As previously mentioned an exterior grade door works well for dog rooms that have continuous outdoor access. If the room is used to keep the dog out of the rest of the house while you are home then you might consider a gate, or a Dutch door that is split into two halves, a top and a bottom. They operate on hinges like a normal door and can be locked together to work as one, or separated into two. These are popular for use in dog resorts where dogs are housed in small rooms rather than kennels. They may help with dogs who bark at gates because of barrier frustration.

Stainless steel hinges on doors are more corrosion resistant than other types of steel. Stainless steel is commonly used in pool rooms or other wet spaces. Stainless steel hinges are more expensive but, if your dog is a leg lifter, this will be a good investment. Most interior and exterior doors require three hinges so you will need three pair if you want them to match. You can replace just the bottom hinges if you aren't fussy about them matching.

Needless to say, doors and gates must be constructed of durable materials that will resist jumping, scratching, and chewing. For more on gates and door protectors see Chapter 12.

Dog room floors will be subjected to a lot of stress so rather than replacing it three times, go with ceramic tile, concrete, or even a poured epoxy floor. However, if this space is used for training it must have a softer surface such as rubber, foam or carpet. Walls can be painted or covered with ceramic tile, plexi-glass panels or FRP, fiberglass reinforced plastic panels. FRP is a sanitary choice that is often used in dairy parlors and restaurant kitchens. FRP panels are more durable than plexi-glass and come in many styles and colors. Some of them are cut and scored to resemble tile. Paint finishes should be durable, a minimum of semi-gloss or eggshell.

Your garage, basement or attic may need to be insulated, heated and/or cooled. Heating or cooling can be as simple as using a freestanding electrical space heater, window air conditioning unit or a more costly installed space heater or AC unit. This may entail a new heating system if your current system cannot handle the additional load. Adding a fan can supplement HVAC by circulating air through the space. Dehumidifiers and adequate ventilation may resolve minor issues of dampness in a basement or garage, but more effective and costly solutions include roof gutters and drainage systems around the outside of the house. Even then, some basements will be damp which may prohibit the use of some types of flooring such as carpet or cork.

Ventilation is essential to eliminate dog odors and maintain air quality if multiple dogs spend much time in this room. Operable windows are the obvious way to improve ventilation. If the space requires the addition of windows consider placing them above dog height to eliminate the problem of dogs barking at the window. An extracting fan can be added to remove odors. Air cleaning units with HEPA filters will help remove dust and dog dander from the space. These units work best when used for several hours per day. See Chapter 4 for more on air cleaning and HVAC.

Your dog room will potentially include storage for food, veterinary supplies, toys, training equipment and seasonal dog items such as winter coats or dog flotation devices. Storage should be out of your dogs reach but easily accessible for humans. Closed storage with drawers and doors is preferable. However, bins on open shelves might work fine. The storage space should be easy to clean, especially if your dog sheds a lot. Determine exactly what you need to store and that will help determine the type of storage that best suits your dog room. For example, drawers are very suitable to store dog coats, boots, and towels. In multiple dog homes it may make sense to store each dog's toys separately. A bin or drawer for each dog is ideal or toys could be separated by type; a separate unit for squeaky toys, balls and tug toys. Tug toys are also great to hang on the wall because it makes them immediately accessibility. Be sure to hang them out of your dogs reach though!

MULTIPLE DOG HOUSEHOLDS
Dogs are social animals and enjoy each other's company. Generally in multiple dog homes dogs coexist in relative harmony, but this may or may not happen on its own. A routine that reinforces structure, supervision, and exercise is essential. Each dog needs to be treated and trained individually, as well as learn to integrate into a group. Owners of multiple dogs understand the value of management tools like crates, gates, doors and even rooms to create temporary isolation if a dog is ill or if two dogs don't get along.

Storage should be tailored to your own needs. A ladder doubles as an exercise tool and a place to store training toys within easy reach for the trainer. Bins store more toys and pegs keep tug toys accessible.

Designated drawers can be used for specific dogs. The dog shaped leash holder was found in the children's department of a major home goods store. Show ribbons are displayed on a cork board.

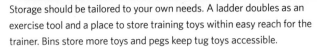

Even if your dogs spend most of their time in a communal area each one will need an individual space for eating and sleeping. Crates or modular cage units are the most common means of confining dogs but they are only suitable for temporary confinement. Crates can also become a nuisance if they need to be moved a lot for mopping and cleaning. In homes with large numbers of dogs, such as breeders or those involved in dog rescue it may be necessary to create more permanent features to separate dogs. Solid walls work well for dogs in need of a sense of security or who are prone to barrier frustration that results in barking or destructive behaviors. The barriers don't necessarily have to be typical stud wall construction. Many boarding kennels today use FRP instead of traditional chain link fencing between kennels because they have discovered that dogs are less likely to bark and become frustrated if they can't see each other. Metal, stone or other solid plastic panels can also work for this. If you are planning on partitioning the space into multiple kennels whatever you choose should be fastened securely to the walls and floors. Kennels with large numbers of dogs should have individual floor drains within each area for sanitary reasons. Key issues with multiple dog homes include:

- They require more maintenance and cleaning because more dogs mean that there will be more general wear and tear on your home.
- Durable materials take on a new level of importance.
- Routine cleaning chores may happen daily rather than weekly.
- Organization is critical for owners of multiple dogs.
- Drugs, medications and equipment must be kept separated.

For example if you have three different size dogs that require three separate quantities of topical tick and flea treatment these must be clearly labeled to prevent a potentially dangerous dosage mix up. Color coding using paint, colored stick-on dots, stick-on letters, tape or labels, is a simple and valuable organizational technique that can be used for everything from leashes and collars to dishes, foods and meds.

PUPPY SPACES

A puppy and whelping area should be free of drafts and enclosed so that it can easily be maintained at a warmer temperature without running up your heat bill by heating the entire house. This may require an individual heating sys-

FRESH, CLEAN AND LIGHT: A PERFECT
START FOR PUPPIES...

The dog breeder who owns this space divided it into
three distinct rooms. *All photos on this page are courtesy of
Windsong Kennels, G. Godbout*

TOP LEFT AND RIGHT the nursery includes whelping boxes, storage,
a dutch door, and a bed where the breeder sleeps for the first few
weeks of the puppies' lives. All floors are poured epoxy with floor
drains so the rooms can be hosed and scrubbed daily.

LEFT The puppy room includes a washer, dryer,
dishwasher, refrigerator, microwave and deep sink for bathing dogs.
It also has plenty of storage and space to showcase dog related
collectibles. Note the ramp that leads to other spaces.

ABOVE The adult dog room has plenty of room and light with multiple
pens built with custom fencing. Note that all the rooms are visible to
each other with dutch doors and/or windows.

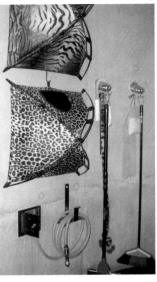

A DOG ROOM FIT FOR A PRINCE...

Lucky are the dogs (and cats) who share this well-designed kennel space! Instead of traditional wire cages each dog has a soft sided crate placed within a cubicle. Artwork and other supplies are safely placed out of reach.

Equipment is stored in an easy to find system. Even dog tents are artfully stored (*above right*).

The Pee Post (*top middle*) is made from stainless steel which prevents rust. The post is refreshed with real tree branches. A drain sits below the pebbles and a hot water retractable hose (*above right*) is used to flush urine down the drain. The drain is disinfected on a regular basis. Concrete floors are easy to keep clean.

All photos on this page are courtesy of The Labyrinth Kennels, M. Fluckiger, White Rock, BC, Canada

tem or separation of the heating system by the use of zones. A zoned system has individual thermostats that control separate zones or spaces in the house. For example it may be common to zone the second floor separately from the first floor. Zoning can be done to most types of heating systems including radiant, baseboard and forced-air. Costs will vary depending on the system and in any case this will require the help of a heating contractor.

Dog room flooring must be durable and in a puppy/whelping area it also needs to be regularly disinfected which requires a smooth and non-porous surface that is easy to clean. The best choices include seamless floors such as sealed concrete or poured epoxy.

Young puppies also require a potty area. Most commercially available dog potties are not suitable for a space with multiple puppies. The best solution is an in-floor drain hooked directly up to the sewer line. (See Chapter 8)

LAUNDRY AND GROOMING

Breeders or multiple dog homes may require a special kitchen, laundry or grooming facility to easily maintain their canine family. For ease of maintenance the best type of flooring in these spaces is concrete, ceramic tile or poured epoxy.

WASHERS AND DRYERS

There is no polite way to say it, dog laundry stinks. Along with hair and dander, it often includes plenty of unsavory canine bodily fluids. Conventional laundry hampers won't do the trick. It should be stored in an airtight container. This is especially important if you have problems with fleas.

There are three basic models of washing machines: top loaders with agitators, high-efficiency front or top loaders.

Front loading machines are the best option for dog owners. They have the best washing capabilities, largest capacity, and most energy efficiency of all types. Their high speed spin cycle expedites drying time. Horizontal axis technology used in front loaders means the clothes are tumbled through a smaller pool of water than a typical top loading machine. They use less water and energy, which really adds up if you do two or three loads of dog laundry per day. Many front loaders can be stacked with dryers to take up less floor space. Front loaders can be placed under counters or in cabinets. For better accessibility, some frontloading models are equipped with an accessory base.

Dryers are the simplest appliances in the home. They are divided into two types, based on the type of energy used to heat them: electric or gas. Gas dryers cost more than electric dryers, plus a gas line may need to be installed, which further increases the price. Dryers shut off when loads have dried by one of two mechanisms: thermostat or moisture sensor. Moisture sensors recognize when the laundry is dry. Machines that shut off at the right dried moment are easier on fabrics. Overheating reduces lifespan through shrinkage and fabric distortion.

> Dog laundry is often impossible to fold or stack, and who has time to fold dog laundry! Rather than leaving it in a gigantic heap, sort it into large bins or baskets stored out of canine reach.

GROOMING

If you find yourself grooming your dog often and/or grooming a large pack of dogs, you may prefer to create a separate grooming facility in your home. This seems like a costly luxury but if you own several Portuguese Water Dogs and calculate the expense and time it takes to brush, bathe and trim this breed, a dedicated space with proper equipment may not seem so extravagant. The size will be dependent on the type of equipment, the size of your dog and the space you may already have to work with. Your in-home grooming salon doesn't have to be too complicated and you can take your lead from looking at a professional salon. It may include space for brushing, trimming and bathing your dog. Like other types of dog rooms it is most convenient to locate your groom-room near an outside door. During "mud season" it will be easier to keep both your dog and your home clean. Most of the equipment used by the pros is very durable, so stainless steel bathtubs or heavy duty fiberglass are the preferred materials. All professional bath tubs are raised off of the floor which is much easier on the groomer's back. Most bathtubs are made to be used from one side only. This means that the dog has to be turned around during the bath. While this is not so difficult with a small to medium sized dog it can be problematic for a large or giant breed. One company, New Breed Bath, created a bathtub that solves this problem. It is accessible from both sides and has a rear entry; the dog remains in place and the groomer moves around him. Obviously these take up more space. After the bath, instead of a hand-held blow dryer most professionals use forced-air hose dryers or stand dryers.

Many spaces can accommodate a dog shower, tub or bath but consider these factors to keep it simple and cost effective:

- Do you have a space that could easily be converted or double as a dog bathroom?
- Is there hot and cold water available near this space?
- Is there space to include adequate drains for the wastewater?
- Is it conveniently located near an exterior door?
- Is the space insulated and heated and/or air-conditioned sufficiently?
- What size is your dog?

This shower is raised to make the work easier for the owner. Stairs provide access for the dog. The room also includes a grooming table, storage and areas to display show ribbons and photos.
Both photos courtesy of Constructional Custom Remodeling: www.constructionalremodeling.com

A PRIVATE BATH HOUSE

The lucky dogs in this household have their own private bathhouse/clubhouse dubbed "The Puppy Palace" by their owners. Inside, the tub blends in with the finishes and the sofa provides a comfortable spot to lounge after the bath.

Both photos courtesy of New Breed Dog Baths: www.newbreedtubs.com

For brushing and trimming your dog a good grooming table can be handy. The styles vary from simple folding tables to sophisticated electric hydraulic lift versions. The materials also range from composite wood to steel. Things to consider when selecting a table:

- choose one that is right for your height and your dog's height
- durable materials
- a top surface that is non-slip or a unit that comes with a non-slip removable mat
- if needed, purchase a grooming arm suitable for that table

Don't forget to include storage for all of your tools and accessories including brushes, combs, scissors, fur clippers, nail clippers, hair dryers and towels. Take inventory of everything you will use to determine the type of storage units you will need. If you have multiple dogs you might double everything so that each dog has his/her own accessories. Separate drawers or cabinets for each dog may be necessary. The best solution is a grooming cabinet on casters, similar to something you might see in a medical facility or beauty salon. Other simple solutions would be metal gym lockers or simple wooden cubes with storage bins. Don't forget storage areas for two often overlooked items; garbage and dirty laundry.

Flooring in a grooming space should be a smooth non-porous surface such as linoleum, concrete or ceramic tile. This will make sweeping dog hair easier and handle spills better.

DOG OFFICE

Professional dog people never seem to have enough space for some of the really important stuff, such as records, their computer and a quiet place to talk on the phone without barking dogs in the background. Incorporating a mini office into your dog room can solve these issues. Noise can be further attenuated by adding insulation between the interior walls.

See Chapter 12 for information on dealing with sound. Metal desks, files and chairs are most durable and least likely to be chewed on.

PLAY/TRAINING AND FITNESS AREAS

Fresh air and exercise are great ways to prevent boredom and depression in both humans and dogs. When it's too hot, cold or wet outside, an indoor play area is an ideal alternative. You can easily create an indoor play, training and/or fitness area in an underutilized space in your home such as your basement, garage, attic, outbuilding or an extra bedroom. The process for designing a doggy playroom is the same as any other area in your home. The first step to any good design is to define the problem and then determine how best to solve it. Remember those needs and wants from Chapter 2? Start by creating a list of what you need and what you want. This is not complicated if you plan for your specific dog's needs.

What might those needs be? The breed, size, and age of your dog will dictate the sort of play area you create. Which activities do you and your dog do together? Are you already engaged in competitive sports such as flyball or freestyle? Or do you just need a place to bounce tennis balls off the wall for your overactive canine friend to fetch? Your list should include specific equipment or toys, design elements necessary to use and house them - such as storage, flooring and lighting. If the room needs insulation, heating/air conditioning or other building components include them on your list. If you have a semi-finished or finished space the project will cost much less than building a new space or adding on to your current home. Most additions will require professional help so add that to your budget as well.

Next, ask yourself two questions: where is the best place for these activities and how can I fit them into this space? Thoroughly examine all of the possibilities and don't limit yourself.

If your dreams are big and your budget allows you could build a separate building for dog training. Many competitive dog trainers do just that and supplement the cost by offering building rentals and dog classes. Good flooring is essential and this facility has one of the best. The base is a layer of gravel covered with EVA foam interlocking matts and a layer of specialized foam matting on top. It is great footing for dogs and humans alike and gentle on the body. The color transition between the floors and walls uses minimal contrast to prevent eye strain. Storage for items that are used frequently should be simple. The storage unit shown in the bottom photo holds agility equipment and keeps items visible and out of the way when not in use.

Many world class agility competitors train in a very limited space that may be large enough for only one obstacle at a time, but it can be enough to supplement other training during bad weather. Basements are often underutilized and already heated and electrified. In addition, some do not have wall partitions and make ideal open spaces for a dog training facility. For many people they might be the largest space in their home. Two drawbacks to most basements are their height and limited accessibility. Since basements tend to be 8'-0" high or less this prohibits major pieces of agility equipment such as A-Frames. Basements are normally built below grade and do not have direct accessibility outside which also limits what can be moved into the space. This may be true for a second or third

floor room in your home too. If you are lucky enough to have an at grade basement (walkout) this makes the space more accessible. Basement access doors can be added for a few thousand dollars.

The garage is another room with doggy playroom potential. The advantages to a garage are: the space might already be wide open, free from central supports, have a higher ceiling than the rest of the house, and be at grade level. If your garage is already insulated it might not cost much to create a useable space. The best part is that it's also possible to use this space for your car too. Rubber or carpet flooring will not be harmed by driving on it. One drawback however, is the dirt that will be brought in by your car tires. A hose-bib with hot and cold water would be useful for keeping a rubber floor clean. And of course, any hazardous items stored in the garage such as antifreeze, pesticides, herbicides will need to be stored in a dog proof storage unit.

Good lighting is essential to any work space and that includes a dog play/training area. Natural light is wonderful during the day but even a space with windows will require artificial lighting at night. Lighting in training facilities should be evenly distributed throughout the entire space and should be properly shielded, focused or located to not cause glare. Supplemental light may be necessary in storage areas or if you decide to make the room work double duty as a grooming space or office

Non-slippery, flexible and durable flooring is crucial for your doggy playroom. Strenuous activities, such as jumping and running, must be done on a floor that flexes with your dog. Three types of flooring can serve the purpose for most dog activities in a doggy playroom and include: carpet, rubber and plastic foam. Carpet modules work very well because they are easy to install and can be individually removed for cleaning and after minor flooding. Be aware that some carpet may not provide enough flexible cushioning and be too slippery for high level activities such as jumping and running. Carpet padding or EVA foam under the carpet may provide more flexibility.

If the subfloor is concrete you may need something more resilient such as rubber or plastic foam. These also come in modules, interlocking tiles, mats or narrow rolls for easy installation and removal. Rubber produces VOCs and should only be used in spaces that can be well ventilated preferably not within your home. From an environmental standpoint choose recycled rubber flooring and for comfort a thick, soft but textured surface. For ease of installation, choose mats or tiles that snap together. Most rubber floors can be driven over by cars, but check with the manufacturer first.

Plastic foams are made from different chemical combinations. Two good choices are EVA (ethylene vinyl acetate) and/or PE (polyethylene) foams which are sometimes used individually or in combination. They utilize non-chlorine vinyl and do not contain harmful softeners found in PVC. For a really resilient

CANINE FITNESS ROOM
Keeping your dog fit is no longer weather dependent! Many serious dog competitors have fitness equipment for both their dogs and themselves, as Ambrose and his mom demonstrate. Fitness rooms are also great for post-surgical rehabilitation.

floor consider using two layers of materials. This could be two layers of plastic foam, a layer of plastic foam and a layer of rubber or a layer of plastic foam and a layer of carpet.

Whatever you decide be sure that the color contrast between floors and walls is not too abrupt. Strong contrasts, such as a black floor with a white wall, can cause eye fatigue and make it difficult to see the task at hand. It would be better to have a black floor contrasting with a mid-range gray color, as shown in the photos of the training facility on the previous page. This is most important from floor level to about four or five feet in height. Above that a lighter color is fine.

FITNESS EQUIPMENT
Dog sports are growing in popularity with all sectors of the dog world. Organized competitive canine sports include agility, flyball, schutzhund, dock jumping, freestyle, tracking, obedience and hunting to name a few. Keeping athletes fit is an ongoing need. Some dog trainers create fitness rooms that they can share with their dog. The dog might use a treadmill while its owner uses an elliptical trainer. The equipment will vary but often includes a treadmill, therapy balls and discs, ladders, and cavellettis. When designing the space ensure you have

enough room for these items. Most dogs do not need a special "dog size" treadmill and do fine with a human version. The most important spatial need is surrounding a treadmill. There should be a minimum of two lengths of your dog behind the treadmill (normally about four feet + will work), there should be space in front of the treadmill to allow you to reward your dog with treats while you are training him to use the equipment. And don't forget to add those elements that might make the experience more enjoyable for you like a TV or radio.

See Resources for products and more information.

CHAPTER 10

Dog-friendly Outdoors

Outdoor spaces are great places to spend some fun time with your dog. If you are lucky enough to have a yard, the best thing you can do for you, your dog, and your neighbors, is to put up a fence. Animal shelters, rescue groups and breeders often require potential owners to have a fenced yard. Fencing choices fall into two categories: hard "visible" fencing and electronic "invisible" fencing. Hard fencing includes garden wire, chain-link, decorative wood, wrought iron, aluminum, and plastic. Walls of stone, concrete or brick can also serve the purpose. Your choice of materials will depend on:

- your dog's size and physical abilities
- budget
- installation: DIY vs. professional
- aesthetic considerations
- privacy requirements
- zoning and building codes

The most important consideration is your dog's requirements. For instance, regardless of their size or athletic skill, some dogs respect any barrier, and a three or four foot chain link fence provides adequate security. But if your dog is a nimble athlete, fencing should be at least six feet. Many Toy dogs can clear a four foot barrier, although some can't jump over 18″. Other dogs will choose different escape routes and will climb, tunnel, or learn to open gate latches. Fencing a yard is quite costly and you definitely don't want to discover your dog effortlessly leaping over your newly installed backyard barrier.

Wood, wrought iron and aluminum fencing typically costs more than chain link fencing. Avoid PVC and choose recycled plastic composite fencing as a durable and long-lasting environmentally-friendly choice. While all of these fences can be installed by a competent do-it-yourselfer, a professional will do it most efficiently. Hard fencing is more expensive than electronic fencing, but it is well worth it. Your dog will be safe, able to run free within his confines, and less likely to bother your neighbors. A fenced backyard also makes your home more secure from burglars. Police are often quick to point out that fences deter thieves because they make it difficult to enter and leave a property. Hard fencing also prevents most other animals from getting in. Often a hard fence will add value to your property.

Wire garden fencing, usually with a green plastic coating, is a cost effective option for quick fencing. Installation is simple and fast by hammering thin metal posts into the ground and attaching the wire fence to hooks on the posts. It's useful around play areas or agility areas or in places you rent, as it can be removed easily. It may not be as secure as other types of fencing. Dogs that repeatedly climb the fence will eventually bend it over with their weight, and escape is quite easy. On the other hand some dogs are put off by the instability of garden fencing and this discourages them from climbing. Only you know your dog's personality!

A privacy fence blocks the view in and out of your yard. Open fencing allows a clear view. Privacy fencing will discourage problems like barrier frustration, excessive barking, and fence fighting. A combination of open and privacy fencing may also work. For instance, you may only need privacy fencing on the most active side of your home, facing a busy road or sidewalk.

Fencing can be decorative or simple. The style of your house, personal tastes, neighborhood choices, and cost will all impact your selection. If you decide on chain link or wire for economical reasons, you can easily dress it up with a wide range of materials such as bamboo, split bamboo, willow, or other twigs. These things can be bought pre-made in 3, 4 and 5 foot heights and are easily attached with wire to any existing fence or structure. In addition to dressing up your boring fence they can create quick privacy or help prevent barrier frustration for your dog.

Material selection should focus on your dog's behavior. Is your dog a climber? Textured surfaces and "ladder" style designs that provide good footing will help him on his merry way. Choose a smooth solid material that does not provide any footing or climbing surface such as solid wood or plastic planks. Is your dog a digger? Be prepared to buy extra fencing or wire screen to bury for escape prevention. Is your dog a chewer? Use metal rather than wood or plastic fencing and avoid pressure treated lumber.

Every dog, large or small, is dedicated to investigating his environment. Therefore fencing must not have any openings large enough to tempt your dog to try and squeeze through. In most cases, if a dog can fit his head through the rest will wriggle through as well. Dogs have been killed or injured, often by a neighbor's dog, when they became stuck in a fence.

A very critical and often overlooked aspect of a fencing system is the gate. Dogs learn to open gates and people forget to close them. The best fence in the world is worthless if your dog can simply walk out of the gate. In busy neighborhoods a lock is essential to keep children, strangers and potential dog thieves out. At minimum your gate should have a latch that closes completely. Too many gates have makeshift closers—a rope looped over a fence post, or a chain wrapped around the gate. A locking mechanism, a gate alarm or gate latches labeled as magnetic, for livestock or kennel use are all good choices. Self-closing mechanisms that completely latch closed are safest but you may risk locking yourself out. The latching mechanism should be placed on the outside of the gate so that a human can reach it but the dog can't. Kennel latches and hinges are good choices for chain link fences. A kennel latch requires the user to lift up and turn the latch making it harder for a dog to open. In addition kennel hinges and latches can minimize the distance between the gate and the upright posts.

No matter how safe your fence may be, always spend time observing your dog's behavior when he first encounters this addition to his environment. Dogs are always learning and he may surprise you by displaying innovative behaviors that lead to escape or injury. Boredom, loneliness, frustration, high prey drive, sex drive and learned behavior all play a role in a dog's propensity to escape. Sufficient exercise, training, and neutering may help but none of these measures are guaranteed to reform an escape artist. It can be tricky to gauge your dog's reaction to a particular type of fence if he has never before encountered it. Some dogs seem capable of escaping from any space and they can be quite ingenious about this. Dogs can learn to use other objects as a launch pad. A bench, trash can, compost pile, or snowdrift near a fence can provide

the strategic inches required to jump over the fence. Other dogs take a direct approach and simply chew through wood or plastic fencing. Still others learn to pull wire away from supports. Dogs in the habit of wandering will continually test fencing and it must be checked on a daily basis. It may require limiting your fenced yard to a small area so that you can keep track of both your dog and the condition of the fencing.

> If you own a breed or bloodline known for a propensity to jump, the best approach is to discourage this idea from the start. Young puppies should always be rewarded for respecting barriers. Do not reach into a pen to encourage a puppy to stand up against the side or reach over the top for attention.
>
> If your breed is known as a "problem solver" don't put temptation in the way, such as objects that can be used as a staging area for scaling the fence. Utilize safety measures like dog proof latches from the start. There is no turning back once your dog figures out an escape plan.

Breeds that are prone to digging require a buried barrier of chicken wire, wire mesh, chain link, concrete blocks or the fencing material itself at the bottom of the fence. It must be buried at least 12" deep. This is a big project but it's also an effective barrier against rabbits, fox and woodchucks.

Adding a barrier at the top may be enough to discourage a jumper from sailing over the fence. Solid wooden or concrete block fencing or even adding plants can all be good solutions because the dog can't see what is on the other side. Choose plants wisely to ensure that your dog does not end up using them as a launching pad. Prickly plants, such as roses, or barberry are a good deterrent. Soft plants such as ornamental grasses and most perennials are good choices because they will topple under your dog's weight. A double fence system composed of two fences spaced 12" to 18" apart may do the trick to discourage jumpers. This can create maintenance issues so use a geo-textile with a layer of gravel to prevent weeds from growing between the fences.

Climbers can be discouraged by adding a section of fence at the top that is angled inward at 45 degrees. This makes it difficult for many dogs to complete the final straddle over the top and also makes it difficult for jumpers to judge the height. Another solution is to add a "roll bar" at the top of the fence. When the climber grabs onto the bar it will roll and prevent him from getting a good grip. These roll bars could be homemade from exterior grade PVC pipe.

Certain dogs seem impossible to fence in. They will require leash walking and constant supervision until they become too old and infirm to jump. You can still provide a fenced area for dogs like this but it is a bit more costly. Solutions include a fenced pavilion with a gravel floor or a plain old chain link dog

OPEN STYLE FENCING

ABOVE, TOP LEFT 7 feet tall heavy duty plastic fencing that is easy to install. Keeping deer out is an additional benefit. *Courtesy of Best Friend Fence: www.bestfriendfence.com*

ABOVE, TOP RIGHT This fence was originally meant for swimming pool security and is made of either wire or polyester mesh. It installs over hard surfaces such as concrete and is easy to install or remove. *Courtesy of Guardian Pool Fence Systems, Inc. Toll free: 1-800-366-7233, www.guardianpoolfence.com*

ABOVE, BOTTOM ROW Chain link is a commonly used type of fencing. It comes in many colors that can blend in with your landscape and is suitable for most dogs.

ABOVE, BOTTOM RIGHT Composite fence made of recycled plastic and wood blends well with ornamental iron. Note that the privacy fence faces the front yard and road. *Courtesy of Long Fence: www.longfence.com*

FENCES: GOOD FOR DOGS AND GOOD FOR THE NEIGHBORHOOD
Private and Semi-Private Fencing
Privacy Fencing is a great solution to prevent barrier frustration in dogs. Smooth faced boards make escapes more difficult. *Courtesy of Long Fence: www.longfence.com*

BELOW, LEFT Semi-private fence
BELOW, MIDDLE Wood/plastic composite
BELOW, RIGHT Wood and lattice

ESCAPE PREVENTION

If your dog is a climber avoid fencing that creates a ladder effect.
Or you could consider the system *above right*. Originally made for
cats, it consists of mesh attached to angled metal rods.
Courtesy of Purrfect Fence: www.purrfectfence.com

ABOVE Benches and other objects can be used as a launching pad.
TOP LEFT Dogs can squeeze through relatively small spaces like the
one that exists between the final post and the house. A board has
been attached to the last post to cover this space.
TOP RIGHT A doggy porthole permits a view out of a privacy fence.
Courtesy of Best Friends Care LLC: infobestfriendscarellc@msn.com
RIGHT Dense plantings can be an effective deterrent for some dogs and
might prevent wildlife from jumping into your yard.

run with a cement floor and covered top. The height must be
high enough for you to enter for maintenance and interacting
with your dog. Whether or not you are concerned with aesthetics, a secure, covered dog run is expensive.

ELECTRONIC FENCING

Electronic fencing has three basic components; two are
installed in and around your home: a transmitter unit is
plugged into an electrical outlet in your home, and underground wiring is buried to establish the containment perimeter. The third component is a receiver that is fixed to a dog
collar. The transmitter sends a radio signal through the under-

ground wire, which is transmitted about 10 feet beyond either
side of the wire. The radio collar receiver picks up this signal
and sends a beep meant to alert the dog that he is getting too
close to the "fence" or wire. If the dog goes beyond this point
he will then get a shock. The dog must be trained to recognize
the boundary and regard the beep as a warning.

While it is arguably the cheapest type of fencing, it has some
major drawbacks. First, it is often installed around the entire
house, including over the driveway and near the road or sidewalk. Dogs do get hit by cars in their own driveway. The second
drawback is that it provides no way to prevent animals, such

JUMPING: WEIGHT TO HEIGHT RATIO

One indicator of how high a dog can jump is known as the weight/height ratio. Two different breeds that are the same height at the withers may not be able to jump the same height barrier. To determine your dogs ratio divide his weight by his height at the withers. The closer the number is to zero the more easily he could jump something twice (or more) his height.

For example if we compared two 13" high dogs: a 50 lb. Basset Hound with a 10 pound Chinese Crested, the Bassett's weight/height ratio would be 3.8 while the Chinese Crested's would be 0.7. While this can't predict exactly how high a dog can jump it may indicate the relative jumping potential of your dog.

These enclosures create an escape proof and safe environment for a dog with indoor and outdoor access.
Courtesy of Habitat Heaven: www.habitatheaven.com

as dogs, coyotes, and cats from entering the area. Another disadvantage is that some dogs don't respond well to the fence. They fall into two categories: those that go through it regardless of the shock, and those who become so fearful of being shocked they won't move beyond the door.

Owners also make a few common mistakes with electronic fencing. They may become complacent once the dog appears to be trained to respect the barrier. If you don't bother to put the collar on your dog or turn on the fence the dog will know instantly. Dogs test the fence every time they are outside. Second, because of the low cost, dog owners try to fence in every square inch of their property. It becomes impossible to monitor your dog in an overly large area, making it more likely that he will develop self-reinforcing habits such as chasing wildlife. Third, boundaries often come too close to sidewalks and roads. Drivers in cars might react as if the dog is going to run in front of the car and people walking dogs or with small children can easily be frightened.

ZONING AND LEGAL ISSUES

Before you erect fencing you will have to consult local municipal zoning and/or building codes. Most places allow fences up to a certain height, usually 4' high. If the fence is higher a building permit may be required. The fencing installer will know, but you will be responsible for obtaining appropriate building permits. You also have to ascertain the requirements for setbacks. A setback is a given distance from a lot line boundary that any physical structure or element can be built. The setbacks are sometimes different in the front, sides and back. Often there is no setback for fences, except for at the front of the property which means that the fence can be built right on top of the side and rear lot lines. You will need to be certain of where that lot line is, or you might end up building the fence on your neighbor's property, and that fence could become his property. Some municipalities and home associations do not permit hard fencing so electronic may be the only option. While it is not universally recommended it is certainly safer than no fencing at all.

If your neighbor already has a fence bordering your property on one side, you may reap the benefit of not having to put up another fence. If you need a taller fence, or a privacy fence you may have to get your neighbor's permission, as well as a variance from your town.

OUTDOOR SPACES

Decks are raised wood platforms most commonly made of cedar, pressure treated or plastic lumber. Plastic recycled lumber is dog-friendly because it does not cause slivers that can lodge in bare feet or paws and highly textured varieties are less slippery when wet. Patios are usually at grade and made with masonry materials such as brick or concrete. Both

Quinn and Rich enjoy hanging out in the hammock together. Water-resistant padded fabric provides a safe place to swing.

are permanent features of homes, and therefore regulated by building codes. These codes address human safety, and dog safety is something we are left to figure out on our own. Deck safety focuses primarily on the materials, access, and railings. Local codes dictate such things as whether a railing is required, the railing height and spacing between railing components. Railings are generally required for decks that are 30″ or higher off of the ground which is inadequate for homes with dogs and children. Both humans and dogs could be severely injured jumping or falling off of a deck at less than that height. A more prudent approach would be to add a railing for any deck over 12″ in height for small dogs or 15″ in height for larger dogs. In terms of the actual rail spacing, most codes do not permit any openings that allow a 4″ ball to pass through. This size determination is based on a child's head—not a dog's head. Depending on the size of your dog, you may need to add protective netting over your railing system. Plastic deck shield netting works for most dogs. (See Chapter 3 for more.) Chicken wire or wire garden fencing may be more suitable for dogs that would chew through plastic netting. Some codes require a maximum of 2″ between the bottom horizontal rail and the deck which is an adequate dimension for dogs.

There is nothing better than lying out in your hammock in the shade on a warm summer day with your dog by your side. Dogs can easily jump into the hammock with you, but it's a very different story if you aren't in it.

Store your hammock when it's not in use. It will last longer and be safer for your dog. The safest hammocks are made from solid fabric rather than rope. Dogs can get caught and injured in rope hammocks.

TOP Maddie and Spangle love a good romp in the waters near their home on Cape Cod. *Courtesy of A. Pettito*

MIDDLE Ramps are a necessity in swimming pools and on boats to ensure that your dog can get out of the water. This smart dog is wearing a personal flotation device. *Courtesy of Skamper Ramp: www.gamma2.net*

BOTTOM Pippy drinks from a backyard koi pond. *Courtesy of D. Doran*

WATER FEATURES

Fountains, pools or ornamental ponds enhance our home outdoor experience. Dogs also appreciate them. From the standpoint of dog owners, there are two basic types of water features: dog-friendly features like pools, and ponds and off-limit features such as hot tubs, spas and fountains.

POOLS AND PONDS

Certain breeds, such as Poodles and Retrievers are natural swimmers but plenty of other breeds are equally attracted to water. Regardless of the breed, never assume that this ability is instinctive. Even dogs who are great swimmers can drown, if they become trapped, disoriented or tired while swimming. Like children, dogs should be supervised when they are in and near the water. If your dog will be around water frequently, it's a good idea to purchase a PFDD, personal flotation device for dogs. It may keep your dog from drowning regardless of his swimming skill.

Swimming pools typically have straight edges, making it very difficult for dogs to climb out. Pools used by dogs should have steps or a floating ramp to ensure a safe exit. The better floating ramps are perforated plastic, mesh or highly textured. They attach to the side of a pool, boat or dock. In most areas zoning regulations require pools to be surrounded with a 4' high fence with locking gates for safety reasons. If your dog can easily scale a four foot fence, you cannot consider this a safety feature.

People have drowned when entrapped by pool drains as the water is suctioned into purification units. A federal law now requires anti-entrapment units on all public and new private pools, but millions of older private pools are not in compliance with this safety law. An anti-entrapment cover may save you or your dog.

Dogs have extremely sensitive skin, and pool chemicals, such as chlorine can cause topical burns. Consider newer water treatment systems that eliminate chlorine such as diatomaceous earth (DE) and ultraviolet (UV) or that minimize the use of chlorine such as ozone, copper and silver. A good choice for a dog-friendly pool filtration system is a DE filter that catches hair, debris and very small particles, including algae and some bacteria. Diatomaceous earth is a fine powder consisting of the fossilized remains of sea organisms called diatoms. These filters are more upkeep than traditional filters but are worth the trade-off for better water quality. Another effective and very safe water purification method uses UV light. UV filtration systems do not use chlorine and other harmful chemicals.

A natural swimming pool looks more like a pond than a pool. It uses environmentally-friendly methods, including plants and biological filtration. The pools are naturally balanced, self-cleaning, aesthetically pleasing and the installation cost is comparable to a conventional swimming pool. Maintenance is more efficient and cost effective. In general natural pools are usually lined with a rubber membrane or bentonite clay. Similar in size to a traditional pool, they are divided into separate areas, usually 50% for swimming and 50% for a "regeneration zone" with shallow or marginal plants and a filtration system. Natural swimming pools are a great choice for dog-friendly homes because they do not rely on any chemicals. Being more natural, like a pond or a lake, your dog should not swim in the pool if his immune system is compromised.

PONDS

A pond can be a wonderful play area for your dog. If you have enough land and zoning allows it, in some parts of the US a ½ to 1 acre pond can be created for less than the cost of most in-ground pools. Ponds require very little maintenance, attract wildlife, and don't contain harsh chemicals. Ponds may need annual maintenance to keep them vibrant and clean. Beneficial bacteria is the safest way to clarify water and reduce muck and algae for a dog-friendly pond.

Ponds have their own unique hazards. Excess water flow on a dam or spillway after the snow melts or a heavy rain can be extreme and knock a dog off his feet, pulling him away. Ponds, especially those with very still water, are breeding grounds for bacteria, such as leptospira or insects, such as mosquitoes that

NATURAL SWIMMING POOLS FOR YOU AND YOUR DOG
Chemical free pools are possible. Biological filters, and plants
naturally clean the water. The water is safe for humans and dogs
to enjoy. Initially developed in Europe, these pools are available
throughout the world.
Photos courtesy of Bionova Natural Pools: www.bionovanaturalpools.com

can carry heartworm. (See Chapter 3 for more). Ponds have
other unique parasites. Trematodes, also called flukes, are a
type of worm that can be ingested by dogs when they eat raw
frogs, snakes or fish. Two species of flukes, alaria and nano-
phyetus salmincola can cause severe diarrhea, fever and vom-
iting. In certain regions ponds can attract dangerous snakes
and other hazardous wildlife such as snapping turtles and can
be a source of poisonous algae and plants.

Dogs are rarely considered when water gardens or small fish
ponds are designed. Whether you use one that is a preformed
plastic unit or have one custom made, they often have steep
sides and no slope which makes it difficult for a dog to exit.
Furthermore, fish and other animals such as turtles or frogs
are attractive to dogs. If you don't want your dog and fish to
comingle you will need to create a barrier around or over top
of the pool. Leaf netting, sold through water garden suppliers,
might work to keep dogs out of the water. A fence surrounding
the water garden is ideal.

If a pool or pond is beyond your budget, don't worry. Many
dogs are equally delighted by splashing around in a children's
wading pool. For under $10 your dog can have a private pool to
wade, sit or lie in on hot days. Supervise your dog and empty
the pool between uses.

Partially frozen ice, especially in late fall and spring can be
extremely hazardous. Dogs can fall through ice, become
trapped and drown. A person attempting to save a dog
could drown as well. Keeping your dog away from frozen
bodies of water or better yet, on a leash, can save more
than one life.

Hot tubs, spas and fountains should be off limits or out of
reach of your dog. Hot tub and spa water can be too hot for a
dog. If your dog likes drinking from a fountain you will need to
keep it clean 100% of the time.

Mosquito "dunks" are small solid pellets used to kill
mosquito larvae and are ideal for small bodies of water.
The main ingredient is BTI, a type of bacteria that is
harmful to mosquitoes. The dunks float on water and
slowly release the BTI over time. Dogs are attracted
to the pellets and while they won't kill your dog they
could make him sick. Place the dunk in a plastic food
container punctured with multiple holes so that it will
sink to the bottom.

OUTDOOR PLAY AREAS
When designing a dog-friendly play area consider specific
needs first and foremost. Does your dog love to chase you,
fetch balls, or run? Are you training your dog for a competitive sport? Does your dog have specific breed related needs or
behaviors? For example a greyhound might love a place to run,
a Dachshund could enjoy a digging space, a Labrador might
love a bit of water, and a Pug may need an exercise area that is
cool and well shaded. Playgrounds could be a combination of
a sand box or digging area, a small water feature and space for
games. If you have enough space you can create a racetrack or
hiking trails.

DALMANIA: A PRIVATE DOG PARK
These lucky Dalmatians have their own dog park. Their owner
purchased six acres of rural land, built a pond and fenced in the entire
acreage to create Dalmania. Ambrose, Beau and Pippy share the land
with wildlife, such as the geese shown above and other dog friends.
At right, Beau and Eha splash in the water. *Courtesy of D. Doran*

Is your dog an excavator? Your home and garden would benefit from a doggie sandbox or sandpit. Sand drains water rapidly
and is more easily rinsed off than the soil. Place it in a shady
place, because sand can get pretty hot in a sunny location.
Make sure you have a place to clean the sand off before the dog
enters your house to prevent damage to your floors.

It is possible to create spaces for your dog to run and still
maintain flower beds. Since dogs will often run the perimeter
of a yard, especially if it is fenced in, it may make sense to create islands of plant beds, rather than concentrating planting
beds along the perimeter. This way, your dog can race around
without destroying your beds. When planning the layout,
consider your dog's breed. Some breeds such as Rottweilers or
German Shepherds instinctively guard the perimeter of their
territory. Others prefer broader paths to sweep back and forth,
such as Border Collies or Pointers.

If you love hiking or walking with your dog, and have one or
two acres of land, you can create a trail through your property.
With 10 acres or more you can create loops that are a ½ mile
or more in distance. Let the natural flow of the land determine
the trail, taking you through varying landscape. Allow some of
your land to revert to natural growth; whether prairie, desert
or forest, so you and your dog can watch these changes over
the years. Trails are easily made with a tractor and bush hog
but they can also be made with hand tools. If you run with
your dog trails provide a softer surface and safer place than
running on the road. To balance muscle development when
you and your dog run, running tracks are best if they include
opposing curves and bends.

TRAINING AREAS
Clear spaces could be created for playing games or to practice
conformation, agility, rally, flyball or disc dog. Any flat, dry level area can be converted into a home training space. It should

have good drainage so you don't have problems with standing
water, especially after a heavy rain. The ground should be free
from rocks and the consistency should soften the impact on
your dog's joints and muscles. Select a site that provides am-
ple shade and wind protection. Because most competitors rest
their dog in a crate between turns artificial shade cover may
be necessary if natural is not available. Training areas should
be fenced to accommodate dogs off lead, avoid accidental
escapes and unnecessary distractions. Temporary wire fence
or ring gating can be used to enclose a portion of your yard.
Training areas should be separate from the rest of your yard
to prevent the dog from using this area as a toilet.

Tracking and Nose Work are competitive dog sports that rely
on a dog's innate sense of smell. Tracking requirements may
include tests on different surfaces but initial training can be
taught in your backyard with minimal equipment or space.
A field of medium height grasses and wildflowers can be a
great place to practice simulated tests. Since the actual tests
are done in areas that are five to seven acres it may be hard to
simulate the entire test in your back yard.

Earthdog or "go-to-ground" events are devised to test small
terriers and Dachshunds' natural abilities to detect quarry underground. The test consists of manmade underground "tunnels" with quarry, usually rats in a cage that the dog must find
and alert their owner. Competitors start with minimal equipment consisting of homemade wooden, PVC or corrugated
cardboard tunnels. Serious competitors may need a backyard
space that could accommodate buried tunnels or space to simulate buried tunnels by covering them with straw. This could

PLAY AREAS

Outdoor areas are great places for your dog to play and get the exercise they need.

TOP LEFT Agility fields don't need to be large. This one is located on a septic field and is only 60' x 60'.

TOP RIGHT Winter wonderland is fun for young pups. *Courtesy of D. Doran*

ABOVE Teddy and Quinn enjoy winter as much as summer. A shoveled path helps them get around in deep snow.

RIGHT Exercise is physically and mentally stimulating for your dog. *Courtesy of A. Pettito*

ABOVE LEFT Beau and his ball. *Courtesy of D. Doran*

ABOVE MIDDLE Geddy plays king of the rock! *Courtesy of A. Meagher*

ABOVE RIGHT Smiling friends enjoy a moment of rest in between play *Courtesy of J. Sahrle*

be construed as unsightly by neighbors so it is best in an area that is remote or can be fenced in.

STORAGE

If you find yourself with a growing number of toys and equipment for your dog, you might want to think about where you will store those things. Plastic cones can be easily stacked and stored in a small place, but agility equipment may need a room or a shed for storage. This, of course, will depend on where you live and what other uses your yard serves. To store these items efficiently it may require shelves or racks that are built specifically for each piece or pieces of equipment.

OUTDOOR LIGHTING

Lighting may be necessary to supervise your dog or work with him after sunset. Good lighting will also help to discourage predatory wildlife. In general outdoor illumination should enhance your use of outdoor space after dark. Ideally you should be able to see into the far reaches of your fenced yard so that you know where your dog is when you take him out at night. Beyond that you may wish to light your outdoor agility field so that you can easily train after a long day of work. Outdoor lighting for training areas can be a very expensive proposition so be sure that you absolutely need it. You will need to obtain a building permit for this type of lighting plan. There are many zoning ordinances relative to outdoor lighting, including preventing glare and light spillage on your neighbor's property.

The best type of outdoor lighting for dog training is adjustable metal halide sports fixtures affixed to poles. Metal halide will produce the most efficient light with the best color rendering capabilities currently available for outdoors. The fixtures should be fully shielded or full cut off types. This will prevent light pollution and reduce glare. The quantity, height and spacing will be dependent on the size of your space and what you need to light. If you are lighting an agility field you will need evenly distributed light with very few shadows. This will allow your dog and you to see the ground and the obstacles. The fixtures will need to be placed high enough to reduce shadows and glare. The higher they are the shorter the shadows. To maintain good neighbor relations the fixtures should be no closer to the property line than four times the mounting height.

Keep the following in mind for outdoor lighting:

- light only areas you need to use
- select the most energy efficient lamp, with the best color rendering capabilities
- use adjustable fixtures
- select fixtures specified for Sports

To prevent light pollution and promote good neighbor relations:

- turn off the lights by 10:30 p.m.
- use fully shielded or full cut off fixtures

TRAILS

Trails that wander through the woods or fields are enticing and enriching places for dogs. Taking a leisurely walk on your own trails with your dogs and friends is a wonderful way to relax. It can also be another great way to exercise.

GENERAL TIPS FOR OUTDOOR SAFETY

- store tools, construction materials, sports and lawn equipment securely
- limit access to garages, workshops and garden sheds
- rock walls and woodpiles can be dangerous because they can:
  - topple on your dog
  - harbor dangerous snakes and bees
- bird baths can be contaminated with bacteria and harmful algae
- bird feeders should be placed out of your dog's reach, the ground surrounding it will be contaminated with moldy birdseed and bird droppings
- fence in vegetable gardens, use wire hoops to keep dogs out of flower beds
- compost bins should be placed out of your dogs reach, they can contain harmful neurotoxin laden mold
- mulch can cause gastric upset and obstruction if your dog eats too much
- power tools and equipment can:
  - seriously injure your dog, i.e. lawn mowers throw stones
  - frighten dogs with their loud noise and vibration.
  - prevent you from monitoring your dog
- children's toys should be picked up
- supervise dogs around anything that moves, swings or involves jumping and climbing

See Resources for products and more information.

This beautiful facility is used for agility classes and events. The covered shelter/viewing stand comes in handy to crate dogs out of the sun or rain. This field is approximately 100 x 100 feet and four evenly spaced light fixtures illuminate it at night.
Courtesy of Robert O. Eggleston, Architect: roeggleston@hotmail.com

DOG PROOFING YOUR GARDENS

ABOVE A wire cage made from concrete reinforcing wire protects plants from dogs (and deer). The wire cage is nearly invisible and blends in with the plants.

RIGHT Low fencing helps keep dogs and rabbits out of the raised beds in the vegetable garden.

CHAPTER 11

Dogs and Humans with Special Needs

A Hoyer Lift is a very handy tool for paralyzed or post-surgical dogs. They can be bought or rented.
Courtesy of Thera Vet Acres: www.Thera-vet.com

Dogs with special needs require physical modifications to their environment to ensure their comfort and safety. These dogs may be disabled, very young or elderly, or simply not the average shape and size. Pregnant bitches and very young puppies also have special needs that are similar to the dogs described in this chapter. Whether the situation is temporary or permanent, a few modifications can make life far easier for both dog and owner. Design solutions for disabled or injured dogs should take into consideration the individual dog. Keep in mind that your dog may need a gradual introduction to accept any changes to his routine and environment.

Dogs may become temporarily disabled or non-ambulatory due to illness, injury or surgery. This can have a major impact on your household, especially if the dog is too large to be easily lifted and carried. Some things that can make it easier include:

- a new sleeping arrangement may be necessary during his recovery time.
    - You can create a bed on the floor to make it easier for him to get in and out of.
    - Arrange a ground floor room where you can sleep comfortably near your dog.
- some dogs will require confinement; an ex- pen can be easier than a crate. See Chapter 7 for more on ex-pens.
- large dogs may need special equipment such as: lifting harnesses for front and/or rear end, dog "wheelchairs", a hydraulic patient lift, stretchers or ramps.

CONVALESCENCE ROOMS

A dog recovering from an illness, injury or surgery requires a safe, quiet and comfortable space. Prepare the space before you bring him home from the vet. Depending upon the illness or injury, your dog may require complete separation from other human and canine members of the household. It should be close to household activity, so your dog feels connected to his family. On the other hand you will want to close off this area to limit noise, distractions and unwanted visits from other pets. There should be adequate space and if your dog is able to eat, he will probably be fed in this room. In a home with many dogs, a canine sickroom may require a permanent space.

When designing a space for convalescing dogs consider how hospital rooms are designed for humans. The primary considerations are comfort, cleanliness, and minimal stress for the patient. The room must have good temperature control and ventilation. A thermometer can help you monitor the room temperature and make adjustments; to maintain a range between 70 and 72 degrees. Operable windows or an exhausting fan are ideal for odor removal and fresh air. The floors should be easily cleaned surfaces such as: ceramic tile, concrete or linoleum. Materials like wall to wall carpet or wood floors can be temporarily covered by linoleum or thick plastic sheeting cut to fit and taped at the edges. If your dog is photosensitive or stressed by light or movement, windows should have window treatments. Use a very low wattage lamp or shield the lighting to prevent direct glare. When shielding the light do not place anything directly on the lamp and use non-flammable materials. Even fluorescent lamps can overheat.

Lillie's big smile is proof that dogs with disabilities lead happy lives. *Courtesy of L. Blick*

Convalescing dogs must be monitored. Personal supervision is best, but this can be augmented with video cameras and audio monitors to keep you aware of his status. Monitoring also means keeping charts of his progress and medication schedules, so be sure to include a convenient place for a clipboard or notebook. Medical equipment and supplies should be stored in a convenient but safe space out of the reach of children or other pets. IV bags need to be held at a high point so a hook on the wall, door handle or coat hanger hung from a door work well. If your dog requires strict bed rest or has drains, open wounds or bandages, other dogs will attempt to investigate and potentially contaminate the sickroom. Do not assume that pain or depression will curb your dog's activity level for very long. Enticing sights, sounds and scents will perk his interest, making it increasingly difficult to keep him calm and quiet. Dogs will get bored just as humans do, so you should plan to keep him occupied with appropriate activities, toys, and treats. Needless to say, you will need a place to store these items when you aren't around to monitor him.

Convalescing dogs often need to eliminate indoors for a variety of reasons. If this is a temporary situation for a normally housetrained dog, you may have no contingency plan in mind. Hard surface flooring is obviously the best choice. Plastic sheeting is a very effective, economical solution for floors needing protection. It can be used under a dog's bed to protect the floor, but be sure that the dog won't be left for long periods of time lying on soiled and wet bedding. Use either 4 ml thick clear plastic or lightweight 8 x 8 cross woven polyethylene tarps. If either is too thick they are more difficult to wash and store. Both can be bought at DIY or discount stores. Cut it into convenient sizes, fold and store it so it is ready to use when necessary. It can be washed in a washing machine with laundry detergent in warm or cold water and hung to dry. Hydrogen peroxide based bleach can be used to sanitize.

For non-ambulatory and incontinent dogs you may need washable waterproof bed underpads, disposable bed pads (cheaper than puppy training pads), thick fleece pads that allow urine to pass through while keeping the dog dry, and/

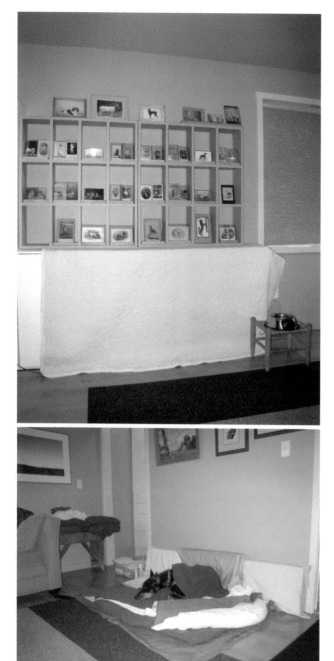

A CONVALESCENT ROOM
Elderly, injured or post-surgical dogs require a quiet space where they can be easily attended to by their owner.

TOP Bookcases covered with padding to prevent a dog from injuring herself if she fell.

ABOVE The converted den where Lena recuperated after major spine surgery. The surgery left her temporarily paralyzed for 2 months. This condition meant that she could not always urinate or defecate outdoors or on schedule. Her temporary bed was a series of layers directly on the floor. From the bottom up they were: a large sheet of plastic, a thin foam bed with removable nylon covering, three layers of old quilts cut into Lena sized pieces and resewn, a twin size waterproof bed pad (underpad) and a layer of thick medical fleece made for pets. Disposable waterproof pads were used as necessary. Three foam pillows padded the space behind the bed.

or special cots made with a wide weave and a plastic tray below to catch urine. Bedding should be kept to a minimum for hygienic reasons, but it must be sufficiently comfortable. For a cost effective efficient solution use a fairly thinly padded foam bed, covered by one or two layers of quilts that are cut and stitched to appropriate size. Smaller quilts are much easier to wash, and one king size quilt will yield several, which can be rotated while others are washed.

Small white cotton sheets, towels or blankets can be boiled to thoroughly sanitize them.

Recovering dogs are more likely to fall due to difficulty with balance, proprioception and general weakness. Furniture moving pads or quilts can be used to pad sharp and hard edges on furniture. Remove objects that can be knocked over or become a tripping hazard. Slippery floors should be covered with rubber backed area rugs. If your dog will wear them, special boots can also improve his footing.

Treadmills, cavaletti work, ladder work, therapy ball work, or hydrotherapy treadmills are typical features of canine rehab. They can be used at home, although some are more complicated or expensive to design and use, depending on the size of your dog. For small dogs, a bathtub or hot tub can be utilized for hydrotherapy. Larger dogs can be exercised in a shallow pool. If funds permit, you can add additional modifications like an underwater treadmill

PERMANENT DISABILITIES
Until recently, most disabled dogs were euthanized. Today thanks to changing attitudes and advances in veterinary technology, disabled dogs are not only given a chance, they can lead surprisingly satisfying lives. Caring for your disabled dog requires a big commitment of time, patience and extra supervision. He may be accustomed to free run in your home or yard, but a disability will produce new risks in a familiar environment. Solid fencing or leashing your dog may be necessary outdoors.

All dogs need a safe retreat and this becomes especially important for disabled dogs. Beds should be situated in a quiet spot away from the main traffic of the house. If he can't see or hear you coming, he will not be able to move out of the way. It is not unusual for blind or deaf dogs to become wary and defensive due to these constant surprises, which can lead to growling and snapping. At the same time disabled dogs need to feel and be a part of the household.

You must determine the actual scope of the problem to implement an effective design solution. Try to imagine what your dog is doing, feeling, hearing, smelling, and seeing as he negotiates your home. If his problem is hearing loss, keep in mind that hard surfaces reflect more sound making it difficult to know where the sound is coming from. If his problem is mobility, consider where he encounters the greatest difficulty walking, turning, and lying down.

Ramps can assist dogs as well as humans. This ramp was built for a dog that was temporarily paralyzed and had to be moved in and out of the house on a cart or a hoist. The low wall of plywood was intended to keep the cart wheels from falling off the edge. There is no handrail, which would be required for a human ramp, because the handrail would have interfered with the cart handle.

Carpet, rubber, interlocking EVA foam tiles or cork flooring are good choices for optimal footing and traction. Since many paraplegic dogs may also suffer from incontinence, use washable modular carpet or carpet runners with rubber backing, rather than wall to wall carpet. Other safety measures include gates, crates and barriers to prevent falling down stairs, off furniture or out windows.

Most residential stairs have a riser height between 6″ and 8″. Lower step heights are easier for the dog. Carpeted stairs, or carpet stair treads improve traction. Slings can also be used to assist a partially ambulatory dog up and down the stairs.

Ramps can help dogs with mobility problems negotiate changes in height encountered with stairs or furniture. Human wheelchair ramps are typically built with a slope of 1:12 minimum but disability experts recommend a slope between 1:16 to 1:20. A 1:12 ratio means you would build 12 inches of ramp length for every inch the ramp rises. While some sources recommend a 3:12 ratio for dog ramps, 1:12 or at least 1.5:12 is preferable. Ramps should have a vertical lip along the edge to prevent a paw or cart wheel from slipping off the edge. A railing is important but be sure it does not interfere with dog carts or stretchers if there is a turn in the ramp. Most manufactured dog ramps are too steep and you may want to consider building your own. See Resources for where to find plans.

A disabled dog's bed should be at a comfortable, accessible height. Thick, soft beds may be difficult for a disabled dog to climb in and out, and a firmer thin foam cushion may be a better choice. This is especially important if you have multiple dogs, another dog could potentially smother an immobile dog by lying on top of him in a very soft bed. Paraplegic dogs have a particularly acute need for multiple beds. Strategically placed beds throughout your home are helpful if your dog can move short distances.

Dogs with spinal cord and disk problems benefit from having their dog dishes elevated. Water pails can also be hung from fences or porch rails to provide extra water sources. These are nearly impossible for an uncoordinated dog to tip or spill.

WHEELCHAIRS OR CARTS

Many dogs live happy lives with the assistance of "doggy wheelchairs" or carts. There are carts for dogs with rear leg problems, front leg problems and quad chairs for dogs who are weak or paralyzed in all four limbs. Carts are typically made to order based on the dog's measurements.

Carts are meant for exercise and potty breaks, and dogs should always be supervised when they are in their carts. They are fairly stable but can tip or flip, causing injuries. Dogs can also get stuck trying to maneuver them under furniture, and over doorsteps. Not all dogs automatically adapt to a cart, and some time and training may be necessary. Home design issues to be considered before you purchase a cart include:

- Is your home on multiple levels? In that case, you may need to restrict your dog to one floor when he is in his cart. Preference would be a floor with outdoor access at grade.
- Some dogs in K-9 carts or wheelchairs can climb up and down stairs, especially breeds with a lower center of gravity such as dachshunds. A ramp may be necessary for other dogs.
- Most doors, hallways and kitchen aisles are wide enough to accommodate the cart, but many dogs are reckless drivers. Walls may need to be protected from the cart. Ready-made wall, corner and door guards work very well.
- Dogs in carts do best on hard surface flooring, but some surfaces may need protection from dogs that are particularly active in their carts.

VISUAL IMPAIRMENT

Rapid vision loss often becomes evident through the dog's resulting confusion and frustration. He may run into doorways or suddenly refuse to go down the stairs. A dog suffering from gradual vision loss will often show no indication of his increasing handicap because he has learned to adapt to the situation. Three important things that you can do to make it easier for him: evaluate the space to remove hazards, maintain consistency in his environment and create navigational cues.

Block access to stairs, outside doors and bodies of water. Are there computer wires or electrical cords that could trip him? Remove unnecessary objects from the floor, such as shoes, clothing or toys. Think of it as another way that owning a dog helps you keep a neater home!

Try to avoid rearranging the furniture. If you add furniture, or move to a new home, you will have to retrain your dog to navigate the space before you can let him roam freely again. Blind dogs should be supervised when outdoors with hard fencing. A hard fence can help a visually impaired dog learn to navigate around an area by walking along the fence.

Close your eyes and try to notice changes in temperature, air circulation, smells and textures. These are a few of the things a visually impaired dog uses to navigate his environment. Create navigational surface, scent or sound cues to help him become more independent. Changes in flooring texture can help a blind dog orient himself to his location in the home. This can be done by adding area rugs to his familiar pathways between rooms. Surface cues can also be added to stairs. A raised rubber or metal stair tread on the top step helps him sense where the stairs begin and end. A cutout pattern on a stair tread is best, the more textural the better.

Dogs normally rely on scent to navigate, and vision loss increases a dog's dependence on this skill. A small amount of vanilla extract, perfume, or essential oils on surfaces can provide olfactory landmarks to help your dog negotiate his way around. The scents help to alert him to an object's presence and help him locate familiar things like his bed, crate or favorite toys. Audible beepers, beacons or sound devices attached to objects can also be used to alert your dog of obstacles. Some emit constant beeps while others can be operated remotely. Humans and other pets can wear bells to alert the blind pet of their location.

Dogs with failing eyesight can benefit from adding contrast to the environment to help them locate items, navigate and differentiate changes in height and depth. This can be especially helpful on steps, at door openings and outside corners of halls or rooms. Adding a dark piece of tape on a light surface or a light colored piece of tape on a dark surface often does the trick. However, some dogs are wary of large dark patches on flooring and will avoid going near these areas, so test a sample first.

Textured stair tread alerts a blind dog where the stairs begin. *Courtesy of L. Wolf*

Lighting is another way to improve contrast. Well placed lighting can assist a visually impaired dog to negotiate dark or difficult spaces such as stairs or corridors. Lighting should never be directed into a dogs eyes, dogs may avoid areas because of the glare. It is important to avoid strong lighting contrasts between spaces because aging dogs may lose visual adaptability between bright light and dark spaces. Normal vision loss or poor night vision due to aging can make it difficult for a dog to negotiate areas that he was formerly comfortable with. If you notice that your dog is avoiding the stairs, hesitating at the bottom of the stairs, or waiting for you to take the lead on the stairway, these behavior changes can be due to vision loss. Try adding more light to the stairway. If he starts to move once you turn on the lights, this is probably the reason. Dogs with glaucoma or cataracts can develop oversensitivity to light. For dogs that have sensitivity to light it is important to create dimmer light and to remove anything that could cause harsh glare—typically reflective surfaces.

HEARING IMPAIRED DOGS

Since deaf dogs can still see, smell and navigate space easily, there are few design accommodations necessary for them. Hearing impaired dogs can become disoriented in spaces that reflect too much sound or produce echoes. Soft surfaces, such as upholstered furniture, fabric window treatments and rugs can reduce echoes and sound reflection. Deaf dogs are more reliant on visual cues, so rooms where they spend most of their time should have good lighting and an unobstructed view at their level. Like blind dogs, deaf and hearing impaired dogs tend to sleep very soundly and rouse slowly. A secluded sleeping spot will prevent the dog from being startled and becoming nervous or defensive as a result. Profoundly deaf dogs should be kept safely indoors or confined with a solid fence.

> Deaf dogs may benefit from a vibrating collar that is used to get your dog's attention. This pager-like unit has two parts, a hand-held remote for the owner and one on the collar. When the remote is activated the dog feels a vibration.

ELDERLY DOGS

Regardless of breed, every dog eventually develops age-related physical changes. These include changes in muscle strength, joint mobility, stamina, hearing and eyesight. Some develop age-related mental problems including confusion, "memory loss" and dementia. All these factors cause elderly dogs to sleep more and awaken more slowly once they have fallen asleep. Although they may have done so for years, elderly dogs often become reluctant to jump onto beds or furniture for a nap. They develop less tolerance for temperature extremes, household commotion, and disturbances in their routine. Incontinence is a common problem in elderly dogs. Old dogs need a sleeping area that is easily accessible, safe, comfortable and quiet.

Design modifications for elderly dogs include:

- gates, doors and fences to ensure adequate safety and supervision
- restrict incontinent dogs to easily cleaned areas, rather than trying to prevent accidents
- AC or portable heaters may be necessary to ensure your dog's comfort and minimize stress. (See Chapter 4 for more on HVAC)
- rubber backed machine washable area rugs to prevent slipping
- ramps and shallow steps to help with mobility

> Fresh, clean water should always be accessible. If it is difficult to reach, elderly dogs may not drink enough to stay hydrated. You may also want to switch to a raised, tip proof, or shallow dish to prevent the dog from constantly spilling his water, fouling it, or falling in the dish and becoming chilled. Again, if you change his routine, do it slowly.

PHYSIOLOGICAL DESIGN ISSUES

Dogs at different ends of the size spectrum have unique characteristics and may benefit from modifications to their environment. Design for breeds with special qualities does not need to be complicated. You can live a comfortable and harmonious life simply by being aware of your dog's needs.

Extra large or giant breeds weighing 100 lbs to 200 lbs obviously require more space. Before you bring home that adorable Mastiff puppy, be prepared to accommodate his needs. He'll need a larger crate, bowl, bed and automobile! Some giants require more exercise while others are quite sedentary or exercise intolerant. Areas that need special attention for larger dogs are hallways and kitchen aisles. A galley kitchen or narrow hall may not be large enough for a giant breed to turn around. Think vertically too. A 42" high bistro style table might be a better choice in the breakfast nook. Most big dogs can easily jump up on 36" high countertops, and their heads and tails are often at table level. A wagging tail can become an implement of destruction!

Larger breeds tend to mature slowly. They often retain puppy-like behavior for a few years, despite their size. Furniture, screen doors, fences, dog pens and the like must be sturdy enough to withstand the stress of a very big, very strong, playful puppy. They are prone to joint, spine and bone problems as they age which can lead to mobility difficulties, such as climbing stairs, getting into and out of cars or jumping on furniture. Large dogs are often heat intolerant, for more on cooling your big dog see Chapter 4.

Small breeds are becoming increasingly popular and they have many advantages. Although they typically enjoy a longer lifespan and lower costs for care and maintenance, they also bring their share of complications. Toy breeds are more fragile and can be easily injured by common mishaps like falling or jumping off a bed or table. Because of their lower body mass, they have less tolerance for cold, and may spend limited time outdoors. Like some large dogs, small dogs may also suffer from structural problems. They may have trouble climbing stairs, getting into and out of cars and furniture. Ramps or stairs can provide easier, safer access to high areas in your home. Small dogs are also a lot easier to lose indoors and outdoors. Tiny dogs have accidentally fallen through grates, been locked into cupboards and gotten stuck behind kitchen appliances. Minimize these problems by eliminating the number of hiding spaces inside and outside your home. Clean up the clutter and remove extra items you don't need. Keep tabs on your dog by keeping him close at hand through the use of doors, crates or gates.

Dogs with long bodies and short legs such as Basset Hounds, Dachshunds, Pekingese and Welsh Corgis may benefit from design modifications to minimize stress on their backs and joints.

Design needs for long bodied, short leg breeds include:
- stairs may be difficult to use; keep dog on one floor
- slippery floors may contribute to injuries; use area rugs or modular carpet
- jumping off beds or furniture may cause serious back injuries; use ramps or lower beds

Flat faced breeds (known as Brachycephalic) have a limited tolerance for heat because their head structure does not efficiently dissipate excess heat. These dogs begin feeling uncomfortable when the temperature is in the 70s. In addition, many are more prone to breathing problems because their nostrils are smaller. Examples of breeds in this category include: Boston Terrier, Boxer, Bulldog, Pekingese, Pug and Shih Tzu.

Design needs for flat faced or short nose dogs include:

- provide adequate shelter, shade and water during warm weather
- add AC
- window treatments to reduce heat from sun

ALLERGIC DOGS

Like humans, dogs can suffer from environmental allergies to practically anything in their living space. Dogs can be tested for many environmental allergens which commonly include dust mites, mold, pollen, chemicals and dander. Allergy testing is time consuming but finding the source of an allergy often alleviates the problem. If this is not possible a veterinary dermatologist can offer suggestions to help you manage your dog's condition, including environmental modifications.

Dust mites are microscopic spider-like insects found anywhere where humans and/or animals live. They prefer warm temperatures and fairly high humidity levels, above 60%. In the home, they inhabit house dust, bedding, carpets and other textiles. While people typically suffer respiratory symptoms to a dust mite allergy, dogs are more like to exhibit skin problems such as itching and rashes. To control dust mites in your home vacuum once or twice a week, keep the temperature below 77° F, maintain humidity levels below 60%, manage moisture problems, launder bedding in hot water, purchase special barrier covers for mattresses and pillows, and keep areas under furniture clear and clean.

Pollen from grasses, flowers and trees as well as mold are the most common outdoor allergens. Minimize your dog's exposure by keeping him indoors during times when pollen levels are high. Humans and dogs may find some relief by installing air conditioning units or HEPA air filters to trap and prevent allergens from entering the living space.

ALLERGIC DOG OWNERS

Approximately 15% of the population is allergic to dogs or cats. Many of these individuals live with dogs, even after being advised by their physician to give them up. There is no such thing as a non-allergenic breed even though many people claim to obtain a particular breed because it doesn't shed or cause allergies. If you have allergic symptoms and already have a dog it's very important to confirm whether you are allergic to dogs. Have your allergist specifically test for allergies to pet dander to know for sure.

Any dog can trigger a serious reaction in an individual suffering from a serious, confirmed allergy to dogs. The culprit is a protein in the skin and saliva known as Can F-1. Dander from dogs contains both skin and saliva cells and this is the cause of irritation. Obviously, small dogs with less skin surface will produce less dander. However, some breeds have more or less potential to trigger allergic reactions. Hairless dogs such as Chinese Crested and Xoloitzcuintli and dogs with soft constantly growing hair such as poodles or Portuguese water dogs are good examples. The AKC, www.akc.org, maintains a list of breeds recommended as good "lower dander" breeds.

Allergy sufferers considering one of these breeds should be prepared to do their own investigating to ensure that they are indeed able to tolerate living with a dog. Never rely on advertising claims or anecdotal evidence when making this important decision. Ideally, find a breeder who is willing to bring a dog to your home to test for a possible allergic reaction. This will rule out the possibility of encountering unknown allergens in an unfamiliar environment. If this is not possible, arrange to visit a breeder who only breeds the breed you are interested in. If they have other animals in the home, such as cats, you will not be able to assess whether the dog or breed caused your allergic reaction. Do not visit more than one breeder per day. This will also make it difficult to determine the source of a reaction. Be prepared to spend enough time with the dog to really know whether you will have a reaction or not. Looking from across the room will not suffice. Pick the dog up, hold it, pet it, cuddle it, and make sure the visit lasts long enough to potentially trigger a reaction.

If you cannot find any breeders in your area, you may be able to conduct a remote allergy test. You could send an article of clothing (a shirt) or a pillowcase and plastic bags that can be sealed. Ask the breeder to have one of her dogs lie on the article to saturate it with dander and ship it back to you. Wear it or sleep on it and note the reaction.

If you are allergic to dogs, it is essential to control the amount of animal dander in your home, especially places that you spend the most time. This approach focuses on the dog, the environment and you.

Control the dog's dander:
- bathe your dog once or twice a week to reduce dander by up to 84%
- dogs with allergies or skin problems may shed more dander so keep his skin healthy
- wash dog bedding, toys and dog clothing regularly

Manage the environment:
- keep it as clean and sparse as possible.
- vacuum and damp mop floors frequently
- get rid of clutter where dust can settle
- minimize upholstery and carpet
- use smooth upholstery finishes such as leather
- keep your dog out of your bedroom and off of upholstered furniture
- cover furniture with sheets and wash them frequently
- ventilate when weather allows.
- use HEPA air cleaners (see Chapter 4)

Take care of yourself:

- wash your hands and clothes often
- don't touch your face after petting or playing with your dog
- talk to your allergist about medications and or drug therapies that might work for you

DISABLED DOG OWNERS

Trained assistance dogs can facilitate independence for many people with disabilities. They have been used as guides for the blind for many years and more recently they have been trained to help deaf or hard of hearing individuals, non-ambulatory people, people with seizure disorders and other life threatening illnesses. Dogs can alert their owners to fire alarms, telephones, and doorbells. They can turn on lights, bring items to their owner or alert others in the home of a medical problem. These are specially trained working dogs and often may be the first dog ever owned by this person. However, not every disabled person relies on a trained assistance dog. Plenty of disabled people come to depend on their pets to help them both physically and emotionally. These dogs may not do the same jobs as their trained counterparts, but they do provide services, security and comfort for their owners.

Most people living with disabilities don't require any special changes to accommodate their dog care routine. If there is a sudden change in your physical condition, it may take time for the dog to acclimate to it. Wheelchairs and other medical equipment may initially scare your dog, especially anything that moves or makes noise, but dogs cope and adapt.

The Americans with Disabilities Act (ADA) was intended to facilitate access to public buildings for people with all disabilities. While it does not cover private residences it is an excellent resource for building information for people with disabilities. The ADA offers its guide "Architectural Barriers Act Accessibility Guidelines" free to the public at www.access-board.gov. Homes already modified to accommodate the needs of a disabled person will most likely accommodate a dog very easily.

WHEELCHAIRS, RAMPS AND ACCESS

Wheelchairs require access ramps with a gentle and wide slope for easy access. See previous information on ramps in this chapter. The width of the ramp should be a minimum of 36″ and the maximum height for any given run of ramp is 30″ high. If you want your dog to walk beside you, you will require a wider ramp. Otherwise, your dog must learn to walk in front or behind you on the ramp.

The ramp location is critical. If you want to go outside with your dog consider the most logical place for this access. Obviously, you need access to terrain that your wheelchair can negotiate. Some people opt to have a ramp into their garage or covered porch. If your garage is accessible to an on or off lead exercise area for your dog, this might be a great solution. As long as the area is fenced, you will still be able to sit in the garage or porch while your dog goes out on his own to do his business during bad weather.

Garages can work well as a dog potty area if you are confined to a wheelchair. The weather will not be a factor. A hose bib can be placed in your garage, a floor drain to a sewer line in the middle, a slight slope in the floor to the drain and you've got yourself an indoor potty that you can flush with the hose! Be sure to place the hose bib at a height that can be reached from a wheelchair. (See Chapter 8 for more info.)

You will also need access for feeding, grooming and bathing your dog. Sinks and countertops should be no higher than 34″. A clear space below the countertop will allow for a wheelchair to pull under the countertop surface. Shelving units for storage should be adapted according to your reach. For grooming and bathing a wheelchair accessible shower is best. A table or platform for the dog will place the dog within your reach.

HEARING OR VISUALLY IMPAIRED HUMANS

If you are hearing or visually impaired it is likely that your dog will easily adapt to your condition and learn to react to your environmental needs. Hearing impaired humans utilize hearing devices to amplify sound. Some use cochlear implants that are surgically placed in the inner ear to improve hearing. Background noise, like barking dogs, can be a problem with both of these devices so it is important to minimize hard surfaces that reflect sound unnecessarily. A major concern for visually impaired humans is knowing where your dog is to avoid tripping over him or just to know he is safe. A bell, jingling collar tags, or an audible motion detector can all help you keep tabs on your dog's whereabouts.

See Resources for products and more information.

Canine Behavior Problems

Multiple dogs can multiply canine behavior problems.
Barrier frustration is a common problem with windows.

Living with dogs can be a joyful experience. A peaceful lifestyle is achieved by utilizing three important means: training, environmental management and design. First, train your dog to live in your home. A good training school will teach you "life skills" to ensure a well mannered dog at home. Consistent training prevents your dog from developing a multitude of common problems like jumping on visitors, guarding food and toys, stealing from countertops, and barking at deliverymen. Along with training your dog, you must learn how to manage his environment. This includes keeping valuables out of his reach, using crates or gates to prevent him from dashing out of a door, and blocking his view of the street to curtail needless barking. The third step is to recognize potential problems and design a living space that will work with you and your dog. The ideas in this chapter are general guidelines. If your dog has serious behavior issues, you should seek professional guidance.

Terriers, especially short legged ones, can be notorious barkers because this trait is essential to their working function. Until the invention of GPS and radio transmitting dog collars this was the only way to locate a dog underground. Trail barking is highly desirable in some hound breeds and many Dachshunds, Beagles and Bloodhounds respond vocally to any interesting scent. Guarding dogs are often bred to be stealthy rather than sounding an alarm.

A dog's potential volume can be estimated by a combination of muzzle length and size. For instance, Pugs are notorious barkers but rarely get called into question for this because their head shape and size works against them. On the other hand, a comparably sized Beagle can create quite a racket.

BARKING

Studies show that noise contributes to stress in both humans and dogs, but you probably won't need to consult a study if your barking dog has enraged your neighbors. In urban neighborhoods or apartment buildings noise will impact more people, and noise tolerance reaches a low point at night when people are trying to sleep. Nuisance barking is usually defined by the duration, time of day and how often it occurs. Municipalities have different ordinances so it is your responsibility to be aware of this. Barking can be controlled by training, although it is one of the most difficult behaviors to extinguish.

Nearly all dogs will bark at strangers arriving at your front door, and the presence of dogs or other animals in your yard. All dogs possess this natural instinct to protect their territory, and obviously there is a time when barking is appropriate. Unfortunately, many dogs engage in unjustified barking for reasons ranging from anxiety to boredom. This type of barking can quickly become a self reinforcing habit, triggered by an increasing number of cues. Some dogs bark in response to sudden environmental changes. In your home this might be something as simple as a new piece of furniture or a plastic bag blowing across your lawn. In these situations, behavior modification can become a full time occupation. Keep your dog indoors, especially when you aren't home and limit access to entries and windows, especially those facing a street or sidewalk. Design solutions are the easiest way to prevent barking and include: soundproofing, window treatments, barriers, windowless front doors and solid fences in front of your property. In addition, air conditioning makes it possible to keep windows shut in warm weather and also creates a distracting background hum for vigilant dogs. All offer effective ways to cut canine noise pollution.

Soundproofing is an excellent solution. It utilizes both absorption and transmission to contain noise at its source. Ideally, it should be done during new construction or a total renovation of your home. Hard smooth surfaces reflect sound, and soft, textured surfaces absorb it. Sound also moves from room to room through openings in walls, floors, or ceilings. Your soundproofing plan should take both issues into consideration. The primary objectives are twofold: to control noise within a room AND prevent it from leaving through walls, ceilings, roofs, doors and windows. Your noise control strategy should include:

- source reduction or elimination
- sound absorption
- sound blocking
- sound masking

Eliminating the source of the sound, your dog, is not a practical or desired outcome. But you may be able to effectively remove the triggers that cause barking in the first place. First, establish what makes your dog bark. Is it the mailman, people on the street, certain noises, the doorbell, the telephone or a squirrel outside of the window? You may not be able to eliminate these sources but you might be able to restrict access to these things. For example, if it is a squirrel that sets off the barking restrict your dog's view to those areas. If the squirrel is there to feed at your bird feeder either eliminate or move the bird feeder out of the dog's sight.

Before you think about soundproofing materials it helps to understand the concepts of decibels and frequencies. Sound vibrations are transmitted through air or other medium (liquid or solid), and measured in units called decibels. A barking dog can generate between 40 and 100 decibels. Multiple barking dogs can reach an impressive range of 70 to 115 dB. To keep this in perspective a car horn is 90dB; a jet taking off is 140dB. OSHA considers anything above 90 dB within the harmful range for human hearing.

Sound is also defined by frequency, characterized as either low or high. A Chihuahua's bark would be considered high frequency, while a St. Bernard has a low frequency bark. This frequency helps to determine the best soundproofing solution. Walls with a high rating for reducing sound transmission will block sounds at the high end, but not at the lower end. To prevent the transmission of low frequency sounds material density is important. Solid masonry, such as concrete block, is a good example of a dense material.

Construction materials either reflect or absorb sound. Understanding their properties, helps determine the best materials to control noise. Two measurements are used, and many construction components, such as doors, windows or walls receive ratings of noise reduction coefficient (NRC) and sound transmission class (STC). Most materials are good at one or the other, but not both.

The NRC measures how effectively a material absorbs sound rated on a scale of 0 to 1. 0. A rating of 1 means that the material absorbs 100% of the sound, so a rating of .8 means that the material will absorb 80% of the sound and reflects 20% of it. Sound absorption is helpful to reduce sound within a space.

The noise control of a particular room is only as good as its weakest link, and sound transmission class or STC is a measurement of how much sound is transmitted. STC rating is based on frequencies within the human speech range. For instance, loud speech can be understood through a wall with an STC rating of 30, but will not be audible through a wall with an STC 60 rating. STC rating does not provide an evaluation of a material's ability to block low frequency noise, such as musical bass tones or the bark of a St. Bernard!

Noise travels between spaces through any opening, under doors, around windows or through an electrical outlet. The STC of a wall is meaningless unless these paths of travel are addressed. To reduce noise under doors a door sweep can be added. If the door itself is the problem consider replacing it with a door that has a higher rating or adding acoustical materials on the face of the door itself. If your walls have an STC of 44 but the windows are only 30, then the walls won't be as effective. Typical wall construction falls in the 30 to 40 STC range, doors in the 20 to 30 STC range and windows 20 to 28 STC range.

Windows are the weakest link in the noise control structure, but there are a few things that can be done. Replace old single pane windows with newer insulated glass or acoustical window units. Storm windows are a simple, effective and less expensive solution. They provide an air space that dissipates and reduces sound transmission. Gaps around windows should be completely sealed with caulk and/or foam insulation. Fill any empty cavities as well. The same is true for trim where the floor meets the wall or ceiling. To effectively limit noise transmission in walls, they must be continuous and extend to the structural deck at the floor and the ceiling.

Electrical outlets and plumbing lines can also be sources for sound transmission. Staggering electrical outlets on two sides of a wall can help prevent a direct path for the sound. Be sure to insulate around these features as well. Insulation is always helpful for reducing noise transmission. Insulated walls have higher STC ratings than non-insulated walls. Walls that are built with staggered studs and insulation are better but two

Many dogs are fearful of loud noises. Thunderstorms and fireworks are the most common problems. But sound sensitive dogs can react to a range of loud sounds. Behavior modification will help many of these dogs overcome their noise phobias but in the mean time they should have a safe retreat from frightening sound. For sound sensitive dogs storm windows and air conditioning may make sense for year round comfort and noise reduction.

separate walls with a 3″ to 6″ space in between will have an even higher rating. Any type of insulation will work but consider the newer more environmentally friendly types such as recycled fiber or soy. In addition to reducing sound transmission insulation has the added benefit of making your home more energy efficient so it is good for you and your dog all around.

Don't overlook cracks and small openings. Insulation seals can be placed behind electrical outlets and switches. Expanding foam insulation can be sprayed into small spaces in walls that aren't easy to fill with other types of insulation. It can also be sprayed behind trim at doors, windows and floors.

Sound can be absorbed by soft and/or textured materials, such as cork, fabric, carpet or foam cushions. However using these alone will only produce minimal results. To be effective these materials must cover at least ¼ of the room's surface area and work best when they are spread throughout the room rather than concentrated on just the ceiling or floor. Suspended acoustical ceilings can help absorb sound and could be a good choice in a large dog room, such as one used for training or housing multiple dogs.

If you are designing or remodeling, keep in mind that a direct path makes any sound more audible. This factor is especially important to keep in mind when designing a dog room or kennel space. Sound will escape outside more easily if doors, windows and other openings are placed in a straight line, across from one another. Solve this by staggering or offsetting the location of these features.

Soundproofing materials can be added under flooring, on walls, inside of walls, in between floors and in the ceiling. Acoustic foam, recycled foam, mineral wool and cork can be used under flooring. For walls you can add a sound absorbing material (see resources) over the existing drywall covered by another layer of drywall. If you can do it to both sides the benefits are even better. Existing ceilings can be soundproofed by adding steel channels perpendicular to the ceiling joists and

DOG GATES

Metal gates are the most durable and best for potentially destructive dogs. The gates above have pass through elements that make them easier to use. The "ring gating" at bottom left is very inexpensive and covers a large open space. It serves as a deterrent to most respectful dogs but would not stop "jumpers" or persistent dogs. The main benefit is that it is easy for humans to step over as is the wooden gate pictured at right. These can conveniently be used at doorways or at the bottom of stairs. Note: Ring gating is not suitable for small children or some dogs as it may cause injury. It comes with a warning that it should not be used with children as it poses a strangulation hazard.

Top row images courtesy of Kidco: www.kidco.com.

Bottom right image courtesy of Cardinal Gates:www.cardinalgates.com

directly on the existing ceiling. Drywall can be attached to these strips. In new construction fiberglass insulation can be added between the floors.

Soundproofing outdoors is more challenging because the sound can't be contained. Soft materials generally absorb sound while hard materials reflect sound. A combination of the two can help. Plants, buildings, solid walls or fences and earthberms will absorb and reduce sound transmission to some extent. If you have a solid fence, planting trees and shrubs in front of it can reduce noise through absorption. Earthberms, which are basically large mounds of dirt with plants on them, are the most effective control.

AROUSING BEHAVIORS

Food, doors and windows are considered three of the highest arousal stimuli in dogs. These are only some of the things that could cause contentious behavior between dogs or overactive

and troublesome behavior. Solutions for problems with food are covered in Chapter 5.

ENTRIES AND OTHER DOORS

There are several problems that can arise at door entries which lead outdoors. They include:

- overzealous greetings when visitors arrive at the door
- barking at everything outdoors when visibility is high— glass doors, sidelights, etc.
- escaping when the door is opened

Dogs are natural compulsive greeters and should be visually involved or included in the greeting process. The best thing would be to train your dog to sit politely at your side and not move until you allow them to. But this is easier said than done for most of us. One management method that works is containing your dog somewhere else until your guests are in your front entry. This could be simply placing your dog in his crate or using a gate between the front entry and another space, and is best if the dog is able to see the guests.

Gates come in a variety of sizes, materials and prices. They can also be custom made but there are many readily available for every size dog. A metal gate attached securely to the wall is best. Make sure that the gate is screwed into a structural element and not superficial items such as door and floor trim. The trim will pull away from the wall over time with use. A gate made for children usually works very well. It should have a hinged side to allow it to swing and the opposite should have a latch at the top and bottom. The latch should be easy to open. A gate that sits in a door opening with only pressure fittings may be your only option if you rent, but it will not withstand the efforts of a determined dog. While plastic, wire mesh and wood may be cheaper, they will not last as long as a metal gate. Dogs can easily chew wood or plastic. They can bend plastic or push through it. A good metal gate should have bars that are close enough together so that a dog cannot get his head stuck in it. If you have a very small dog or puppy you may need to add something over the gate. Metal chicken wire, plastic coated garden fencing or decorative screens work well and need to be secured with wire. Cut ends on the wire should be bent so that the dog will not injure himself. The height of the gate is an important consideration. Although a tall gate is an inconvenience because it is more difficult to step over, the gate should be high enough to keep an adult dog contained. If your puppy is able to jump over the gate try to anticipate the height of your dog as an adult and buy the appropriate height from the start. If you only add on small increments at a time, you will only succeed in teaching the dog to jump each subsequent higher height. Open plan homes present a special problem but there are gates that can span large spaces. For determined dogs these gates must be durable and strong. For dogs who easily respect barriers the options are greater. Ring gating, commonly used for dog shows, is a less expensive alternative and because it can be folded to a compact size is easier to store when you need to. Ring gating is traditionally made of wood, but lightweight plastic versions are available.

BARRIER FRUSTRATION

Doors, windows and window treatments are important and unavoidable design elements in homes. They provide access, ventilation, natural light, and security. They might provide views onto a beautiful rural landscape or a busy city street. Either way, there will always be some activity that might draw your dog to the door or window. Humans think that being able to look out a window is important to our wellbeing and enjoyment so we assume that dogs like to do this too. Outdoor activities that can be seen by a dog may be a source of behavioral problems in an otherwise well behaved dog. Windows with an active free view can lead to something known as "barrier frustration". While dogs may enjoy looking out windows, many are actually frustrated by what they can see and can't get to. A good example is a dog that looks out a window and spots a squirrel at the bird feeder. Often this behavior occurs when we are not at home, and we might not realize it until a neighbor

complains about a dog barking or howling. Barrier frustration is worse in areas with the highest level of outside activity. Barrier frustration can also happen outdoors with fences. Refer to chapter 10 for more information on fencing. In an urban or suburban setting this is typically the front of the house facing a sidewalk or street. In rural areas it could be any part of the house especially if wildlife is present. Barrier frustration may cause a dog to bark, howl, whine, growl, snap, lunge, claw at or hit the barrier. Dogs have gone through screens, windows, and even doors or chewed through walls or jumped over fences because of barrier frustration. Some dogs will bark more than others. Dogs with a high prey drive may want to give chase, but of course, can't. Others are positively reinforced for their barking when the object moves away. Guarding breeds may go on "high alert"; some have been known to be so stressed their fur begins to fall out.

Barrier frustration can also happen at doors inside your home. It can be triggered by food, a need to be with you or another pet. Because of this it is important to consider the type of door, door locks and door pulls that you will use. Most doors inside our homes are hinged doors with a door pull that latches when closed. Certain doors, such as bi-fold doors or lightweight pocket doors are problematic with dogs as they are fairly easy for a dog to open. Both doors are convenient space savers often used for closets and are a bit more difficult to keep closed and locked. Hook and eye closures or deadbolts can help to keep them closed but a persistent dog will still scratch at the door in an attempt to open it. If your dog can manipulate a cylindrical door pull, door pull locks that are meant to foil small children might work. They are made to spin continuously making it difficult for the door pull to turn.

The solutions to doors and windows that cause barking, stress or "barrier" frustration might be temporary or more permanent depending upon how bad the problem is and whether you rent or own. For a new house, design the space so that a door or gate separates the busiest view or highest arousal space from the rest of the house. Other solutions would be a windowless front door, a door with high windows or a door without sidelights. Sidelights (windows immediately adjacent to a door) are not a good idea with dogs. These windows are often at or near floor level activating and exacerbating behavior problems. With an existing space there are a few things you could do. If your dog is not overly destructive you could cover the glass with a window shade, blinds or cover it temporarily with cardboard. If none of these work because your dog will rip it off, try placing a cover over the outside. If you need a more permanent solution consider changing the door, if this is not feasible you might want to screw on a piece of plywood to cover the door glass. Another alternative to block the view is to cover it with glass film overlay, a translucent or opaque plastic film with an adhesive that adheres to glass.

Windows facing an active view require some of the same solutions. Closing drapes or doors and/or adding a gate can go a long way to prevent your dog access to these views. If that isn't possible, consider keeping him in a crate when you aren't home.

Dogs that bark at people or wildlife often benefit from closed window treatments. While for some dogs it is "out of sight, out of mind", it is not so for others. There are dogs that will bark at the window all day and if their owner put up drapes and closed them, the dog rips them down. This is another example of the individual nature of dog problems. If you have a destructive dog that loves to chew soft things avoid soft window treatments like drapes, curtains or soft fabric shades. A better choice would be roller shades, wooden or metal blinds or wooden shutters. Shutters are a good option for the dog who is prone to bark at the window or who would be most likely to destroy draperies. Shutters can be designed so that they are stacked two high. This way, you can leave the top half open to let in light and close the bottom half so that your dog can't see out the window. Which brings up another point, if you can't bear to keep your drapes closed all day, consider putting a window treatment on the lower half of your windows so the dog can't look out but light will come in from above. Another more costly solution would be to install exterior blinds or shutters that are electronically controlled. In some cases resolution may only occur if the dog is removed from the room, changing the window configuration, or by moving to a home with higher windows.

ESCAPES

Dogs will attempt to get outdoors whenever they can because outdoors is a fun place to be. Doors and windows must be secured to prevent escapes. Front doors seem particularly vulnerable to dog escapes because of the excitement caused when the doorbell rings or a new person arrives at the door. You are likely to move in response which sets off a chain reaction within your dog. If your dog is not under control or contained the likelihood of him running past you as you open the door is great. Once free, your dog may be very difficult to get back. In addition, too often, arriving guests have no idea whether it is okay for your dog to go out, nor do they ask, and many will open the door and let him go!

If a specific door poses a particular risk for escape train your dog not to use that door. By limiting the dog's access to other doors instead, some dogs eventually lose interest in the problem door. Until that happens, consider using a barrier to keep the dog out of that particular room whenever the door will be opened frequently.

> Some very clever dogs easily learn to turn handles and open doors. One solution to this is a lever styled locking door pull installed upside down. If the dog jumps on it the door locks instead of opens. Of course this should only be installed in places that you have a key for and access to.

WINDOWS

Windows are classified by the way they operate or open. There are several basic types of windows including casement, double-hung, sliding, awning, fixed and jalousie. Of these, casement and double-hung are the most common. Casement windows open like a hinged door by means of a crank or lever. Double-hung windows consist of two sashes which slide by each other vertically. Double-hung windows open from both the top and bottom. Awning windows hinge at the top of the window and the window opens out. One advantage to these windows is that they can be left open during mild to moderate rain. Most windows come in a variety of sizes and configurations, both standard and custom depending upon the manufacturer. There are manufacturers that will combine different types of windows in one unit so you could order a casement window with an awning window as part of the same unit. The possibilities are endless and an architect or designer can be of great help in creating the right look for you.

When selecting windows for a remodeling project or new construction in a dog friendly home you should consider the most common problems or issues associated with windows in homes with dogs which include:

- escapes through windows
- the need for adequate ventilation
- window treatments are destroyed
- screens scratched or destroyed
- window treatments with dangling cords pose a choking hazard to your dog

Always buy quality windows and screens with adequate latching devices. This can help prevent potential problems with your dog and will improve the general security of your home.

Dogs can break through older single-paned window glass that is more fragile or missing glazing. These windows should be replaced with newer and stronger double or triple paned glass. In addition to actually breaking through glass dogs can escape through windows without screens, or push out screens that are weakly attached to the window opening. Tactics to avoid escapes through windows include:

- use awning windows or operable windows placed out of a dog's reach
- never leave your dog alone with fully opened windows
- open windows minimally
- AC can keep your dog cool when you aren't home
- hinged metal dog gates placed over the window will prevent escapes and access to the screen

SCREENS

Casement windows have screens on the inside of the window which means they have the potential to be damaged even when the window is closed. To minimize damage limit access to windows of highest arousal, remove screens during months when they are not necessary or remove screens from windows you never open. In new home construction or renovation, consider another window type or plan windows to be out of your dog's reach. Consider using a combination of casement windows with awning windows above. If the problem occurs with double hung windows make sure both top and bottom sashes are working and only open the top portion. Or, you could consider retractable screen systems that disappear into the framework around the window when you don't need them.

Screens on windows and doors can easily be ripped and shredded by a dog. It doesn't matter whether the screening is made from fiberglass, plastic or metal. The dog can still put holes in it. The problem occurs mostly with doors or windows that are low to the ground. It only takes one time for a dog to jump up and damage the screen. Screen material does vary in strength and durability. Most screens in today's homes are made from fiberglass or aluminum. Aluminum is stronger and more durable than fiberglass but it is prone to denting and it can be ripped by a dog's claws. Bronze/copper is stronger and more durable than aluminum but it costs more. Avoid screens made from plastics or synthetic fibers such as nylon. These tend to be too lightweight and more easily ripped.

Other than constantly replacing the screen there are a couple of products that can help. One is used for doors and windows as a replacement screen. It is a heavy duty vinyl coated polyester screen that is pet proof and seven times heavier than traditional materials. Its major drawback is that the mesh is thicker and heavier so it impedes the view.

Another solution for exterior doors consists of a screened curtain hung from a tension rod at the top of the door opening. The screen is divided in half and has a series of magnets in the middle and bottom where the two halves meet. This allows dogs and people to pass through the door very easily as the two edges close upon each other. The bottom edge is weighted. The sides are adhered with tape and Velcro to the side jambs of the door. It is scratch resistant, inexpensive and will last a few years. Because it is meant to be a pass-through screen it does not function as containment. Therefore it is used only when you want your dog to have access inside and out.

On exterior doors, screen/storm doors that are half glass/half screen are better than if they are full screen. If you have a dog that has any aggression, a strong prey drive or frustration at the front door, then it is probably best to leave the main door closed at all times.

Another great solution for protecting screens, especially screens on doors is to add a rigid decorative screen directly to the bottom half of the door. Rigid decorative screens have a perforated pattern to let light and air in, but are strong enough to protect the actual screen mesh underneath it. Choices include perforated steel or aluminum panels or hardware cloth. Perforated metal panels may have an anodized finish typically in copper, gold or silver finishes or powder coat paint in nearly any color. Hardware cloth is a wire grid that is also very strong, protective and available in a variety of colors, patterns, shapes. An added bonus is that these materials are more difficult for an intruder to cut than regular screening. Decorative screens and hardware cloth are readily available at DIY or online stores.

See Resources for products and more information.

A simple and inexpensive solution for door screens.
This unit hangs on a pressure fitted rod and can easily be removed.

CHAPTER 13

Maintenance, Repairs and Construction

Dogs require more housecleaning. That is certainly one of the concessions you have to make when you get a dog. You may need to vacuum and mop your floors more. All of the surfaces in your home may take more of a beating. One dog may not make a significant difference, but multiple dogs will. While all dogs can do damage, in general larger dogs will do more damage than smaller ones. Some people adapt and resign to live with a slightly messier home, others become super cleaners and still others hire outside help. There are other solutions that work. Keep in mind that there is no such thing as maintenance free materials or finishes including flooring. All floors have to be maintained whether it is daily or occasional vacuuming, sweeping, damp mopping or scrubbing.

> Proper maintenance will contribute to the lifespan of a product which is good for the environment. So, always obtain a copy of the manufacturer's maintenance instructions and save it in a folder.

Some general tips include:

- Use materials and finishes that are durable and easily cleaned.
- Keep dirt out in the first place.
- Create files for copies of manufacturer's cleaning and maintenance guidelines
- Bathe your dog regularly. A clean dog will promote a cleaner home and your dog will be welcome anywhere.
- Wash dog bedding and toys on a regular basis.

Beware of materials that are described as "hiding dirt, such as carpet designed to trap and hide dirt. Unfortunately, the dirt is still there, along with dog hair and possibly flea eggs. Materials that release dirt are preferable. According to popular advice, matching upholstery colors to your dog makes shed hair less noticeable. Unfortunately, color selection becomes a challenge if you happen to own a predominantly black dog, a blonde dog and a medium gray dog. Although the idea of "hiding soil" may not be ideal, it can be practical to select colors based on your maintenance schedule. If you are willing to vacuum or brush your upholstery everyday or wash your dogs' paws (or more) daily then maybe it doesn't matter what color you choose. On the other hand, if you own a group of active dogs, who are apt to run through mud and track it in the home, make your life easier by selecting colors and fabrics that won't show the dirt as quickly. Keep in mind that when you select flooring based on your dog's color, your socked feet may become dust mops!

STOP DIRT AT THE FRONT DOOR

The best strategy for keeping your home clean is to never let dirt it in. This is much easier said than done. Things that help include:

- Always use the same entry door for your dogs. This limits the dirt to one specific area and minimizes cleaning.
- Use hard surface materials such as stone, concrete, tile or decking outside the doors you use most.
- Use walk-off mats outside and inside your home.
- Remove your shoes at the entrance to your home. This will eliminate potential hazards tracked into your home such as lead, chemicals and bacteria.
- Store shoes in floor to ceiling shelves that you can install in your front closet. An added benefit will be no more chewed shoes!
- Store old towels near the door to wipe off your dogs paws.

- If you can't sweep or vacuum other rooms in your house on a fairly regular basis, at least do the entry everyday or as often as necessary. It is helpful to store a vacuum cleaner or broom nearby.

MUD CONTROL

Rinsing and drying your dog's feet to remove mud, sand or ice can go a long way to keep floors, dogs and the house clean. Prepare a dishpan of warm water inside the doorway to clean his paws before he sets foot in the house.

VACUUM CLEANERS

"What is the best vacuum cleaner?" With a little consumer products research and reviews it sounds like an easy question to answer. But it isn't that simple. Everyone has a different reason for buying a specific type of vacuum cleaner and sometimes it has nothing to do with how well it cleans. Some people love their vacuum cleaners because they're lightweight and easy to carry up and down stairs. Other people like theirs because it is quiet or easy to empty. Other vacuum cleaners are favored because of their HEPA filters. There is probably no such thing as a perfect vacuum cleaner for every purpose, so you will need to determine which one meets your needs best. More importantly, following proper vacuum cleaner maintenance may be the key to a better vacuum.

Vacuum maintenance will promote optimal function and longevity. Brushes can wear out and need to be replaced. Air flow is important so hoses may need to be cleaned out periodically. Perhaps the most important recommendation for vacuum cleaners is that you empty them frequently. Whether you have a bagless vacuum cleaner or one that requires a bag don't wait until the bag or container is more than half full, change it before then. Dog hair, dander and dust is often very fine and can quickly clog a vacuum cleaner, making it work much harder, and therefore reducing its lifespan.

Several basic vacuum cleaners are available on the market today. Selection will depend on the type of floors you clean, air filtration you desire, weight, ease of use and storage. Most vacuum cleaners work well on bare floors, but not all work equally on carpets. Upright vacuum cleaners are a good choice for carpet, but they tend to be noisier than canisters, can't reach under all furniture and are not easy to use on stairs. Some come with hose attachments for these specific conditions. Canister vacuum cleaners are good for tight spaces, bare floors, stairs, upholstery and under furniture, but they can be more expensive and difficult to carry and store. Different types of brushes and heads can be added depending upon the type of work you are doing. Cordless vacuum cleaners are good for small jobs or light cleaning and the category includes cordless uprights, or those considered "robotic" such as the Roomba®. Central vacuum systems are preferred because they are quiet and have no messy bags to contend with. Instead they have a large central-

WALK-OFF MATS

The best walk-off mats have a highly textured surface and choices include rubber mats with "fingers", artificial turf and highly textured coarse nylon. Resist the temptation to buy one large mat. Walk-off mats are heavy so buy a few smaller ones instead.

Walk-off mats used in front of doors, outside or in, should overlap the door by 8 to 12" on the opening side of the door. While humans may be diligent about stepping on a mat, dogs typically veer towards the opening door.

Commercial style walk-off mats help keep dirt out of your home.

ized container, usually in a utility space, often in the basement. A series of hoses connect to the container through the walls and/or floors and outlets are placed strategically throughout the house. A portable hose is connected to these outlets. One drawback is that the hose is cumbersome and requires storage.

All vacuum cleaners have containment systems to trap dirt particles. Disposable bags are the most common but bagless vacuums have permanent containers. In addition to trapping dirt and dust particles, bags act as filters. One drawback to using a bagless container is that they are difficult to empty without exposing yourself to dust and spilling dirt. Newer systems claim to be spill-proof and easier to use. Bagless containers are more environmentally responsible but bags may be preferable in homes with flea problems because the bags can be sealed with the vacuumed fleas inside and thrown away.

Air filtration has become a major concern for indoor air quality today. Many vacuum cleaners have HEPA filters that are the most effective means of reducing fine particles and dust. This is particularly helpful in a household with people and/or pets who may have allergies or asthma. See Chapter 4 for more on HEPA filters.

Vacuuming removes dog hair, dander, dust and other dirt from your floors. Removal of these items will help prevent abrasion, scratches and generally preserve your floors. All floors benefit from regular vacuuming at least once per week. Areas of high traffic, such as entryways, hallways or stairs may need to be vacuumed more frequently, daily or every other day. This frequency may also be dependent upon where you live and the type of weather you experience. Seasonal changes, such as rainy or snowy periods will require more frequent vacuuming. Proper vacuuming means moving the vacuum back and forth over a surface several times. Once is not enough and this should require physical effort on your part.

CLEANING

Carpet should be vacuumed once or twice per week, especially areas that are used most frequently. Vacuum cleaners should have adjustable and rotating brushes to loosen dirt. Deep extraction cleaning can be done periodically but different carpets and fibers will require different methods so it is important to check with the manufacturer first. Modular carpets are ideal because they can be removed and cleaned in a large deep sink using enzyme cleaners followed with laundry detergent and then air dried thoroughly.

In general most hard surface and resilient floors can be vacuumed, dust mopped and periodically damp mopped with water and a cleanser. Other guidelines include:

- Use neutral ph cleaners for linoleum, concrete and cork. Liquid dishwashing soap is considered neutral.
- Water should not be left to dry on linoleum, wood or cork.
- Soap-based cleaners can leave a dull film on cork, wood, and ceramic tile, rinse thoroughly.
- Wood and bamboo floors with a hard finish, as opposed to wax, can be cleaned with a homemade mixture of 1 cup cider vinegar to a gallon of warm water.
- Wax finishes need to be buffed, stripped and reapplied periodically.
- Ceramic tile should be damp mopped with a non oil-based cleaner. Ammonia-based products will discolor the grout and too much use of acid based products such as vinegar can remove or wear down the grout.
- Grout can be sealed to help keep water and dirt out. It needs to be resealed every 6 to 12 months depending on the amount of foot traffic in that area.
- Unsealed grout can be cleaned every few months with non-abrasive non-chlorine bleach cleaners. Apply a small amount, brush the grout with a soft brush and rinse with water.

Bare wood stairs are vulnerable to dog damage. One solution is to embrace the abuse and make your finish choice work with it. The oak stair treads on these front stairs were purposely painted with deep green milk paint. As the paint is worn down it contrasts nicely with the "red" of the oak beneath it.

Dog urine is problematic for all types of floors. If left to dry it can leave permanent stains on carpet, linoleum and wood. It can penetrate grout and concrete always leaving a little bit of odor that may be detectable by other dogs if not by you. It is important to use an enzymatic cleaner in these situations to remove odor.

On walls, vacuuming or dust mopping prior to washing helps remove surface dust, dog fur and loosens dirt. Walls made of wood paneling can be cleaned in a similar fashion to wood floors but do not need to be cleaned as frequently. There are many cleaning products made specifically for wood cabinetry and furniture and these work well on wood walls too. The type of product will depend on the type of finish that has been applied to the wood. Oil wood finishes benefit from the use of oil based cleaners, such as linseed, almond or lemon oil.

Painted surfaces can be cleaned by vacuuming or dusting. The type of paint finish is critical and should be one that can easily be washed without removing pigment. Choose eggshell, semigloss or washable matte finishes, and avoid flat paint. However, too much scrubbing or rubbing on any paint finish can result in removal of the paint. Sometimes it is easiest to repaint large areas periodically.

Dog owners often complain about the grimy residue left on the walls or trim by their dogs. It appears as a black streak that runs horizontally along a wall, most evident at wall corners. Certain breeds, with more oily coats, tend to leave this more than others. Other than washing your dog frequently, what else can be done? A solution of hot water and dishwashing soap works very well on painted surfaces. Another product that works well on these streaks is a type of sponge, usually with the word's magic or eraser (or both) in the name. Simply dampen the sponge and the streak will disappear. These sponges contain alkaline chemicals that may burn skin so care must be taken when using them.

Vacuuming regularly is helpful in increasing the lifespan of your furniture and fabrics by removing dirt, dust, dander and dog fur. Once per month for each piece of furniture is probably enough, but if your dogs lie on the furniture, you will want to do those pieces more frequently.

Removing pet fur from upholstery will depend on the type of dog hair, fine or coarse, long or short and the type of upholstery and fiber content. Experiment by using the most low-tech and cheapest methods first. There are several different products on the market that specifically remove pet hair from upholstery. They are either made from rubber or use adhesive tape. The rubber works by creating a static charge and the hairs attach to the adhesive. Both types work fairly well, but you may not need to purchase a special item to use.

Here are some solutions that might work for you:

- vacuum with a brush attachment
- wet sponge
- your dog's brush, especially rubber brushes
- latex or rubber dishwashing gloves
- masking tape wrapped around your hand so that the sticky side is out
- lint remover brush
- rubber brushes made for this purpose

The best way to deal with a spill is to blot it immediately with a towel or paper towel. Upholstered furniture can be cleaned by hand using an approved upholstery cleaning solution. If your upholstery is badly soiled hire a professional. This may seem like an expensive alternative, but it is certainly cheaper than replacing your furniture.

Upholstery manufacturers have their own voluntary cleaning standard labeling code that is printed on fabric samples, on a tag under the seat cushion or on removable tags. This code is intended to be used as a guide for spot removal and overall cleaning. It is fairly simple and straightforward, and knowing whether something is easy to clean may help you make a decision about buying it in the first place.

W   Use a water-based cleaner.
S   Use a solvent cleaner.
S-W Use either a water-based or a solvent cleaner.
X   Vacuum only. Use of any cleaning solution could damage or alter the fabric.

WASHING DOG ITEMS
Your home and dog will stay cleaner if you wash his toys, clothes and bedding on a regular basis. Toys can be washed in dishwashing liquid and bedding can be washed with your normal laundry detergent as long as your dog is not allergic to it.

SAFE CLEANING PRODUCTS
If we are going to live in environmentally friendly homes made from sustainable materials, it makes sense to use cleaning supplies that are less toxic to people and pets. While there may be times that you may need to occasionally use a stronger cleaning solution, chlorine bleach comes to mind, most of the time harsh, toxic chemicals are not necessary. There are steps you can take to select and use safer products. Read the label. If it contains single words like Poison, Danger, Warning or Caution it should cause you to pause and think twice about the product. Poison or danger means that the product is highly toxic, warning means it is moderately toxic and caution means that it is less toxic. In addition a more specific word may follow—such as Corrosive or Caustic, and refers to the chemical's ability to burn body tissue. Often a phrase will be associated with these words that describe the type of hazard such as "Causes burns on contact", "harmful or fatal if swallowed" or "vapors harmful."

A number of very good environmentally friendly cleaning products are available on the market today. There are also many good sources for information on how to make your own cleaning products. See Resources for where to find recipes or organizations that recommend or test products.

When using any cleaning product, especially if it is used in places where your dog will eat, sleep and walk, it is important to thoroughly rinse any residue that might be left from the cleanser. Homemade products are generally safer, but they still might contain things that could irritate your dog's skin. Dogs will lick the floor if food falls on it and if a harsh chemical was used on it, he'll be ingesting that too.

CLEANING UP BODY FLUIDS
"Accidents" always occur at the most inconvenient time: in the middle of the night or just before you leave for work, but must be dealt with immediately. Accidents happen for a number of reasons, forgetting to take your dog out late enough before bed time, your dog ate something they shouldn't have or they are ill. There are times, when a dog is elderly or ill, that this process may seem endless.

Keep the process fairly simple. First, make sure you always have a supply of the following items on hand:

- Old towels
- Toilet Paper
- Paper Towels
- Enzyme cleaner or white vinegar
- Safe cleansers
- Bucket
- Sponge or Mop
- Small shovel, wide putty knife or spatula for cleaning up feces

The key to dealing with accidents is to act immediately. The process is simple for hard surface floors. Feces are picked up with toilet paper, as long as it is solid enough, and thrown down the toilet. Loose stools may require a combination of things, toilet paper and a small flat shovel, spatula or putty knife. Sprinkling sawdust, kitty litter, or even flour on the loose stools may help to consolidate them. Urine may be picked up with an old towel or paper toweling. The towels can be washed and used again. Vomit can be picked up with toilet paper, paper toweling or the shovel and thrown away in the garbage. After everything is picked up clean the area with an enzyme cleaner. This works to prevent stains and odors. Depending on how bad it was, you may need to wash the floor again with a disinfectant or sanitizer. A disinfectant is a product that kills 100% of intended germs; a sanitizer will kill 99.9%. Chlorine bleach is considered a disinfectant while hydrogen peroxide is considered a sanitizer.

Carpet, upholstery and bedding are tricky to clean. If your dog urinates on carpet, upholstery or your mattress, the first thing to do is blot it with paper towels or towels. Bedding can be removed and washed. After the initial blot use enzyme cleaner or white vinegar, let it seep in a bit (or follow label instructions), then blot it and let it dry. Make sure that you never rub or scrub fabric because this will only serve to embed the soil into the fabric structure. See Chapter 7 for more on cleaning beds.

ODOR BUSTERS

METHOD	RATING
Open Windows	Best
Extracting Fan	Best
Enzyme Cleaner at Source	Very Good
Air Cleaner w/Activated Charcoal Filter	Good
White Vinegar	Fair to Good
Baking Soda	Fair

STAINS

We can't always be there when an accident happens. It is much easier to clean a stain on a hard surface then to remove it from a soft surface like upholstery or carpet. If a stain sets in carpet there are a few things that you can do to help remove or at least reduce the stain. Remember that natural fibers, which readily absorb water, will more likely release the stain when a water-based cleaner is used. If the fabric or carpet is made from a synthetic fiber it may require a more specialized cleaner recommended by the manufacturer. Area carpets that can be removed are best cleaned by a professional. Carpets made from wool, such as Oriental carpets, can be cleaned very well in this manner. Professional cleaners typically have facilities that allow the whole carpet to be cleaned and dried thoroughly. Nearly all stains, including dog urine and vomit, can be removed. In the worst case, the carpet may be repaired.

A simple cleaning solution of 2 tablespoons dishwashing liquid mixed with 1 quart lukewarm water works well for urine and feces stains. On carpet it helps to add 3 tablespoons of white vinegar to the solution. The best method is to take a clean cloth and "sponge" the liquid solution onto the surface and blot it with another absorbent cotton cloth until the stain disappears on the surface. For items that can be washed under the sink or in a washing machine, such as sheets, pillow covers and small rugs run the water over it until the stain disappears. Blood that is fresh is very easily removed by placing the fabric under cold running water. Vomit stains are sometimes more difficult to deal with. Strong acids in vomit will destroy finish surfaces, such as wood, and may leave a permanent stain if not caught immediately. Enzyme cleaners work well on some old stains. They can be used on most surfaces, fabrics, carpet, wood, linoleum or tile. Dark stains in unfinished wood floors can be bleached out with oxalic acid, available at DIY stores.

DOG DAMAGE REPAIRS

Damage from dogs is something all homeowners, landlords and tenants worry about. All materials will wear out over time, so it is important to select durable materials and finishes. Planning and prevention are key to avoiding damage, but even the best planning won't prevent all damage. Common damage caused by dogs occurs to surfaces that they come in contact with. Claws and teeth do the most damage, followed by stains from feces, urine, food and blood. The majority of damage is limited to scratches on various surfaces such as wood floors, gypsum board on walls or exterior doors. Once in awhile a dog might chew through a door, rip up vinyl flooring or carpet or tear trim off of a wall. The information in this section provides some general tips on how to deal with damage, but keep in mind that some things may need to be replaced or repaired by a professional.

Wood furniture, doors, trim, and cabinets that have a natural color and/or finish may become scratched by a dog's claws. Major scratches, dents, and chew marks may require a professional, and minor scratches or dents can be repaired dependent on several factors. The size of the damage, the location and whether the surface has a finish on it or not will all impact

DOOR PROTECTION

ABOVE Little Wilbur didn't cause the damage to this door protector! *Courtesy of K. Gagliardo*

RIGHT A clear plastic door protector is less visible and keeps the door free of scratches. *Courtesy of Cardinal Gates: www.cardinalgates.com*

PREVENTING DAMAGE

- Use window sill, door, wall, and trim "guards"
- Use durable finishes and materials in the most vulnerable locations
- Protect floors by utilizing modular carpet or area rugs with slip resistant backs

the way that it will be repaired. Very small scratches and dents in unfinished wood can be repaired by putting a few drops of water on the surface. This will raise the grain of the wood as it swells. Another option is to place a clean damp white cotton cloth on the surface and put a hot iron on top of it. Don't let the iron touch the wood directly as it may scorch. Avoid this procedure on wood finishes which may become permanently "cloudy" as a result. Scratches can be hidden with a wax furniture repair stick or permanent ink marker that closely matches the color of the wood. This doesn't fix it but makes it more difficult to see the scratch. Scratches and dents in wood finishes can be repaired but require more skill or the help of a professional.

Outside corners on walls are vulnerable to damage. Wall guards made of plastic or metal offer excellent protection. Scratches or chew marks in painted surfaces are easy for a novice to repair. Holes in gypsum or plaster walls, especially if they are larger than 1" in diameter are a bit more difficult but it can be done. Scratches and chew marks will require a putty knife, filler, sandpaper, primer and paint or other finish. For drywall and plaster, joint compound or spackle are excellent fillers. Today there are specialized spackles so read the label

to determine which one is best for your job. The first step is to spread the filler over the damage and cover the area. Don't overfill; it is much easier to build up layers than it is to sand through them. Let it dry before sanding it. Apply more spackle and feather it to the edge of the damage. Use primer and paint to finish it. Large holes in drywall will require cutting out a portion of the wall, adding a support behind the hole and drilling new drywall into the hole. Filler is applied over the new patch in the same manner as outlined above.

Wood surfaces that have been painted and damaged can also be repaired in a similar manner as the walls. While wood filler is recommended for repairs, spackle can work in a pinch. It might take longer to build up the surface, especially if it is trim that has curves and angles, but it can be done by a novice. Scratches in natural wood floors and trim can be filled, sanded and refinished, but will likely be noticeable. Severely damaged floors and trim may have to be replaced rather than repaired.

Window sills are a common place for damage to occur from dogs. If the surface is not painted it will be more difficult to repair the wood. One solution is to cover the sill with sill protectors which are pieces of plastic adhered to the sill with double stick tape. These products are available to purchase but it would be easy to make your own. In new construction you might consider using stone or metal sills.

Window screens are also commonly damaged. Window screening can be replaced with minimal tools and skills. Small holes can be temporarily covered with window screen repair tape—or duct tape. You will need to use the tape on both sides of the screen.

Wall damage is common near doors or gates from leaping dogs.
The good news is that this type of damage is easily repaired with spackle, sand paper and paint as can be seen in these before and
after photos.

Doors that are frequently kept closed are damaged by frustrated dogs who want to get to the other side. But keeping doors
open is not a practical or desirable solution. To minimize
damage, doors can be covered with metal or plastic protective
covers that can be purchased or homemade. Depending on
the extent of the damage doors can be repaired. If the door is
painted and the damage is minimal, wood filler, epoxy filler or
spackle will work. If the door is wood and comprised of panels,
the damaged panel can be replaced. In severe cases the door
may need to be replaced.

CONTRACTORS AND REPAIRMEN

Contractors are an inevitable part of home ownership at one
point or another. Maybe you have a repair job that is too much
for you to handle or you are interested in renovating or adding
on to your home. Every home construction job becomes complicated when you have a dog in the house. By preparing for
the unexpected and taking a few extra precautions your construction or remodeling job should go smoothly. Part of that
planning includes what to do with your dog. When the job is
done you will be glad you did, in your new dog-friendly home.

Home renovation and construction is typically stressful for
humans but we often overlook its impact on dogs. Some dogs
do not respond well to the presence of strangers in their home.
It is normal for dogs to instinctively protect their territory and
this reaction should be considered the rule rather than the
exception. Hammering, sawing, nail guns and the strange
beeping sounds of construction can be disturbing for a
dog. Calm dogs may become hyperactive, elderly dogs may
become disoriented, and friendly dogs may turn cranky. This
mind frame greatly increases the risk of a dog bite, escape or
destructive behavior. Dogs tend to become suspicious and
territorial under these circumstances. Many dogs will bark
incessantly at workers and some workers will exacerbate this
by teasing the dogs or trying to play with them. It may seem
irrelevant but make sure your dogs are completely up to
date on their vaccinations before starting a construction job.
If someone is accidentally bitten this may be the only thing
preventing your dog from being impounded. Regardless of the
circumstances, laws rarely favor the dog owner in cases like
this. During initial interviews with contractors or workers
ascertain whether they like dogs. This is good to know, but

even if they love dogs plan accordingly to minimize any contact between your dog and the workmen. Be careful who you give your house keys to. Prevention is always your best option.

Construction sites are often a minefield of hazardous materials such as paint, glue, caulk, solvents, fuel, nails, screws, saws, drills, ladders, open holes, and glass. Even small, indoor projects such as painting a room can pose hazards for your dog. Construction workers often leave personal debris, such as cigarette butts, food wrappers and candy bars.

Construction disrupts a dog's normal routine, temporarily preventing access to regular locations for eating, sleeping, elimination or exercise. This can be especially difficult for senior dogs. They have less tolerance for changes in routine and the resulting stress can exacerbate existing health disorders. If you intend to remain in your home during construction, consider your dog's health, personality and habits. If you have concerns about his ability to cope, the best alternative may be to remove him from your home for the duration. For a long term job consider other arrangements. The dogs will need to be exercised and you may need to enlist someone to do this. Temporarily hiring a dog walker or dog sitter when you are away from home is beneficial.

Home renovations also represent one of the most common situations leading to dogs escaping and running away. If your dog disappears during a home renovation project first ascertain whether he could have gotten out of the house. If you don't think this was possible thoroughly search your house from top to bottom. Frightened dogs can hide in improbable places.

Inform your workmen that you have a dog but assure them that the dog will be confined during work hours. Ideally crate the dog in a room that is off limits to workmen. Keep the dog occupied with some highly appealing and safe toys or chews and turn on a TV or radio to distract them from the construction noise. Workers can and do wander about the house regardless of whether they need to be in certain rooms. They also leave gates, doors and windows open despite instructions to the contrary. You should always have at least two barriers between your dog and the street when workers are present. During external construction keep your dog in a fenced area, or on leash at all times when he is outdoors. Workers often throw heavy materials like wood, roofing, bricks, and concrete from roofs, decks, and upper stories without concern for who, or what, might be below. Construction vehicles come and go, including large delivery trucks, concrete trucks, and bulldozers. Visibility in these larger vehicles is often poor and they may not see your dog in the yard.

Here are some simple rules to prevent problems:

- Never leave your dog unattended when you are not home and workmen expect to have free run of your house
- Never leave your dog unsupervised in a fenced yard during home construction
- Check and double check all exits before allowing your dogs out into your yard at the end of the workday
- Make sure the construction site is picked up inside and outside before allowing your dog to roam after the workers go home for the day

See Resources for products and more information.

Resources

USING THE RESOURCE GUIDE

This guide is meant to provide information for ideas and solutions mentioned throughout the book. It is not an endorsement of any particular product. Product websites are listed by manufacturer or distributor only. Retail outlets are too numerous and often change. In any given category there may be many more products available.

Some products may have been left off of the list because they contain harmful chemicals or may be dangerous to you or your dog. Please do your homework when researching products and use the book as a guide to help.

Remember: not all products are suitable for every dog. Size, age, behavior and other factors all have an impact on suitability.

*Products with an asterisk are featured in the book.

INTRODUCTION

Benefits of Dogs
Delta Society
www.deltasociety.org

Professional Organizations for architects, interior designers and contractors
The American Institute of Architects
www.aia.org

International Interior Design Association
www.iida.org

American Society of Interior Designers
www.asid.org

The National Home Builders Association
www.nahb.org

Codes and Regulations, Building Codes
International Code Council (ICC)
www.iccsafe.org

Zoning
www.generalcode.com

ADA
American's with Disabilities Act (ADA)
www.ada.gov

Sustainable Design
There are many excellent resources for sustainable design.

Environmental Building News
www.BuildingGreen.com

Environmental Protection Agency
www.epa.gov

Environmental Working Group
www.ewg.org

Environment and Human Health, Inc.
www.ehhi.org

Leadership in Energy and Environmental Design (LEED)
www.usgbc.org/LEED

National Association of Home Building
www.nahb.org

National Resources Defense Council
www.nrdc.org

Rocky Mountain Institute
www.rmi.org

US Green Building Council's Green Home Guide
www.greenhomeguide.com

Whole Building Design Guide
www.wbdg.org

Sustainable Certification or Green Certification Organizations Green Labeling
A number of independent organizations have begun to certify products according to specific criteria relative to the type of product. Beware of "green washing" where products make claims of being "natural" or "green". There are other organizations that certify products but they are usually trade organizations who may have a more biased view of their own products or members. If you want to be sure to get an unbiased perspective, look for the following labels on products.

Wood Products
Forest Stewardship Council
www.fscus.org

Finishes, furniture, products and cleaners
Green Seal™
www.greenseal.org

GreenGuard®
www.greenguard.org

Energy
www.energystar.gov
www.eere.energy.gov

Socially Responsible Certified Products
Products and manufacturers are analyzed and scrutinized by an independent third party agency that investigates labor issues such as child labor, unsafe working conditions and abuse of workers.

Care and Fair
www.care-fair.org

GoodWeave™
www.goodweave.org

Socially Responsible Design
www.sociallyresponsibledesign.org

Product Reviews
Consumer Reports
www.ConsumerReports.org

CHAPTER 1
The Logistics of Living with *Canis familiaris*

Dog Breed Registries
Canada
CKC (Canadian Kennel Club)
www.ckc.ca

Great Britain
KC (Kennel Club of Great Britain)
www.thekennelclub.org.uk

International
FCI (Federation Cynologique Internationale)
www.fci.be

United States
AKC (American Kennel Club)
www.akc.org

UKC (United Kennel Club)
www.ukcdogs.com

Rescue and Adoption
Many purebred dogs are available through rescue organizations that are affiliated with each breed club. Mixed breed dogs can be found through local animal shelters and rescue organizations. Use the following websites to find a shelter or group near you:

www.animalshelter.org
www.theanimalrescuesite.com

CHAPTER 2
What the Dog Needs and Wants

Water Drinking Systems
Indoors
*HDuo™ Water Dispensing System
www.hduo.com

Outdoors
Contech Water Dog®
www.contech-inc.com

Elimination
Pet Waste Septic and Outdoor Composting Systems
(see Chapter 5 for indoor composting)
*Doggie Dooley®
www.doggiedooley.com

*Pet Poo Converter Worm Compost Bin
Tumbleweed
www.tumbleweed.com.au

Worm-e-loo
WormsRus™ in New Zealand
www.wormsrus.co.nz

Do-It-Yourself Composting
www.cityfarmer.info

Dog Waste Composting Guide (PDF)
www.ak.nrcs.usda.gov/publications.html

Biodegradable Poop Bags
The BioBag for Pets®
www.biobagusa.com

Flushable Poop Bags
FlushDoggy™
www.flushdoggy.com

CHAPTER 3
Health & Safety

Poisons in your home
Toxic Plants and Poisons
Animal Poison Control Center
www.aspca.org/pet-care/poison-control
888-426-4435
(private fee based consultation available by phone)

Cornell University (list of toxic plants)
www.ansci.cornell.edu/plants

Veterinary Partner
www.veterinarypartner.com

Parasites, Bacteria, Viruses and Tick Borne Diseases
Companion Animal Parasite Council
www.petsandparasites.org

Centers for Disease Control
www.cdc.gov
www.cdc.gov/niosh

National Institutes of Health
www.nih.gov

Wildlife
Living with Wildlife Foundation
www.lwwf.org

Humane Society of the United States
www.humanesociety.org/animals/wild_neighbors

Bird Mites
www.medent.usyd.edu

There are many other state by state internet resources
that relate to living with wildlife.

Dangerous and Poisonous Animals
List of poisonous snakes, lizards, spiders and
scorpions in the USA
www.venombyte.com

De-Skunking Preparations
Nature's Miracle® Skunk Odor Remover
www.naturemakesitwork.com

Skunk-Kleen – GG Bean
No website

Skunk-Off® – Thornell Products
www.thornell.com

Stairs and non-slip resources
Slip resistant additives
Bondex Skid® Tex ST-30
www.zinsser.com

Griptex
www.spratex.com

Coatings with additives in them
Eco-Safety Products, LLC
www.ecosafetyproducts.com

Anti-Slip Latex Coating M55, Anti-Slip Aggregate M67 and
Superspec HP® Anti-Slip Aggregate P67
www.benjaminmoore.com

EasyTread and HardPave
www.phoenixpaints.com

Clear Coatings
Skid Safe and ND Aggregate
www.ndclean.com

Non-slip tape for rugs
HOLD-IT for rugs™
www.duckbrand.com

Safety products
Electrical Safety: cords, cord covers and
concealed surge protectors
CritterCord™
www.crittercord.com

Metal Braided Sleeving
www.glenair.com
www.techflex.com

Belkin Conceal Surge Protector
www.belkin.com

Deck/Balcony/Railing Safety
*Deck Shield Outdoor Safety Netting
Banister Shield Protector
www.cardinalgates.com

Window Safety
Guardian Angel Window Guards
www.angelguard.com

Safer Anti-freeze
Sierra
www.sierrantifreeze.com

CHAPTER 4
Air, Ground, Water and Light

Air purifiers
Ozone free systems
California Air Resources Board (CARB)
www.arb.ca.gov

"Air Cleaners in the Home" (PDF)
www.epa.gov/iaq/pdfs/aircleaners.pdf

"Ozone Generators that Are Sold as Air Cleaners"
www.epa.gov/iaq/pubs/ozonegen.html

Indoor Air Quality and Indoor Toxins
Aerias
"Clearing the Air on Indoor Air Cleaners/Purifiers"
www.aerias.org

Agency for Toxic Substances and Disease
www.atsdr.cdc.gov

Building Green News
www.buildinggreen.com

Environmental Protection Agency
"Indoor Air Pollution: an introduction for
Health Professionals" (PDF)
www.epa.gov/iaq

Environmental Working Group
www.ewg.org

Carbon Monoxide, specific guides
"Carbon Monoxide Poisoning"
www.cdc.gov

"Carbon Monoxide: The Silent Killer"
www.aerias.org

"Protect Your Family and Yourself from
Carbon Monoxide Poisoning"
www.epa.gov

VOC Testing and information
Air Quality Sciences
www.aqs.com

Indoor Air Quality Association
www.iaqa.org

Mold Testing and Removal
American Industrial Hygiene Association (AIHA)
www.aiha.org

Environmental Protection Agency: Mold and Moisture
www.epa.gov/iedmold1/

National Association of Mold Professionals
www.moldpro.org

Radon Testing and Remediation
Environmental Protection Agency: Radon
www.epa.gov/radon

National Environmental Health Association
www.radongas.org

National Radon Safety Board
www.nrsb.org

Mercury Information
Environmental Protection Agency: Mercury
www.epa.gov/mercury

Environmental Working Group
www.ewg.org

Oceans Alive (for safe fish to eat)
www.oceansalive.org

Arsenic Removal
Edenfern™
www.edenspace.com

Formaldehyde free products
AdvanTech® OSB
www.huberwood.com

U.S. Architectural Products
www.architecturalproducts.com

Weyerhaeuser
www.weyerhaeuser.com

Water
General Information
Environmental Protection Agency
www.epa.gov/safewater

This is an excellent resource about drinking water:
www.cyber-nook.com/water/solutions.html

Water Purification Systems Certification and Consultants
NSF International
www.nsf.org

Underwriter's Laboratory
www.ul.com

Water Quality Association
www.wqa.org

Safer Antifreeze
Sierra®
www.sierraantifreeze.com

CHAPTER 5
Kitchens and Dining Rooms

General Info
National Kitchen and Bath Association
www.nkba.org

Countertops
General Info (for all types of countertops and names of manufacturers)
International Surface Fabricators Association
www.isfanow.org

Concrete Resources
"Concrete Countertops", Fu-Tung Cheng (with Eric Olsen), Taunton Press, 2002

Concrete Network
www.concretenetwork.com

Flooring
Ceramic Tile
Tile The Natural Choice (Tile Council of North America, Inc.)
www.tilethenaturalchoice.com

Tile Contractors
Tile Contractor's Association of America
www.tcaainc.org

Cabinets
There are numerous cabinet manufacturers.
For environmentally friendly cabinets look for companies that use FSC certified lumber (for FSC certification see Chapter 1 resources)

General Info
Kitchen Cabinet Manufacturer's Association
www.kcma.org

Sustainable Cabinets
Green Cabinet Resource
www.greencabinetsource.org

This cabinet manufacturer is featured in the book:
*Heritage Cabinetry
www.heritagecabinetry.biz

Cleaning Products (see Chapter 13 Resources)

Garbage Cans and Indoor Composting Units
*Doggy + Safe®
www.doggy-safe.com

*Nature Mill Composting Units
www.naturemill.com

Sinks and Faucets
American Standard
www.americanstandard-us.com

*Elkay Sinks
www.elkay.com

Franke Group
www.franke.com

*Kohler USA
www.kohler.com

Safety Products
Stove Guard
www.cardinalgates.com

Fabric for Tablecloths
Sunbrella®
www.sunbrella.com

CHAPTER 6
Living Rooms, Offices and Libraries

Furnishings
*The Livable Home Store
www.livablehomestore.com

Carpet General Info
The Carpet and Rug Institute
www.carpet-rug.org

Modular Carpet
FLOR™
www.flor.com

Upholstery
Leather and Vinyl Alternatives
Boltaflex®
Omnova Solutions Inc.
www.omnova.com

Ultraleather™
Ultrafabrics® LLC
www.ultrafabricsllc.com

Sustainable Fabrics
Climatex® Lifecycle™
www.climatex.com

Paint
Master Painter's Institute
www.specifygreen.com

Fireplace and General Safety
Gates, hearth bumpers, furniture bumpers, furniture brackets etc.

*Cardinal Gates
www.cardinalgates.com

*Kidco
www.kidco.com

Mommy's Helper Inc.
www.mommyshelperinc.com

CHAPTER 7
Bedrooms

Dog Beds
There are too many to list. Read Chapter 5 for ideas on types of beds. These resources will include specialty beds only.

Custom Dog Beds
The Furniture Society
www.furnituresociety.org

Designer Dog Beds
*Pre Fab Pets
www.pre-fab-pets.com

Max Comfort® Dog Beds
www.bigdogbeds.com

Heated Beds
Electric heated beds
K & H Pet Products™ (Thermo-Bed, Thermo-Pet)
www.khmfg.com

Pet Safe™ (Universal Bed Warmer, Heated Wellness Beds)
www.petsafe.net

Microwaveable Heating Pads
Snuggle Safe® (stays warm for 8 to 12 hours)
www.snugglesafe.co.uk

Cooler Beds
Canine Cooler ™
www.chillow.com

Comfort Breeze Pet Cot
www.petcot.com

Waterproof Pet Blankets for your Bed
*Mambe Waterproof Blankets
www.mambeblankets.com

Water Resistant Fabric (without PFOS)
Crypton® Super Fabrics
www.cryptonfabric.com

Crates
Folding plastic crates
Nylabone® Cozytime (for small dogs only)
www.nylabone.com

Pet Gear The Other Door®
www.petgearinc.com

Soft Sided Crates (avoid products with PVC)
General Cage
www.generalcage.com

*Midwest
www.midwesthomes4pets.com

Pet Gear
www.petgearinc.com

Precision Pet Products
www.precisionpet.com

Solid Plastic Crates
See Pet Gear and Precision Pet Products above and:
Kennel-Aire®
www.kennel-aire.com

Pet Mate Vari-Kennel®
www.petmate.com

Specialty Crates (security, strength)
High Country Plastics Deluxe Dog Kennel
www.highcountryplastics.com

Wire Crates
See General Cage, Kennel-Aire, Midwest, Pet Gear,
Pet Mate, and Precision Pet Products above

Custom Crates and Crate Furniture
Aluma Den (aluminum)
www.alumaden.com

Classic Pet Beds (wood)
www.classicpetbeds.com

Crate Haven (wood covers for wire crates)
www.cratehaven.com

*Den Haus (wood and metal)
www.denhaus.com

Dynamic Accents (wood)
www.dynamicaccents.com

Kustom Krates® (aluminum)
www.kustomkrates.com

Mr. Herzher's™ Pet Accessories (wicker and wire)
www.mrherzher.com

Pro Dog Crates (aluminum)
www.prodogcrates.com

Richell (wood and wire)
www.richellusa.com

Steps (see ramps under Chapter 11 Resources)
Mr. Herzher's™ Pet Accessories
www.mrherzher.com

CHAPTER 8
Bathrooms

House Training
Pee Post™ by Simple Solution®
www.simplesolution.com

Indoor Dog Toilets
Litter Boxes and Trays
PETaPOTTY
www.petapotty.com

Pet Loo
www.petloo.com

*Pet Patio Potty™
www.doggysolutions.com

Pooch Potty
www.poochpotty.com

UgoDog®
www.ugodog.net

*Wizdog™
www.wizdog.com

Outdoor Covered Toilets
*Elevated Canopy Potty
www.doggysolutions.com

*Covered dog kennels
www.shadenthings.com

Dog Litter and Pads (see Chapter 11 Resources for more)
Nestle Purina Petcare Company
www.purina.com
www.doglitter.com

Portable potty for RVs and boats
Pup-Head™ portable dog potty
Pup Gear Corporation
www.portabledogpotty.com

Plumbed dog toilet
The Pet Potty
www.thepetpotty.net

Do-It-Yourself Indoor Toilet
The Ultimate Dog Litter Box Instructions
www.kturby.com/showerlitter/index

Do-It-Yourself Outdoor Toilet
Washing Machine overflow trays or pans with or without
drainage holes. Most washing machine manufacturers make
them or check out the following:

Driptite™
www.driptite.com

Floodsaver®
www.floodsaver.com

Artificial Turf for outdoor toilets
K9 Grass®
www.k9grass.com

Toilet lid locks
Kidco, Inc.
www.kidco.com

Toilet Paper Holders, Canisters and Cabinets
*Blomus® – Tarro enclosed toilet paper holder, canisters
www.blomus.com

*Hidden TP (buy direct from this site)
www.hiddentoiletpaper.com

Polder® – Stainless steel canisters
www.polder.com

TPSaver™
Mom Inventors, Inc.
www.mominventors.com

Zenith Country Cottage Toilet Paper Holder
www.zenith-interiors.com

Commercial toilet paper dispensers, soap dispensers
Bradley
www.bradleycorp.com

Bobrick Washroom Equipment
www.bobrick.com

Hidden Plunger storage
Hy-dit® Hidden Toilet Plunger Storage
www.hy-dit.com

Showers, Bathtubs, Shower Wands and Whirlpools
Fiberglass tubs
*New Breed Bath Tub
www.newbreedtubs.com

Galvanized and Stainless Steel Tubs
Edemco Pet Tub
www.edemco.com

Shor-Line®
www.shor-line.com

Pet Lift® Equipment Corp.
www.petlift.com

Angel Touch Bathing Systems
www.angeltouchbathing.net

Plastic bathtubs, showers and sprayer wands
Booster Bath
www.boosterbath.com

Rinse Ace®
www.rinseace.com

Scrub a Dub Dog Tub
www.scrubadubdog.biz

Poly Pet Tubs®
www.polypettubs.com

Shower Wands
Siroflex (handheld trigger nozzle)
www.siroflexshowerhead.com

Zoe Industries (dog shower)
www.showerbuddy.com

Whirlpool Spas
*MTI Whirlpools – Jentle Pet® Spa
www.mtiwhirlpools.com

Handmade Ceramic Tiles of Dogs
*Sondra Alexander
www.sondraalexander.com

Laundry and Utility sinks
American Shower and Bath Corp.
www.mascobath.com

Elkay®
www.elkay.com

*Kohler®
www.kohler.com

E.L. Mustee & Sons, Inc.
www.mustee.com

Swanstone
www.swanstoneproducts.com

Hair Traps
Pet Lift® Smartway Hair Interceptor
www.petlift.com

. . . .

CHAPTER 9
Dog Rooms

Dog Doors
Pet Safe™
www.petsafe.net

PlexiDor®
www.plexidors.net

Hi Tech Pets (Electronic Pet Doors)
www.hitecpet.com

Laundry Appliances Ratings
www.consumerreports.org
www.greenerchoices.org

Basement Access Doors
Bilco
www.bilco.com

Specialty Flooring for Dog Training
EVA Foam
AgiliFlex™
www.groupsummit.com

Dog Agility Foam Mats
www.greatmats.com
www.getrung.com
www.softtiles.com

Fitness Equipment
Therapy Balls
Dyna Discs
www.exertools.com

Fitness Balls - Physio Roll (Gymnic®)
www.gymnic.com

Treadmills (human treadmills can work but here are some made just for dogs)
Dog Tread™
www.petzenproducts.com

Fit Fur Life
www.fitfurlife.com

Jog a Dog®
www.jogadog.com

Pawwws Pet Treadmills
www.pawwws.com

CHAPTER 10
Dog-Friendly Outdoors

Fencing
American Fence Association
www.americanfenceassociation.com

*Long® Fence
www.longfence.com

Specialty Dog Fencing
*Guardian Pet Fence
www.guardianpoolfence.com

*Best Friend Fence
www.bestfriendfence.com

Fencing solutions for diggers to hold fencing down
Ground Stakes (can be used for mesh, wire or chain link)
www.bestfriendfence.com

Fencing Solutions for climbers
These products are made for cats but work for some dogs.
Cat Fence-In™
www.catfencein.com

Katzecure
www.katzecure.com

Kitty Klips
www.kittyklips.com

*Purrfect Fence
www.bestfriendfence.com

Pet Enclosures
Little Doggie Digs, Escape-proof totally enclosed modular unit for small dogs.

Habitat Haven
www.habitathaven.com

Gate Latches
Co-Line (livestock latches)
www.surelatch.com

D & D Technologies (magnetic latches)
www.ddtech.global.com

Mason Company (kennel and gate latches)
www.masonco.com

Northern Industrial Tools (livestock latches)
www.northerntool.com

Pool and Gate Alarms
PoolGuard (Pool and Gate Alarms)
www.poolguard.com

Water features
Floating dock ramps
*Skamper Ramp®
www.skamper-ramp.com

Doggydocks™ Ramps
www.doggydocks.com

Pool Safety and Pool Filtration
The Association of Pool and Spa Professionals
www.apsp.org

Safe Kids USA
www.usa.safekids.org

Info on pool barriers and entrapment hazards:
US Consumer Product Safety Commission
www.cpsc.gov

Pools
Natural Swimming Pools
*BioNova Natural Pools
www.bionovanaturalpools.com

Total Habitat LC, (USA)
www.totalhabitat.com

Pond Design, Builders
Guidelines for pond design and construction are available through many US State Cooperative Extension services or state conservation departments. Many excavators claim to build ponds in addition to other work they do. Not all excavators are knowledgeable in pond design. Be sure that the person you hire has success in building ponds or is only in the pond building business.

Natural Resources Conservation Service
www.nrcs.usda.gov
www.in.nrcs.usda.gov/pdffiles/PONDS.PDF

National Association of Pond Professionals
www.nationalpondpro.com

Outdoor Play Areas
Trail Construction Resource
American Trails
www.americantrails.org

Play and Training Spaces
Clean Run Magazine (articles on designing and building training spaces)
www.cleanrun.com

Outdoor Lighting
International Dark-Sky Association
www.darksky.com

Musco Lighting – Sports Lighting
www.musco.com

Outdoor Garbage Containers
Critter Proof Garbage Cans
Bearicuda® Bins
www.bearicuda.com

CHAPTER 11
Dogs and Humans
with Special Needs

Resources
General Info on Disabled Dogs and Support Groups
www.dogdisability.com
www.petswithdisabilities.org
www.spanna.net

Yahoo Groups (search by specific issue; two good groups are Neuro Dogs and Able Dogs)
www.groups.yahoo.com

Rehab and Physical Therapy Veterinarians
There are many veterinarians who specialize in sports medicine, physical therapy and rehabilitation for dogs. They can be found through the following websites:

American Association of Rehabilitation Veterinarians
www.rehabvets.evetsites.net

American Canine Sports Medicine Association
www.acsma.org

Canine Rehabilitation Institute
www.caninerehabinstitute.com

International Veterinary Academy of Pain Management
www.ivapm.org

University of Tennessee Certified Rehabilitation Practitioner
www.canineequinerehab.com

Veterinary Rehab Facilities - a few places to look at:
*Thera Vet Acres Rehabilitation and Fitness
www.thera-vet.com

TOPS Veterinary Rehab
www.tops-vet-rehab.com

Scouts House
www.scoutshouse.com

VetHab
www.vethab.com

Products and info for post surgery, rehab, disabled and elderly dogs
Animal Ortho Care
www.animalorthocare.com

Dog Leggs® Therapeutic and Rehabilitative Products
www.dogleggs.com

Dog Mobility
www.dogmobility.com

Handicapped Pets
www.handicappedpets.com

Orthodog™
www.orthodog.com

Scouts House
www.scoutshouse.com/store/

Products
Anti-slip paw sprays
Show Foot™ Anti-Slip Spray
www.biogroom.com

Firm Grip®
www.cramersportsmed.com

Boots
Neo Paws™ Dog Boots
www.neopaws.com

Pawz
www.pawzdogboots.com

Thera-Paw Boots
www.therapaw.com

Beds and Bedding
Beds for paraplegic dogs and orthopedic support
Kuddle Kots™
www.kuddlekots.com

Beds for incontinent dogs
Pet Cot "Dry as a Bone" Incontinent Bed
www.petcot.com

SleePee-Time Bed®
www.sleepeetimebed.com

Fleece Bedding for incontinent dogs and to prevent bed sores
Palace Bedding
www.scoutshouse.com/store/

ProFleece®
www.pro-fleece.com

Vet Bed
www.vetbed-canada.com
www.petlifeonline.co.uk

Harnesses and slings
Walkabout™ Harness (separate front, mid and rear harnesses)
www.walkaboutharnesses.com

Web Master™ Harness (front and mid section)
www.ruffwear.com

Bottoms Up Leash™ (rear end only)
www.bottomsupleash.com

Help 'Em Up Harness (for dogs over 60 pounds, supports front and rear ends)
www.helpemup.com

Hydraulic Patient Lifts
Hydraulic lifts are either manual or electric. They can be found at medical supply stores, purchased new, used or rented. A few are being made specifically for dogs. It is important to purchase a sling attachment used specifically for dogs even if you buy a human version lift.

Hoyer Lift
www.hoyer.com

Vet Lift
www.vetsystems.net

Ramps
Plans for building a wheelchair compliant ramp
The Home Wheelchair Ramp Project
www.wheelchairramp.org

ADA Guidelines
www.access-board.org

Ready-made dog ramps for beds, cars and furniture
Dog Ramp
www.dogramp.com

Mr. Herzher's™ Pet Accessories
www.mrherzher.com

Pet Classics
www.petclassics.com

Wheelchairs and carts
Dewey's Wheelchairs for Dogs
www.wheelchairsfordogs.com

Doggon' Wheels USA
www.doggon.com

Eddie's Wheels for Pets
www.eddieswheels.com

K9 Carts
www.k9carts.com

Wall and Door Protection (see Chapter 13 Resources)

Visually Impaired Dogs
Resources and Books
"Living with Blind Dogs", by Caroline D. Levin R.N. is an excellent resource.

Websites
www.blinddogs.com
www.blinddogs.net
www.blindpets.com

Products
Audible Orientation Devices
Sound devices can be used to orient dogs.
Search these sites for suitable devices.
Beacons, Beepers, Crickets
www.abledata.com

Wireless Sound Beacon
Beeping Frisbee
www.braillebookstore.com

Beeper Sound Tracker®
www.braillegifts.com

Audible Water Bowls
Drinkwell®
www.vetventures.com

Body vests for blind dogs
Littlest Angel Vest
www.angelvest.homestead.com

Protective Eyewear
Doggles®
www.doggles.com

Creations and Eyeshields
www.angelvest.homestead.com

Hearing Impaired Dogs
Resources
"Living With a Deaf Dog: A book of advice, facts and experiences about canine deafness" Susan Cope Becker. 1997

Deaf Dog Education Fund
www.deafdog.org

CHAPTER 12
Canine Behavior Problems

Animal Behaviorist and Dog Trainer Organizations
Association of Pet Dog Trainers
www.apdt.com

Canadian Association of Professional Pet Dog Trainers
www.cappdt.ca

Certification Council for Professional Dog Trainers
www.ccpdt.com

International Positive Dog Training Association
www.ipdta.com

National Association of Dog Obedience Instructors
www.nadoi.org

Humane Training Devices
Manner's Minder
www.premier.com

Sound
General information
www.acoustics.com
www.stcratings.com
www.nrcratings.com
www.nonoise.org
www.soundproofing.org

Canada Mortgage and Housing Corporation
www.cmhc-schl.gc.ca

Canine Noise Control Specialists
(The following engineering firm specializes in animal care facilities—and provides a lot of great info on its website)
Design Learned Inc.
www.designlearned.com

Sheathing and wall finishes
A web search on soundproofing will find many more products

BlueRidge™ Fiberboard
www.blueridgeboard.com

Quiet Rock® and Quiet Wood®
www.quietsolution.com

RPG Diffuser Systems
www.rpginc.com

Windows and Doors
Protective covers
*Pet Door Shield Scratch Protection
www.cardinalgates.com

Door Grilles and perforated metals
CR Laurence
www.crlaurence.com

Diamond Manufacturing Company
www.diamondman.com

Lansing Housing Products
www.lansinghousingproducts.com

McNichols
www.mcnichols.com

M-D Building Products
www.mdteam.com

Temporary Screen Doors
Bug Off
www.bugoffscreen.com

Replacement Screens
*Phifer Pet Screen
www.petscreen.com

Retractable Screens
Phantom Screens
www.phantomscreens.com

Rollaway™
www.rollaway.com

Gates
Metal Gates and Expandable Gates
Cardinal Gates
www.cardinalgates.com

Kidco, Inc.
www.kidco.com

Ring Gating
Max 200
www.max200.com

Retracting Gates
www.retract-a-gate.com

CHAPTER 13
Maintenance, Repairs and Construction

Resources for safer cleaning supplies
Aerias AQS IAQ Resource Center
www.aerias.com

Environmental Protection Agency
www.epa.gov

Design for the Environment
www.epa.gov/dfe

Homemade Cleaning recipes
Safer Cleaning: an A to Z resource guide of safe alternatives to household cleaning supplies (PDF)
www.epa.gov/region7/citizens/safercleaning.pdf

Environmental Working Group
www.ewg.org

Cleaning Products
Consumer Reports Greener Choices
www.greenerchoices.org

Green Guard (certified products)
www.greenguard.org

Green Seal (certified products)
www.greenseal.org

Wall, Corner and Door Protection
Acrovyn® Wall and Door Protection
Construction Specialties™
www.c-sgroup.com

Boston Retail
www.bostonretail.com

MISCELLANEOUS INFO

Dog Laws and Regulations
Books
"Dog Law" Mary Randolph, Nolo, 2001

Housing Resources
"Pets In Urban Areas: A guide to integrating domestic pets into new residential developments"
www.petnet.com.au

Homemade Products
Make and Build Dog Stuff
www.make-and-build-dog-stuff.com

Pet Loss
The Association for Pet Loss and Bereavement
www.aplb.org

Index

For products and more information refer to Resources, pg. 122–134

CPSIA information can be obtained
at www.ICGtesting.com
Printed in the USA
242173LV00006B